History Goes to the Movies

Can films be used as historical evidence? Do historical films make good or bad history? Are documentaries more useful to historians than historical drama?

Written from an international perspective, this book offers a lucid introduction to the ways films are made and used, culminating with the exploration of the fundamental question, what is history and what is it for?

Incorporating film analysis, advertisements, merchandise and Internet forums; and ranging from late nineteenth-century short films to twenty-first-century DVD 'special editions', this survey evaluates the varied ways in which filmmakers, promoters, viewers and scholars understand film as history. From *Saving Private Ryan* to *Picnic at Hanging Rock* to *Pocahontas*, *History Goes to the Movies* considers that history is not simply to be found in films but in the agreements and arguments of those who make and view them.

This helpful introductory text blends historical and methodological issues with examples to create a systematic guide to issues involved in using historical film in the study of history.

History Goes to the Movies is a much-needed overview of an increasingly popular subject.

Marnie Hughes-Warrington is Senior Lecturer in Modern History at Macquarie University, Sydney. She is the author of *Fifty Key Thinkers on History* (2000), *'How Good an Historian Shall I Be?': R. G. Collingwood, the Historical Imagination and Education* (2003) and editor of *Palgrave Advances in World Histories* (2005).

History Goes to the Movies

Studying history on film

Marnie Hughes-Warrington

Routledge
Taylor & Francis Group

LONDON AND NEW YORK

First published 2007
by Routledge
2 Park Square, Milton Park, Abingdon, Oxon OX14 4RN

Simultaneously published in the USA and Canada
by Routledge
270 Madison Ave, New York, NY 10016

Routledge is an imprint of the Taylor & Francis Group, an informa business

Typeset in Times by
RefineCatch Limited, Bungay, Suffolk
Printed and bound in Great Britain by
Antony Rowe Ltd, Chippenham, Wiltshire

British Library Cataloguing in Publication Data
A catalogue record for this book is available from the British Library

Library of Congress Cataloging-in-Publication Data
Hughes-Warrington, Marnie
  History goes to the movies / Marnie Hughes-Warrington.
      p. cm.
  Includes bibliographical references and index.
  1. Motion pictures and history. 2. Historical films—History and
criticism. I. Title.

PN1995.2.H84 2007
791.43′658—dc22   2006014053

ISBN10: 0–415–32827–6 (hbk)
ISBN10: 0–415–32828–4 (pbk)

ISBN13: 978–0–415–32827–2 (hbk)
ISBN13: 978–0–415–32828–9 (pbk)

For Jill, Helen V., the State Cinema and my parents

Contents

Figures

Acknowledgements

How is it possible to unravel the ideas and arguments presented in a book? If I cast my mind back, the starting point for this book may have been a late summer's day in 1999, when Professor Jill Roe encouraged me to design an undergraduate unit that combined my interests in film and historiography. I thank Jill for her supportive and thought-provoking comments over the past seven years, and I hope that this publication marks not the end but the continuation of our good-natured banter over visual culture and history. Looking back even further, though, this book might have begun with the many outings that my school friend, Helen Verrier, organised to the State Cinema, Hobart. In that time and place, I caught sight of worlds that I have never forgotten. And as with some of the viewers whose experiences are described in this book, the films that I saw continue to organise and keep vivid my memories of friends. Or going back further still, this book might have its origins in my parents' act of naming. With thanks to them, I have spent a lifetime wondering about how people draw upon and are drawn into films. In recognition of these beginnings, I dedicate this book to Jill, Helen V, the State Cinema and my parents.

But a book is not just about beginnings; it is also about the many people who tug, prod and argue it into shape. I would like to thank those individuals who read and commented on the proposal for this work, including Professor Robert Rosenstone and Associate Professor Judith Keene. I am deeply appreciative of the advice they offered, though of course any responsibility for errors is entirely my own. Thanks again to Bruce, whose efforts as a proof-reader continually inspire me to do better. Additionally, I would like to thank Vicky Peters, Philippa Grand and Anna Hines at Routledge for their support and patience with this project.

I am also grateful for the support provided by Macquarie University, Sydney, including the generous financial support provided for this project through the Macquarie University Research Development Scheme. I thank the Department of Modern History, now led by Professor Angela Woollacott, for supporting my explorations of film in teaching and research. More particularly, I would like to thank Michelle Arrow for her invaluable help with locating print and online resources in the early stages of this project and for bringing new dimensions to the topic through her lectures, talks and papers. Helen Groth in the Department of English prompted me to think about special effects in novel and promising ways. Thanks are also owed to Mary Spongberg and Bridget Griffen-Foley, whose comments and encouragement never cease to help and bring a smile. Acknowledgement must be made of the document supply staff in the Macquarie University library, which processed countless requests for materials with efficiency and great patience. Thanks are also owed to Nicola Myton for her work on the filmography. Additionally, an enormous vote of thanks is owed to the hundreds of students who have now completed HIST243: History on Film. I thank each of you for allowing me to test out my ideas and for stimulating me to explore ideas and issues.

I cannot finish without noting the support of family and friends: to the folks at St David's Lindfield for their interest and words of encouragement; to Cath, Andrew, Bronwyn and Evan for their calls, messages and enduring support; to the Warringtons, whose love and support for one another never cease to amaze; and to Bruce and Alice, at whose side I can find no greater happiness.

Permissions

The author and publisher gratefully acknowledge the permission granted to include the following images in this book: the Australian Film Commission for the frame enlargement from *Picnic at Hanging Rock* (1975) and promotional posters for *Rabbit-proof Fence* (2002); Touchstone Pictures for the advertisement for *Pearl Harbor* (2001); Gen Productions for the frame enlargement from *Hadashi no Gen* (1983); Akiyuki Nosaka/Shinchosha for the frame enlargement from *Hotaru no Haku* (1988); Screensound Australia for the frame enlargements from *The Story of the Kelly Gang* (1906); Dreamworks SKG for the frame enlargements from *Saving Private Ryan* (1988) and *Gladiator* (2000); the British Film Institute for the frame enlargement from *Distant Voices, Still Lives* (1988); Centropolis Effects for the 'before' and 'after' shots from *The Patriot* (2000); the USC Shoah Foundation Institute for Visual History and Education (www.usc.edu/vhi) for the promotional poster for *The Last Days* (1998); the Australian Broadcasting Corporation for the frame enlargement from *Mister Prime Minister* (1966); Disney Corporation for the promotional poster for *Pocahontas* (1995); 20th Century Fox for the frame enlargement from *Anastasia* (1998); Sony Classical BMG for the advertisement for the *Titanic* soundtrack sequel (2000); the Franklin Mint for the advertisement for the Rose portrait doll (2000); Max Factor Cosmetics for the *Titanic* promotional advertisement (2000); and Simplicity Patterns for the cover of the *Titanic*-inspired sewing pattern (2000).

Every effort has been made to trace copyright holders and to obtain their permission for the use of copyright material. The author and publisher apologise for any errors or omissions in the above list and would be grateful if notified of any corrections that should be incorporated in future reprints or editions of this book.

Introduction
Why history on film?

Why, may I ask, devote an entire issue to film when there are serious issues to discuss? . . . In the future, please try to be serious.[1]

Why devote an entire book to history on film? The answer to this question might at first sight be obvious: for many people, 'history' is what they see in films and television programs. In the US-based 'Presence of the Past' project, for instance, 81 percent of the 1500 people interviewed indicated that they had watched films or television programs about the past in the previous year. The number of people engaged in that activity was second only to taking or looking at photographs and much higher than the number of people who read books about the past (53 percent) or who participated in a group devoted to studying, preserving or presenting the past (20 percent). Moreover, respondents registered a stronger connection with the past when they watched films and television than when they studied history in school.[2] Similar results have been reported in the 'Australians and the Past' project.[3] As one respondent in that study reported:

> [on] a monthly basis I can see documentaries on the Second World War. . . . History has come out of the little box it was in [in] primary school. I feel connected to the past all the time.[4]

While far from global in scope, these studies suggest that in terms of popular presence alone, the study of historical films is significant. Yet those same surveys also revealed that people trust historical films and television programs far less than books, academic historians and museums. Moreover, respondents in the Australian study held that objects and places were better evidence for the past than books and films. How can film and television be so popular but at the same time less persuasive than other historical media? The challenge of these findings, as Roy Rosenzweig and David Thelen have argued, is that 'History professionals need to work harder at listening to and respecting the many ways popular history makers traverse the terrain of the past that is so present for all of us'.[5] But there is another challenge: that of explaining people's ambivalence towards history on film.

It might be objected that we should not confuse popularity with significance. Popularity, it may be argued, does not bestow on a topic importance, or as Marshall Poe put it in the quote that opens this book, 'seriousness'. How has it come to be that we might think of a popular medium like film as something less than serious? We start with the observation that viewers—including film scholars—are often described as being engaged in a form of 'escape' and consequently interested only in mere entertainment. This Noël Carroll puts down to the very nature of 'mass artworks'. They are, he argues:

> intentionally designed to gravitate in [their] structural choices (e.g. [their] narrative forms, symbolism, intended affect, and even [their] content) toward those choices that promise accessibility with minimum effort, virtually on first contact, for the largest number of relatively untutored audiences.[6]

Similarly, Northrop Frye holds that 'the most obvious conventional fictions are the easiest to read'.[7] At work in these definitions are two key untested assumptions: that films offer access with minimum effort, and that they are accessible to 'mass', 'untutored' audiences. By contrast, certain 'specialised' skills are assumed to be required to access academic monographs. And, sometimes, it is even assumed that with training, viewers will move beyond or outgrow film or some kinds of film.

If these accounts are to be believed, the charges against history on film as a serious endeavour are charges against both the medium and its audience. It is possible to rebut these charges without going to the other extreme and uncritically valorising the efforts of filmmakers and their audiences. It is argued that history on film provides little scholarly satisfaction because it can be understood, as Carroll puts it, with 'minimum effort'. Similarly, Max Horkheimer and Theodor Adorno have credited films with the production of boredom, because they 'do not demand any effort. . . . No independent thinking must be expected from the audience . . . [and] anything calling for mental effort is painstakingly avoided'.[8] The problem with this view is that it conflates 'effort' with 'mental effort' and 'mental effort' in turn with 'independent thinking'. By what means did we arrive at this view of effort, and is it immune to change? Does 'mental effort' allow for emotional effort, for example, and if not, why not? And why do we assume that sharing or following the ideas of others is necessarily an effortless act? In raising this last question, we move on to the assumption that film, by its formulaic nature, is a barrier to independent thought and action. At the very least, empirical evidence from studies of film and television watching suggests otherwise, although many more studies of viewers' responses to historical films in different historical and cultural contexts remain to be done.[9]

People are not born with an ability to interpret film, and filmic conventions have not remained static over time. We have yet to chart the effort involved when a viewer first encounters a construction of history on film, whether that construction is novel or conventional. Moreover, novelty may be generated in the relation and juxtaposition of even the most hackneyed of conventions. Far from being transparent and universal clusters of conventions, films are characterised by multilayered and nuanced meanings. Failure to recognise these may be more a reflection of a lack of willingness or training on the part of critics to understand them than anything else. Finally, it is important to disentangle the concept of a 'mass audience' from 'multitudinous audience' or even 'everyone'. As Shusterman explains:

> A particular taste group sharing a distinct social or ethnic background or specific subculture may be clearly distinguishable from what is considered the homogeneous mass audience of average Americans or Britons, and yet still be numerous enough to constitute a multitudinous audience whose satisfaction will render an art sufficiently popular to count as popular art.[10]

Particular films may appeal to a lot of viewers, but not to all of them. They are consequently not so popular as to require that their devices and diegeses—ways of 'telling' by 'showing' on screen, or the 'worlds' presented by films—be homogeneous.[11]

If historical films are characterised even in part by conventions, are they unfit for scholarly attention? Quite the contrary if our interest is in acquiring a better understanding of the nature and purposes of history, otherwise known as historiography. Historiography is often portrayed as a tool that can be used to examine and resolve debates between historians, or 'history wars' as they are sometimes called. Put simply, it is believed that where there is disagreement, a historiographer is needed to set things aright. However, historiography can also be used to illuminate, question and modify conventional and uncontested activities. Moreover, historiography is not ancillary to historical practices and cannot be disentangled from them. Every practice associated with the making, communication and reception of histories either establishes or confirms assumptions that define, contract or extend understandings of 'history'. Some historiographical assumptions vary markedly across cultures and times, while others are so persistent and widespread that they appear to be universal or even natural. But all historiographical assumptions, let us be clear, are subject to change and open to question. If, as some scholars maintain, the illumination and study of historiographical assumptions is no easy matter,[12] then the perception of film as a simple or accessible medium—ill-founded or not—might work in its favour. This perception, for instance, may explain an observation I noted above: viewer ambivalence towards historical films. It could be that viewers have more sense of historical films as representations than other history media such as museums or books. That is, their status as the products of particular groups of people in particular contexts—and the limitations of those products and contexts— may be more obvious to viewers. If that is the case, then films might offer a more approachable route to the study of historiography than other media.

Historical film studies

I cannot claim credit for being the first person to note the historiographical potential of historical film studies. Analysis of films representing history is as old as the medium itself, but in 1971 it was put on a new footing with the creation of a specialist journal, *Film and History*. Offering a mixture of reviews, survey articles and pedagogical suggestions, *Film and History* stimu- lated the creation of monographs, film review issues in other journals and eventually, the John E. O'Connor Prize—awarded by the American Histor- ical Association in recognition of one of the founding editors of *Film and History*—for outstanding achievement in historical filmmaking. Notable is the work edited by O'Connor himself, *Image as Artefact: The Historical Analysis of Film and Television* (1990). Addressing researchers, educators and students alike, O'Connor argued for the recognition of film as a 'representa- tion of history' and 'evidence for social and cultural history', 'actuality foot- age as evidence for history' and 'the history of the moving image as industry and art form'. Underpinning these arguments was recognition of the complex relationship between films and the times of both their production and diegeses. A similar view was advanced in Marc Ferro's *Cinema et Histoire* (1977; translated as *Cinema and History*, 1988) and Pierre Sorlin's *The Film in History* (1980), the latter of which defined the historical film as 'a reconstruc- tion of the social relationship which, using the pretext of the past, reorgan- izes the present'.[13] Sorlin and Ferro, though, were insistent that films tell us more about the times in which they were produced than the times represented on screen. Ferro, for instance, saw historical films as divided into those 'inscribed in the dominant (or oppositional) currents of thought and those that propose an independent or innovative view of societies'.[14] As with O'Connor, though, they endorsed the view that, as one of the contributors to *Image as Artefact* put it, 'film is radically different from other and more familiar [historiographical] tools'.[15]

Belief in film as something 'radically different' was reinforced in the 1980s and 1990s with the production of multiple monographs, new specialist jour- nals like *Screening the Past*[16] and new space at conferences and in journals like *The Journal of American History, American Historical Review* and *History Today*. R.J. Raack and Ian Jarvie presented divergent accounts of the poten- tial of film as a medium for history, with the former seeing it as the best way to 'recover all the past's liveliness' and the latter maintaining that it could not represent the past with any complexity because of its 'poor information load'.[17] Many more writers, though, moved beyond debating film as poor or rich and sought to spell out how the medium could best show history. Barbara Abrash and Janet Sternberg took a practical approach, for example looking for opportunities for historians and filmmakers to work together.[18] In a special forum on history and film in *American Historical Review* in 1989, by contrast, Robert Rosenstone directed attention instead to the theoretical assumptions that he saw as a barrier to the scholarly treatment of historical films. The major problem, in his view, was the routine comparison of filmic histories with written histories, as if the latter were an unquestioned and unproblematic standard for history making. To Rosenstone, film offered new ways of thinking about the past and could be studied and appreciated on its own terms.[19] In their responses to Rosenstone's article, David Herlihy, O'Connor and Robert Brent Toplin endorsed the distinction between 'history in images' and 'history in words'.[20] Another respondent—Hayden White— went one step further and coined a term to distinguish the study of visual histories from written history. It was high time, he argued, that historiography was joined by 'historiophoty'.[21]

In subsequent publications, Rosenstone worked with other scholars to sketch out the features of what he called 'new' visual histories. From Ousmane Sembène's *Ceddo* (1976) to Shohei Imamura's *Eijanaka* (1981) and Alex Cox's *Walker* (1987) to Terence Davis' *Distant Voices, Still Lives* (1989), he claimed, we see a move away from the presentation of history as a polished and complete story and towards its being a representation that can and ought to be questioned.[22] *Visions of the Past* (1995) and *Revisioning History* (1995) were part of a new surge of publications on historical films that has not yet lost its force. Drawing on Gramsci and Nietzsche, for example, Marcia Landy connected cinematic uses of the past with the desire to either escape or engage with the present.[23] Toplin suggested that even the most derided Hollywood films 'can arouse emotions, stir curiosity, and prompt viewers to consider significant questions'.[24] Frank Sanello argued the opposite, and Leger Grindon and Deborah Cartmell, I.Q. Hunter, and Imelda Whelehan illuminated the fictional nature of constructions of the past.[25] Finally, Phillip Rosen employed André Bazin's historicised notion of 'reality' to highlight the historicity of all filmic statements.[26]

For every monograph that explores the nature and purpose of historical films in general terms, there are many more that consider particular aspects or kinds of historical films. To take just a small number of examples: Jon Solomon has surveyed representations of the ancient world, and Natalie Zemon Davis, Brian Taves, Guy Barefoot and George Custen have analysed representations of slavery, historical adventure films, films set during the London gaslight period and biographical pictures (biopics), respectively.[27] Aspects of film art have also been of interest: Charles Tashiro, for example, has looked at the use of costumes to represent the past.[28] There are also numerous books on filmic representations of particular events like the Holocaust, the Second World War and the Vietnam War.[29] Furthermore, works like Anton Kaes' *From Hitler to Heimat* (1989) or Sue Harper's *Picturing the Past* (1994) consider historical film production in particular cultural contexts.[30] Finally, there are even more publications that consider the merits of individual films, ranging from Mark Carne's edited collection of sixty reviews, *Past Imperfect*, to the hundreds of articles in specialist and general journals.[31]

This study

Publications on historical films now number over a thousand and are beginning to reflect global interest in and uses of the medium. Why then, you might ask, is it necessary to add another publication to this arguably overcrowded field? Although there is merit in drawing together the information on historical films that is currently scattered across specialised and general print and online publications, this is not my prime motivation for offering *History Goes to the Movies*. I have written this book because I believe that despite the prodigious outpouring of publications on historical films, large and serious gaps in the discussion and therefore understanding remain. I hope to highlight and unpack five in this work.

The first is that relatively few publications explore the impact of technologies—particularly new technologies such as DVDs, the Internet and digital effects—on the production, promotion and reception of historical films. Second, scholars have tended to treat the study of historical films as being synonymous with the analysis of on-screen representations. In this work, I argue that there is more to historical film studies: I combine textual analysis with a study of the evidence we have for the promotion and reception of historical films. Advertisements, merchandise and viewer fan fiction are considered, for instance, as well as editing techniques and costumes. Third, few studies of actual historical film viewers exist to complement the many film and literary studies that construct 'hypothetical' viewers. Fourth, I do not hold that we can understand the claims that historical films make upon audiences if we judge them solely in terms of proximity to historical evidence, or fact and fiction, or photorealism and simulation. Historical films are also aesthetic expressions, and they can be and have been appreciated by viewers as such. Finally, I have endeavoured to unite the often quite separate efforts of film scholars, historical film scholars, historians and historiographers.

I have worked to address these five gaps above all others because I hold them to be symptoms of two fundamental—and limiting—assumptions that scholars routinely make about historical films. The first is that they are synonymous with dieresses. Films clearly cannot be understood apart from their plots, dialogue, effects, costuming, editing and so on: in short, their on-screen worlds. What I question, though, is whether their significance may be exhausted through the analysis of these on-screen features alone. Nor do I believe that historical films can be treated simply as the property of directors, film crews, commercial outfits or governments that inscribe and fix meaning. To begin to understand historical films, we must see them rather as sites of relation, agreement and even contestation among film producers, critics and scholars, promoters and viewers. In this relationship, no single group consistently emerges with the controlling hand. Theoretical studies of historical films therefore need to be complemented by historical accounts of the relationships that they secure and enhance among viewers, promoters and creators. A growing number of reception studies, such as Annette Kuhn's *Dreaming of Fred and Ginger* (2002), have offered us insight into the ways in which viewers are both drawn into, and draw upon, films to organise their experiences.[32] These studies, though, have tended to favour the experiences of British viewers before the 1960s. Moreover, they need to be drawn together with a consideration of how new technologies can be used and with the intellectual and commercial imperatives that shape film production, distribution and promotion.

Second, in routinely stressing the differences between 'history in images' and 'history in words', historical film scholars have assumed a gap between—as Hayden White put it—'historiophoty' and 'historiography'. Arguing for the recognition of film as distinct is taken to be an effective strategy for encouraging us to think of and value historical films on their own terms. However, as I will begin to argue in the next chapter, this strategy is logically unsustainable and does not guarantee that the 'seriousness' of historical film studies will be recognised. Scholars may identify more and more forms of history, and methods for studying them, but this process of identification may do little to challenge or re-articulate the deep-seated historiographical assumptions that explain their treatment as marginal forms. Arguably, the best result is a lively pocket of specialist scholarship, with specialist courses of study and specialist texts. That new specialism may not disrupt understandings of history in other areas of specialist research, teaching and publication. So, rather than arguing for words or images as *forms* of history, it is my claim that they are both history. This book is thus as much about 'history' as it is about particular historical films.

My preoccupation with the assumptions made about historical films and history is reflected in the focus and structure of this book. It is not a collection of film reviews; nor is it an appraisal of how particular historical films, or history on film in general, gets history 'wrong' or 'right'. Rather, it is a reflection on how some of the themes that currently run through historical film scholarship might be used as an entry point to prompt discussion on the features and functions of history.

In every chapter, I have opted to 'go behind the scenes' and to focus attention on the ideas and issues that give shape to the production, promotion, reception and scholarly discussion of historical films. My primary aim in doing so is to highlight judgements about how and why visual histories are made. This explains the thematic focus of the chapters and my decision to analyse a wide range of films. The question of how many films may be addressed in a single work of historical film research is important, yet largely unexplored. John Gaddis and David Christian provide an accessible route to the discussion of this question when they liken histories to maps. Maps are conventionally on smaller scales than the phenomena they represent; maps on the same scale as the phenomena they represent are not very helpful, because to find a feature, we would have to walk as far on the map as we would in the world.[33] Achieving such compression involves selection and thus the omission of particular details. But maps are also available on more than one scale, and maps of different scales serve different purposes. A map of a school or university campus, for example, includes different information to that of a map showing a suburb, or a country, or the world. Histories, like maps, can similarly be on different scales; they may be more or less detailed and can serve different purposes. The scales of histories are those of space and time: a work on historical films may range over global sites of production and consider nineteenth-century actualities as well as current productions. Scholars may also shift scales within works, moving from the analysis of one film through to global patterns of production. In practice, such shifts are unusual, and certain scales have been favoured over others: namely, the analysis of a single or a small number of sound films in a single or small number of cultural contexts. While this approach to historical film studies has highlighted important issues and ideas, others remain obscured from view.

This work seeks not to overturn the efforts of scholars who work on small numbers of sound films but to complement their efforts with a larger view. That larger view, I believe, is like taking a step backwards and being rewarded with a new perspective on familiar terrain. An additional, pragmatic reason for analysing more rather than fewer films is that there is an increased likelihood of reader accessibility. I am personally and acutely aware, for instance, of how difficult and expensive it can be to track down copies of *Ceddo*, or even to replace a well-worn VHS copy of, say, *Distant Voices, Still Lives*. I have also made a deliberate effort to include works that have attracted different audience sizes and that were produced in different cultural contexts. Every now and then, I shift scales and focus on a single work, or even a single element of a single work. Moreover, I have tried to provide plenty of opportunities for the reader to shift scales by identifying specialist resources that may be used in further research. What I have to say in each chapter is thus not a definitive and final pronouncement but the opening of a new and expanded discussion on film and history.

Two more structural features serve to distinguish this work from others in the field of historical film studies. The first is an explicit shift to historiography in each chapter, indicated by the recurring heading 'Images and words'. This should not be read as an attempt to pin historical film studies down to historiography and thus to reify the latter as an unquestioned standard for analysis. Rather, as was suggested above, these spaces will be used to explore the common, and differing, interests of historiographers and historical film scholars and to explore how the insights of each may inform the other. The experiences of both help to illuminate the question running through this work: 'what are histories and what are they for?' Second, I have not assumed that the question 'what is an historical film?' can be answered by a definition with a sharp boundary and a definitive set of necessary and sufficient criteria, or resolved in the space of a paragraph or even a chapter. On the contrary, this work opens up the concept of 'historical film'. This explains my interest in exploring not only film forms and activities that are widely accepted as 'historical' but also those deemed by scholars to be marginal or 'nearly' historical.

It is commonly assumed that films can offer viewers only an impoverished or compromised vision of history. Why? The force of this assumption, as Rosenstone has argued, derives from the lack of involvement of historians in film production and from six perceived shortcomings of 'mainstream' historical films: (1) their routine packaging of history as upbeat comedy or romance; (2) their focus on the actions of individuals to the exclusion of wider contexts; (3) their focus on emotional dimensions of phenomena at the expense of their intellectual dimensions; (4) their conflation of historical meaning with property ('props'); (5) their avoidance of multiple points of view and inconclusive or contradictory explanations of phenomena; and (6) their purportedly poor information load. Chapter 1, 'Words and images, images and words', explores these shortcomings and endorses Rosenstone's questioning of written histories as a standard for judging history making. In addition, however, I turn a critical eye on Rosenstone's and other historical film scholars' attempts to circumvent criticisms of film by separating the efforts of 'historical' filmmakers from the creators of 'faction', 'costume', 'melodrama', 'period' or 'heritage' films. I do this by noting the persistence of a metaphysics that holds one 'form' of history to be a 'solid and unproblematic' foundation against which all other expressions of history should be tested.[34] As I have already intimated and will argue in more detail, historical films and written histories are not forms of history; they are history.

History is not solely about events; it is also about the relationships between those events, the order in which they are presented and the selection of emphases. Historians and historical filmmakers are thus stylists, whether or not they like or even recognise it: they shape their works according to conventional story forms or forms of 'emplotment'. Chapter 2, 'Genre', highlights the varying forms of historical films. It opens by noting a disjunction between the interest of historical film scholars in identifying works that unambiguously sit in an 'historical' genre and that of film promoters in attracting large audiences through an appeal to multiple story forms. Noting that historical films are mixtures of story forms, I seek to explain why some combinations of story form, such as historical animations, musicals and melodramas, have been routinely neglected by scholars. This investigation highlights academic belief about the functions of historical films and leads to the conclusion that histories are not 'things' that can be clearly and transparently classified by scholars. Rather, when they work with films, scholars, like promoters, participate in discursive sites where meaning is circulated, contested and agreed. So history is not just about the relation of events but is also about the relation of various groups who hold, promote and contest the selection, connection and emphasis of events.

Films signal temporal setting in a number of different ways. Titles or a voiceover may set the scene, but even if these are missed, costumes, dialogue and physical surroundings may tell us that the filmed action does not take place in our present. Since the early days of cinema, too, filmmakers have formulated and applied conventions that shape cinematic time. In Chapter 3, 'Pasts, presents, futures', I offer an account of some of these conventions and use them to open up a discussion on what times historical films can show. Rebutting the claim that historical films are simply statements about the present, I argue for the recognition of the temporal heterogeneity of films. Through a consideration of elements such as editing techniques and costume, make-up and props, I note how various time paths open up, diverge and regroup but never in an entirely seamless way. The time paths of historical films, I conclude, fragment 'history' into histories, and foster awareness of their sometimes coalescing, sometimes competing forms and functions.

One of the functions most often connected with historical films is that of establishing, affirming or challenging national identity. In Chapter 4, 'Identity', I note how the transnational dimensions of historical film production, promotion, reception and scholarship make them ill-suited to be lenses for national analysis. Drawing on historical reception studies, I also highlight that other 'imagined' communities, such as family, may occupy more of the attention of film audiences. Moreover, when we study the comments of viewers, we discover that 'identity' is not simply an outcome—the connection of a viewer to a community—but the process whereby that happens. Identification with others is possible in both an intellectual and emotional sense, I argue, because it involves conceptual and not numerical, spatial or temporal identity. Finally, I make it clear that identity is a two-way process, involving both being 'drawn into' film and 'drawing upon' film. Thus films may be historical in two senses: diegeses may draw viewers into an exploration of past activities and be drawn into viewers' lives to delineate and secure understandings of their past.

What kinds of film draw viewers in? One of the terms most commonly used to endorse historical films is 'realistic': the more 'realistic' a picture, the better we assume it to be. What do filmmakers, historians, reviewers and viewers mean by this term, however? Are 'realistic' films the ones that are historical in the double sense mentioned above? The aim of Chapter 5, 'Reality', is to unpack the meaning of 'realism'. I begin by noting the purported division between Jean Baudrillard's vision of films as 'hyperreal' (presenting a world that appears more legitimate, more believable and more valuable than the real) and Jean-Luc Godard and Walter Benjamin's claim that cinema is organised by reality anterior to our world, 'the dream of the nineteenth century'. Looking more closely, I note that these three theorists share a vision of viewers as vulnerable to the illusionary effects that cinema presents, and I argue against it by noting first that the 'reality' presented by films is far from seamless, and second that, as André Bazin holds, realism can never be found apart from viewer constructions of it. Realism is thus a matter of convention:

for example, an historical musical may be considered 'realistic' in some contexts but not in others. This does not mean, though, that 'anything goes', for, as I conclude, the making and shaping of histories is formed by agreed ways of viewing the past.

What then are some of the conventions that organise 'realistic' visual histories? How do some visual histories come to be seen as more realistic than others? In Chapter 6, 'Documentary', I search for the answer to these two questions by examining the case of 'documentary'. 'Documentary' may elicit trust as having a stronger link to the past, but a study of the forms of historical documentaries endorses that it is, as John Grierson puts it, a 'creative treatment of actuality'. Like many other scholars, I start my exploration of historical documentary by applying Bill Nichol's typology of poetic, expository, observational, participatory, reflexive and performative forms and Carl Plantinga's typology of formal, open and poetic 'voices'. In the process of doing so, though, I highlight and question the conventional connection of various filmic techniques with a valued outcome of viewer reflexivity. Certain forms of film may in fact foster particular viewer outcomes, but in the absence of historical studies, we cannot be sure that this is the case. Finally, I argue that perceptions of increasingly permeable boundaries between documentary and fiction are problematic because they also rest on a slight body of historical evidence and philosophical argument.

At a number of points in this book, we will see exposed the persistent treatment of viewers as passive, politically disengaged and vulnerable to filmmakers' effects. This understanding comes under direct scrutiny in Chapter 7, which has as its focus the concept of propaganda. The topic of propaganda in historical film studies is conventionally limited to explorations of state or state-sponsored articulations of national community during times of war and social upheaval, for example in Nazi Germany or the Soviet Union. Furthermore, its presence is generally confirmed through the analysis of filmmakers' intentions, or certain methods or techniques, or kinds of content, or viewer behaviour after viewing. None of these in isolation, I make clear, offers a necessary and sufficient criterion for the concept. Furthermore, I note disagreements about the content and methods thought to be synonymous with propaganda. This leads me to note, and offer a critical response to, the recent expansion in applications of the term to all mass communication practices. This expansion, we will discover, rests upon the characterisation of viewers as the passive or willing recipients of what they see. Looking again to historical evidence, I find examples of informed and critical 'connoisseur' viewers who confound that view through their delight in, and wonder at, the art of visual histories.

The vision of viewers as passive consumers is also called into question in Chapter 8, 'Selling history'. In this chapter, our exploration of historical films broadens to encompass merchandise, tie-in products and viewer activities such as costume creation and the composition of fan fiction. Questioning the reductive treatment of viewer collectors as engaged in a form of nostalgic consumerism, I highlight how many adopt and adapt film materials to their own ends and moderate their own, filmmakers' and other viewers' activities in accordance with the concepts of 'canon' and 'historical canon'. Furthermore, it is clear from an analysis of their activities that 'canon' does not simply mean conformity with accounts that are taken to be 'true' but also indicates that a work has consistent and valued literary and aesthetic qualities. To balance this picture of viewer agents, however, I note how film companies have worked within fan networks to realise commercial imperatives. The picture of historical films which thus emerges at the end of this chapter is that of 'an uneasy dance' in which the hopes and aims of filmmakers, promoters, distributors and scholars 'chafe uncomfortably against fans' resourcefulness'.[35]

In the final part of this book, the uneasy dance of the makers, promoters and viewers of films becomes the cornerstone for my definition of historical films. I also reiterate my argument for the study of historical films on the grounds that they provide an accessible route to key historiographical questions and because they highlight that history does not belong simply to academics. Increasingly, historians are looking to films as evidence of the past. Also offered in the conclusion are some of the key problems and benefits of that shift. Problems considered include past and present judgements about preservation value, material degeneration and accessibility. On the positive side, I argue that evidence means more than dieges. This opens the way for my critical response to Hayden White's call for 'historiophoty', a last act in which I reassert the major theme of this work: that films are not a form of history but are history.

Recommended resources

American Historical Review, 1991, vol. 96(4), and every October issue thereafter includes a film review section.

Cannadine, D. (ed.), *History and the Media*, Basingstoke: Palgrave Macmillan, 2004.

Carnes, M. (ed.), *Past Imperfect: History According to the Movies*, New York: Henry Holt, 1995.

Cineaste, 1971, vol. 1–

Cinema Journal, 1961, vol. 1–

Ferro, M., *Cinema and History*, trans. N. Greene, Detroit: Wayne State University Press, 1988.

Film and History, 1971, vol. 1–

Film Quarterly, 1958, vol. 1–

Grindon, L., *Shadows on the Past: Studies in the Historical Film*, Philadelphia: Temple University Press, 1994.

Hamilton, P. and Ashton, P., 'At home with the past: initial findings from the survey', *Australian Cultural History*, 2003, no. 23, pp. 5–30.

Landy, M. (ed.), *The Historical Film: History and Memory in Media*, New Brunswick, NJ: Rutgers University Press, 2001.

Landy, M., *Cinematic Uses of the Past*, Minneapolis: University of Minnesota Press, 1996.

O'Connor, J.E. (ed.), *Image as Artefact: The Historical Analysis of Film and Television*, Malabar, Fla: Krieger, 1990.

Rosen, P., *Change Mummified: Cinema, Historicity, Theory*, Minneapolis: University of Minnesota Press, 2001.

Rosenstone, R., *Revisioning History: Film and the Construction of a New Past*, Princeton, NJ: Princeton University Press, 1995.

Rosenstone, R., *Visions of the Past: The Challenge of Film to Our Understanding of History*, Cambridge, Mass.: Harvard University Press, 1995.

Rosenzweig, R. and Thelen, D., *The Presence of the Past: Popular Uses of History in American Life*, New York: Columbia University Press, 1998.

Sanello, F., *Reel vs Real: How Hollywood Turns Fact into Fiction*, Lanham, Md: Taylor Trade, 2003.

Screening the Past, no. 1, 1997, available online at http://www.latrobe.edu.au/screening the past

Shusterman, R., 'Popular art', in D. Cooper (ed.), *A Companion to Aesthetics*, Oxford: Blackwell, 1990.

Sorlin, P., *The Film in History*, Oxford: Blackwell, 1980.

Toplin, B., *History by Hollywood: The Use and Abuse of the American Past*, Urbana: University of Illinois Press, 1996.

Toplin, B., *Reel History: In Defence of Hollywood*, Lawrence: Kansas University Press, 2002.

Warren-Findley, J., 'History in new worlds: surveys and results in the United States and Australia', *Australian Cultural History*, 2003, no. 23, pp. 43–52.

Notes

1 M. Poe, 'letter to the editor', *Perspectives*, available online at http://www.theaha.org/perspectives/waves/1999/9905/9905let1.cfm

2 R. Rosenzweig and D. Thelen, *The Presence of the Past: Popular Uses of History in American Life*, New York: Columbia University Press, 1998.

3 P. Ashton and P. Hamilton, 'At home with the past: background and initial findings from the national survey', *Australian Cultural History*, 2003, no. 23, pp. 5–30. See also J. Warren-Findley, 'History in new worlds: surveys and results in the United States and Australia', *Australian Cultural History*, 2003, no. 23, pp. 43–52.

4 P. Ashton and P. Hamilton, 'At home with the past', p. 13.

5 R. Rosenzweig and D. Thelen, *The Presence of the Past*, p. 189.

6 N. Carroll, 'The ontology of mass art', *The Journal of Aesthetics and Art Criticism*, 1997, vol. 55(1), p. 190.

7 N. Frye, *A Natural Perspective: The Development of Shakespearean Comedy and Romance*, New York: Harcourt, Brace and World, 1965, p. 3.

8 M. Horkheimer and T. Adorno, *The Dialectic of Enlightenment*, New York: Continuum, 1986, p. 137.

9 See, for example, J. Fiske, *Television Culture*, London: Routledge & Kegan Paul, 1987.

10 R. Shusterman, 'Popular art', in D. Cooper (ed.), *A Companion to Aesthetics*, Oxford: Blackwell, 1992, p. 338.

11 The concepts of 'diegesis' and 'mimesis' were first used by Plato to denote a distinction between 'showing' and 'telling'. Christian Metz and Gérard Genette have questioned that distinction and introduced the term 'diegesis' to film theory to denote 'telling by showing'. See C. Metz, *Film Language: A Semiotics of the Cinema*, trans. M. Taylor, New York: Oxford University Press, 1974, pp. 97–8; and

G. Genette, *Narrative Discourse: An Essay in Method*, trans. J.E. Lewin, Ithaca, NJ: Cornell University Press, 1980, pp. 162–9.

12 R.G. Collingwood, *An Essay on Metaphysics*, rev. edn, ed. R. Martin, Oxford: Oxford University Press, 1998, p. 44.

13 P. Sorlin, *The Film in History*, Oxford: Blackwell, 1980, p. 80.

14 M. Ferro, *Cinema and History*, trans. N. Greene, Detroit: Wayne State University Press, 1988, p. 161.

15 P.-A. Lee, 'Teaching film and television as interpreters of history', in J.E. O'Connor (ed.), *Image as Artefact: The Historical Analysis of Film and Television*, Malabar, Fla: Krieger, 1990, p. 96.

16 *Screening the Past*, no. 1, 1997, available online at http://www.latrobe.edu.au/screening the past

17 R.J. Raack, 'Historiography as cinematography: a prolegomenon to film work for historians', *Journal of Contemporary History*, 1983, vol. 18(3), p. 418; and I.C. Jarvie, 'Seeing through movies', *Philosophy of the Social Sciences*, 1978, vol. 8(4), p. 378.

18 B. Abrash and J. Sternberg (eds), *Historians and Filmmakers: Toward Collaboration*, New York: Institute for Research in History, 1983.

19 R. Rosenstone, 'History in images/history in words: reflections on the possibility of really putting history into film', *American Historical Review*, 1988, vol. 93(5), pp. 1173–85.

20 D. Herlihy, 'Am I a camera? Other reflections on film and history', *American Historical Review*, 1988, vol. 93(5), pp. 1186–92; J.E. O'Connor, 'History in images/history in words: reflections on the importance of film and television study for an understanding of the past', *American Historical Review*, 1988, vol. 93(5), pp. 1200–9; and R.B. Toplin, 'The filmmaker as historian', *American Historical Review*, 1988, vol. 93(5), pp. 1210–27.

21 H. White, 'Historiography and historiophoty', *American Historical Review*, 1988, vol. 93(5), pp. 1193–9.

22 R. Rosenstone, *Visions of the Past: The Challenge of Film to Our Idea of History*, Cambridge, Mass.: Harvard University Press, 1995; R. Rosenstone (ed.), *Revisioning History: Film and the Construction of a New Past*, Princeton, NJ: Princeton University Press, 1995; and R. Rosenstone, 'The future of the past: film and the beginnings of postmodern history', in V. Sobchack (ed.), *The Persistence of History: Cinema, Television, and the Modern Event*, London: Routledge, 1996, pp. 205–15.

23 M. Landy, *Cinematic Uses of the Past*, Minneapolis: University of Minnesota Press, 1996. See also M. Landy, 'Introduction', in *The Historical Film: History and Memory in Media*, New Brunswick, NJ: Rutgers University Press, 2001, pp. 1–11.

24 R.B. Toplin, *Reel History: In Defence of Hollywood*, Lawrence: University of Kansas Press, 2002, p. 1.

25 F. Sanello, *Reel v. Real: How Hollywood Turns Faction into Fiction*, Lanham, Md: Taylor Trade, 2003; L. Grindon, *Shadows on the Past: Studies in the Historical Film*, Philadelphia: Temple University Press, 1994; and D. Cartmell, I.Q. Hunter and I. Whelehan (eds), *Retrovisions: Reinventing the Past in Fiction and Film*, London: Pluto Press, 2001.

26 P. Rosen, *Change Mummified: Cinema, Historicity, Theory*, Minneapolis: University of Minnesota Press, 2001.

27 J. Solomon, *The Ancient World in the Cinema*, New Haven, Conn.: Yale University Press, 2001; N.Z. Davis, *Slaves on Screen: Film and Historical Vision*, Cambridge, Mass.: Harvard University Press, 2000; B. Taves, *The Romance of Adventure: The Genre of Historical Action Movies*, Jackson: University Press of Mississippi, 1993; G. Barefoot, *Gaslight Melodrama: From Victorian London to 1940s Hollywood*, London: Continuum, 2001; and G. Custen, *Bio/Pics: How Hollywood Constructed Public History*, New Brunswick, NJ: Rutgers University Press, 1992.

28 C.S. Tashiro, *Pretty Pictures: Production Design and the History Film*, Austin: University of Texas Press, 1998.

29 See, for example, Y. Loshitzsky (ed.), *Spielberg's Holocaust*, Bloomington: Indiana University Press, 1997; I. Avisar, *Screening the Holocaust: Cinema's Images of the Unimaginable*, Bloomington: Indiana University Press, 1988; A. Insdorf, *Indelible Shadows: Film and the Holocaust*, Cambridge: Cambridge University Press, 1989; M. Anderegg, *Inventing Vietnam: The War in Film and Television*, Philadelphia: Temple University Press, 1991; J. Basinger, *The World War II Combat Film*, New York: Columbia University Press, 1986; J. Chamber and D. Culbert, *World War II, Film and History*, New York: Oxford University Press, 1996; J.M. Devine, *Vietnam at 24 Frames a Second*, Austin: University of Texas Press, 1999; L. Dittmar and G. Michaud, *From Hanoi to Hollywood: The Vietnam War in American Film*, New Brunswick, NJ: Rutgers University Press, 1990; and T.P. Doherty, *Projections of War: Hollywood, American Culture and World War II*, New York: Columbia University Press, 1999.

30 A. Kaes, *From* Hitler *to* Heimat: *The Return of History as Film*, Cambridge, Mass.: Harvard University Press, 1989; and S. Harper, *Picturing the Past: The Rise and Fall of the British Costume Film*, London: British Film Institute, 1994.

31 M. Carnes (ed.), *Past Imperfect: History According to the Movies*, New York: Henry Holt, 1995.

32 A. Kuhn, *Dreaming of Fred and Ginger: Cinema and Cultural Memory*, Washington Square, NY: New York University Press, 2002.

33 J.L. Gaddis, *The Landscape of History: How Historians Map the Past*, Oxford: Oxford University Press, 2002, p. 32; and D. Christian, 'Scales', in M. Hughes-Warrington (ed.), *Palgrave Advances in World Histories*, Basingstoke: Palgrave Macmillan, 2005, pp. 64–89.

34 R. Rosenstone, *Visions of the Past*, p. 49.

35 S. Murray, ' "Celebrating the story the way it is": cultural studies, corporate media and the contested utility of fandom', *Continuum: Journal of Media and Cultural Studies*, 2004, vol. 18(1), p. 9.

1 Words and images, images and words

Let's be blunt and admit it: historical films trouble and disturb professional historians.

Robert Rosenstone, *Visions of the Past*, 1995, p. 45

I think many historians come at filmmakers with an attitude and with hostility. It's as though history is their territory, and we don't belong.

Oliver Stone, 'Past imperfect', *Cineaste* 1996, p. 33

It seems that every historian has an opinion about historical films. Over the last quarter of a century, their views have spilled out over the pages of the specialised journals *Historical Journal of Film, Radio and Television*, *Screening the Past* and *Film and History* and into more general professional journals, newspapers, books, online forums and television discussions. These opinions are often far from favourable, if Robert Rosenstone and Oliver Stone are to be believed. Historians and historical filmmakers appear to be antagonists, with the former protecting history with the fervour and solemnity of 'chief priests in ancient Egypt protecting the sacred innards' and the latter struggling to produce works that are both engaging and economically viable.[1] The starting point for our investigation into history on film will be this apparent antagonism. Unpacking the means by which Rosenstone and Stone arrived at their view of historians and filmmakers, we will be led towards the common—and as I will argue, limited—concepts that are used to describe the relationship between history and film. This will set the scene for an expanded vision of history on film to be articulated in the chapters that follow.

The problem begins, Rosenstone argues, with the distance between historians and historical film production. Few historians have any direct involvement in, let alone control over, historical filmmaking. Few historical filmmakers have any professional training in history, and if historians are consulted, it is only late in the production process. They are called upon after a workable script has emerged and often even after filming has begun. Conversely, few historians have any training in visual production. Thus historians

appear to sit both literally and metaphorically on the edges of production.
John Sayles, director of *Matewan* (1987), admitted as much when he wrote:

> I probably use historians the way most directors use them: I tend to use
> people who are well versed in historical details, very specifically in the
> details, but not in the big picture. You ring people up and ask whether
> there were phone booths in 1920.[2]

This resistance towards using historians as anything more than fact checkers,
he believes, springs from the fear that they will want the work changed in a
way that will lessen its box office appeal. Money rules historical filmmaking,
leading to the view that history itself is a 'story bin to be plundered' and a
pliable commodity: 'if the test audience doesn't like the way the Civil War
came out, maybe the studio will release another version for Alabama'. In
short, historical responsibility and the movie industry are incompatible.[3]
From the perspective of a consultant like Bill Gammage, the picture of historians contributing late and little to film production also appears to be
confirmed. As he writes of his experience as a consultant in *Gallipoli* (1981):

> what I did and what I was used for varied greatly according to the person
> or the department that was talking to me. Peter Weir [the director], who
> was responsible for having me work on the film, spoke to me often. So
> did some of the departments. The Art department in particular, and the
> Special Effects department, for example, asked many and detailed ques-
> tions, some of which I could answer and some of which I couldn't. Then
> there were a group of departments in the middle, such as Wardrobe,
> which tended to ask me things when they couldn't think of an answer for
> themselves. . . . Finally there were some departments, which perhaps it
> would be best not to name, which considered me in the road and treated
> me as if I were in the road. So my contribution varied, from on rare
> occasions stopping filming, to being flat out getting a lift out to the set.[4]

Finally, Julie Jeffrey has noted that the chief value of historical consultants
may lie in their use as promotional 'window dressing': connecting a well-
known historian with a film may lend the latter an air of authenticity and
authority. This, she reports, was Howard Jones's impression of his role in the
making of *Amistad* (1997).[5]

Adding up all of these examples, we might have good cause to be sceptical
about the possibility of historians and filmmakers ever working together.
Nevertheless, these reflections might be the result of practical constraints
rather than inherent problems with the idea of putting history on film. What
if filmmakers and historians worked in partnership before shooting began
and if filmmakers were open to the 'big picture' changes of the historian?
This need not remain a hypothetical question, for there are a few examples
where historians have played a significant part in the shaping of a production.

An obvious case that springs to mind is that of Natalie Zemon Davis, who helped to bring the remarkable story of Martin Guerre to the big screen. Martin Guerre was a sixteenth-century French peasant who left his village for eight years and returned to find that another man—Arnaud du Tilh—had impersonated him and was living with his wife (Bertrande de Rols). When Davis first read Jean de Coras' 1572 account of the case, she thought that it would make a good film.[6] 'Rarely', she wrote later, 'does a historian find so perfect a narrative structure in the events of the past or one with such dramatic popular appeal'. Two French filmmakers, Daniel Vigne and Jean Claude Carrière, had the same idea, and although opinion differs about whether they sought out Davis or the other way around, by 1980 she had become a consultant to *Le Retour de Martin Guerre*. Davis enjoyed working on the film but soon realised that it 'posed the problem of invention to the historian as surely as it was posed to the wife of Martin Guerre', because aspects of the story were compressed, altered or even left out. Furthermore, she wondered if film was capable of handling and conveying 'the uncertainties, the "perhapses," the "may-have-beens," to which the historian has recourse when the evidence is inadequate or perplexing'.[7] Davis' interest in the uncertainties of the Guerre case led her to write her best-known book, *The Return of Martin Guerre* (1983), and a number of papers on the problem of invention in historical films. Davis' dissatisfaction with perhaps one of the most optimal of filmmaker/historian partnerships is instructive. It suggests that there is something limited about film itself rather than just the arrangements for a particular film. In this next section, we will draw out just how it is that film falls short as a medium for history.

Six filmic sins?

Davis' comments suggest a shortcoming in film as a medium for communicating history as well as in the practical arrangements that see historians and filmmakers drawn together. Rosenstone has expanded on those comments, providing a more systematic appraisal of the six problematic features of 'mainstream' historical films. Each of these problems is worthy of examination, for they open up wider historiographical issues. The first problem with mainstream films is that they package history as romance or comedy, in which individuals escape from, or in the case of the latter triumph over, a particular situation or problem.[8] No matter how apparently tragic the setting, some form of positive outcome ensues. So while, for example, Captain Miller (Tom Hanks) in *Saving Private Ryan* (1998), Guido (Roberto Benigni) in *La Vita è bella* (*Life is Beautiful*, 1997), Jenny (Robin Wright) in *Forrest Gump* (1994) and Donnie (Jake Gyllenhaal) in *Donnie Darko* (2001) die, we are left with the impression that it has been for the good: the liberation of Europe; the end of the Holocaust; the rearing of a child by a good man; and the setting of an increasingly violent parallel world to rights. Even as a frozen Jack (Leonardo di Caprio) is prised off the door by Rose (Kate Winslet) in *Titanic*, we know, as Celine Dion tells us, that 'their love will go on'. However, not all films, Rosenstone concedes, fit this template, as with the downbeat messages of *Radio Bikini* (1987) and *JFK* (1991). And Rosenstone's point loses further ground when we note that it is not based on any substantial historical survey but on anecdotal impression. To date, no extensive analysis has been undertaken to test whether comedy and romance do dominate filmic offerings. We are not in any position to say whether romance and comedy dominate film offerings in all cultural contexts or in some more than others, or whether the valuation of comic and romantic plots has waxed and waned over time. Equally importantly, we are unable to judge whether romantic and comedic plots are more prevalent in historical films than in other forms of history making. Who is to say that the producers of written histories, for example, might not be equally enthralled by romance and comedy?

Second, mainstream film presents history as the story of individuals. Men and women are singled out for attention, and that focus, Rosenstone argues, 'becomes a way of avoiding the often difficult or insoluble social problems pointed out by the film'.[9] This point is echoed in the surveys by Brent Toplin, Marcia Landy and David Cannadine.[10] Taking a more specific example, a number of critics have seen in the 'band of brothers' focus of recent US combat films an evasion of uncomfortable political and social questions such as why the USA was engaged in Vietnam. This particular issue will occupy more of our attention in Chapter 4. Additionally, it might be argued that the use of an individual's experiences to represent those of a wider group—as with Molly and Daisy's struggles in *Rabbit-Proof Fence* (2002) standing for the wider struggles of Aboriginal people in Australia in the 1930s—is problematic. Films that track the actions of large groups of unnamed individuals, like segments of Sergei Eisenstein's *Stachka* (*Strike*, 1925), *Bronenosets Potemkin* (*Battleship Potemkin*, 1925), *Oktiabr* (*October*, 1927) and *Staroye i Novoye* (*The General Line*, 1929) certainly appear to be more unusual. Once again, however, we are able to note the absence of historical studies of the representations offered in historical films. Might print historians be equally enamoured of individuals? It is worth taking stock of David Christian's observation that print historians conventionally work with a range of experiences, from those of individuals to those of national communities. While this may appear to be a broad spectrum, the works of world historians show us that analyses at much larger spatial and temporal scales are possible.[11] At the other end of the spectrum, it is also possible to study a fragment of an individual's 'self' or even of their body. Louis Althusser, like a number of postmodern thinkers, argues that the human self is nothing more than an ideological, imaginary assemblage that society fosters to elicit subjection to the *status quo*.[12] He writes:

> Since Copernicus, we have known that the earth is not the 'centre' of the universe. Since Marx, we have known that the human subject, the economic, political or philosophical ego is not the 'centre' of history—and

even . . . that history has no 'centre' but possesses a structure which has no necessary 'centre' except in ideological misrepresentation.[13]

Human-centred history is at an end for Foucault too: it, and the notion of the creative self that it reifies, can be erased 'like a face drawn in sand at the edge of the sea'.[14] Similarly for Barthes, the individual 'self' is no more than a myth that has become so much a part of our cultural furniture that it has been 'naturalised'.[15] So why are historians so interested in the actions of named individuals that are taken to be single 'selves'? Are they inherently suited to historical analysis? Or are they a 'naturalised' myth? Moreover, anecdotal evidence suggests that historians, like filmmakers, are also prone to using individuals to represent the experiences of a wider group. Are we any more justified in extrapolating from the experiences of individuals in written microhistories such as *The Return of Martin Guerre, Montaillou* or *The Cheese and the Worms* than we are from films?[16]

   Third, film often highlights the emotional dimensions of human experiences. As Rosenstone writes, film

> uses the closeup of the human face, the quick juxtaposition of disparate images, the power of music and sound effect—to heighten and intensify the feelings of the audience. (Written history is, of course, not devoid of emotion, but usually it points to emotion rather than inviting us to experience it. A writer has to be a very good writer to make us feel some emotion while the poorest of filmmakers can easily touch our feelings.)[17]

Rosenstone's comments appear to present a neutral stance on the role of the emotions in history making. Closer inspection, though, highlights his characterisation of written history as 'usually' associated with the distanced consideration of the emotional experiences of historical agents. Furthermore, in asking 'To what extent do we wish emotion to become an historical category?' he suggests that it sits outside historical analysis and that 'we' may sit in judgement on its proposed entry. In reply, we may ask, have the emotions ever been absent from historical analysis? And what might be wrong with our feelings being engaged when we study the past? I do not want to pre-empt the discussion on the role of the emotions in history making that is set out in Chapter 4. Here it will suffice to note that Rosenstone is not alone in his stance, for Marcia Landy, Charles Tashiro and Sue Harper—to take just three examples—all see emotional engagement as sitting outside historical filmmaking.[18]

   Fourth, film is prone to what Rosenstone calls 'false historicity' and Mark Neely 'accuracy in antiques'.[19] This is the idea that the 'look' of the past—as presented through costumes, make-up, property ('props') and sets—takes precedence over any consideration of the ideas, beliefs and actions of historical agents. Or, as Rosenstone puts it: 'as long as you get the look right, you may freely invent characters and incidents and do whatever you want to the past to make it more interesting'.[20] On this view, the past becomes a warehouse that is plundered for aesthetic rather than historiographical reasons, and history making is collapsed into the activity of getting the details right. This challenge opens up a range of historiographical questions. Sets may brim to overflowing with objects, as with the many props in Marcus Aurelius' tent in *Gladiator* (2000) that announce its Roman setting but may consequently also present what Davis calls a 'static' view of the past. Everyday life—past and present—is characterised by a mixture of the new and the fashionable, the familiar and the worn, the dated and the hand-me-down. Yet, as Davis argues, historical films often narrow down the range of objects used to the new, so that there is little ambiguity about temporal setting. Furthermore, she has noted the tendency for paintings to be used by film designers as mimetic records of the past, rather than representations, and for projects to use actual locations and their local inhabitants because they are thought to lend film legitimacy. An example she notes is that of Ermanno Olmi, director of *L'albero degli zoccoli* (*Tree of Wooden Clogs*, 1978), who prefers

> a relationship with reality, not reconstructed in a studio. . . . The real tree is continually creative; the artificial tree isn't. . . . Thus with the actor. Maybe there exists an extraordinary actor, but really, I have always felt in them a bit of cardboard in respect to the great palpitating authenticity of the real character. . . . In a film about peasants I choose the actors from the peasant world. . . . [They] bring to the film a weight, really a constitution of truth that, provoked by the situations in which the characters find themselves, creates . . . vibrations so right, so real, and therefore not repeatable.[21]

None of these things, Davis and Rosenstone are clear, provides viewers with an 'authentic' historical film. Everyday life is characterised by a variety of objects that gain historical meaning only in connection with their relationship with people. History, put bluntly, is not a table, but a table that was built and used by people, a table that can perhaps tell us something about how people understood space, time, the body and social relations. Furthermore, it is not clear that the table—or any prop—is necessary in historical filmmaking, as the example of *Dogville* (2003) demonstrates. Made on a soundstage with spaces designated through chalk markings, *Dogville* shows us that there is more to history than its 'look'—if indeed any film can be characterised by a seamless 'patina' or look, as we will question later—and that not all historical filmmakers are gripped by 'accuracy in antiques'.

Fifth, mainstream film is characterised as offering a closed, completed and simple past. Davis' primary doubt about historical film, we recall from above, was about its ability to handle and convey 'the uncertainties', the 'perhapses', the 'may-have-beens' that historians use when evidence is lacking, inconclusive or contradictory. Numerous other historical film scholars have echoed Davis' claim. Mark Carnes, for one, has complained that

Hollywood history is different. It fills irritating gaps in the historical record and polishes dulling ambiguities and complexities. The final product gleams, and it sears the imagination. . . . Hollywood history sparkles because it is so morally unambiguous, so devoid of tedious complexity, so *perfect*.[22]

Film achieves this by constructing history as a linear story with a clear beginning, crisis point and romantic or comedic resolution. Multiple points of view and argument are winnowed down so that audiences are not 'alienated'. Even in documentary, differences of opinion among participants, narrators or contributing 'experts' are controlled within a prescribed range or even edited out. As Michelle Arrow has noted, visual history is assumed to work best when it offers a limited range of characters, a driving issue and a resolution of one kind or another.[23] While filmic history may, as in the *The Cat's Meow* (2001), announce that history is most often told in multiple whispers, in practice it presents the past as a single story. Multiple viewpoints are not unheard of, but they are often managed by being presented as relatively discrete mini-stories that are nested within a large and ultimately resolved narrative. Such is the case in *Courage Under Fire* (1996), where initially conflicting accounts of the actions of Captain Karen Walden give way to a single favourable one when vested interests and corruption are exposed. However, not all filmic histories are so tidy. The unreliable narrators of the multi-perspective films *Rashomon* (1950) and *Ying Xiong* (*Hero*, 2002) and the historiographically provocative *Memento* (2000) and *The Life and Death of Peter Sellers* (2004) give us good reason to doubt the certainty of anything we see. Moreover, documentaries like *The Trouble with Merle* (2002) foreground the complex, persuasive, strongly held and often irreconcilable beliefs of historical agents and history makers. Nevertheless, commentators see filmic history as nearly always offering audiences a view of history that is more simplistic than the findings of print historians. Again, this assumption is yet to be tested, and tested against print and filmic histories. One of Oliver Stone's major complaints against historians was that they demanded a tidier story than the one he offered in *JFK*.[24] Is this complaint, like that against filmic histories, an assumption rather than a tested claim?

Sixth, mainstream film is perceived as offering, as Ian Jarvie puts it, a 'poor information load'.[25] This is not simply Brent Toplin's point that film scripts fill somewhere between ten and twenty book pages, whereas print histories are normally over two hundred pages long and come complete with bibliographies and sometimes extensive footnotes.[26] Jarvie's point is rather that film cannot teach us anything new about the past. This view rests on two assumptions. The first is that professional producers of written histories— and for 'professional' here we may read academic—are, in Simon Schama's terms, 'hewers at the rockface of the archives'.[27] They are on the cutting edge of historical research, and if we are lucky, their discoveries will filter through to film production. Historical film lags behind breakthrough knowledge, and thus if we want to be up to date in our understanding of the past we should concentrate on the efforts of professional historians.

The second assumption is that film is characterised by the constant recycling of images, or as Jacques Derrida puts it, 'a textual labyrinth panelled with mirrors'.[28] This assumption appears to be supported by three anecdotal observations. To begin, the choice of topics in historical films appears to be quite conservative, with a small number of historical agents, events and phenomena dominating representations. The online movie database www.imdb.com, for instance, lists over a hundred film productions on the life of Adolf Hitler alone. Broaden the search to include the wider concepts of the Third Reich, the Holocaust and the Second World War and the total quickly leaps into the tens of thousands. Indeed, so strong is the perception of visual history as being dominated by representations of the Second World War that it is blamed for high school graduates' apparent lack of knowledge and interest in other historical phenomena.[29] Similarly, it has fostered the satirical treatment of the History Channel as 'The Hitler Channel' in web and television comedy.[30] Yet countless other historical agents, events and phenomena have never been represented on film. This is not simply due to a lack of archival footage or stills—which are often thought to be essential elements in documentary—because if that were the case, then no films could be made on events that happened over two hundred years ago. Furthermore, films made without stills or archival footage—most feature films and documentaries like Claude Lanzmann's *Shoah* (1985)—would be considered a fiction. This point will be discussed in more detail in Chapters 5 and 6. For the present, it will suffice to note that the selection of topics is not due solely to the availability of visual evidence.

A related anecdotal observation is that filmmakers do literally recycle images. It is possible to watch multiple documentaries on the Second World War, to continue with our example, and see the same material used over and over again. Similarly—and this is our final observation—in feature films we may see the same 'icons', as Roland Barthes called them, used time and time again to signify a particular historical setting. So, for example, yellow cloth stars serve as shorthand for a Holocaust setting. As a number of the students I have taught admit, these icons can play an important role in judging whether a film is credible and even 'realistic'. A film that departs from conventional iconic representations is likely to be judged unconvincing. How iconic objects come to signify contexts—even if there are no historical grounds for their usage—is as complex a matter as trying to work out why they are used. The suspicion of some film theorists is that their familiarity reassures and stupefies viewers, rendering them uncritical consumers. Who would pay to see an historical film, it is argued, which presents you with a setting and props that are almost entirely unfamiliar? Who would gain satisfaction from such an experience? One of the primary aims of this book is to challenge the assumption that the answer to this question is a self-evident 'no one'. In Chapter 7, I hope to show that using the same body of visual evidence and icons does not guarantee uniformity either of representation or of audience reception. Importantly, too, I want to stress that my account, like that of Rosenstone, currently rests at the level of anecdote. It remains to be established in historical and cultural studies whether historical film is equivalent to a maze of mirrors.

Words and images

Underpinning the six characterisations of mainstream film listed above is the more or less explicit comparison of filmic histories with written histories. This comparative relation is hierarchical: to written history are attributed the positive qualities of rigour and access to true meaning. Film is given second-ary, derivative status: its meaning is opaque, mediated and open to perver-sion. It 'rarely beats a good book' and is with few exceptions 'execrable'.[31] Film is not a locus of analysis but a redirection towards the analysis of written history. The creators of written histories therefore claim to have the most intimate ties with meaning, and to connect with that meaning film must refer back through written histories. This relation may be represented thus:

historical meaning ← written history ← filmic history

This arrangement is problematic, as Rosenstone has argued, because it rests upon the unquestioned positioning of written history as a solid foundation for history *per se*.[32] Rosenstone's comments reflect the complaints of literary critics about 'graphocentrism', or the privileging of written text over other forms of expression. For Marshall McLuhan, for instance, print 'is a trans-forming and metamorphosing drug that has the power of imposing its assumptions upon every level of consciousness'.[33] Similarly, Walter Ong and Roy Harris have argued that text has become such a 'naturalised' part of our lives that it is hard to think of other ways of expressing ourselves.[34]

In the hierarchical arrangement of written and filmic histories, Derrida's challenges to the concepts of 'metaphysics' and 'logocentrism' appear perti-nent. Metaphysics and logocentrism describe the desire to identify origins, fix points of reference or certify truths. They are

> the enterprise of returning 'strategically', 'ideally', to an origin or to a priority thought to be simple, intact, normal, pure, standard, self-identical, in order then to think in terms of derivation, complication, deterioration, accident, etc. All metaphysicians, from Plato to Rousseau, Descartes to Husserl, have proceeded in this way, conceiving good to be before evil, the positive before the negative, the pure before the impure, the simple before the complex, the essential before the accidental, the imitated before the imitation, etc. And this is not just one metaphysical gesture among others, it is the metaphysical exigency, that which has been the most constant, most profound and most potent.[35]

Consistent with the search for origins, metaphysicians establish hierarchies, relations of domination and subordination and dualisms.[36] In this frame-work, it is in the name of *logos* or truth that the practices of filmic histor-ies are judged, proscribed or prescribed.[37] However, what Derrida seeks to question is whether any mode of representation—books or images—refers to some real meaning external to language, whether it be a transcendental truth or human subjectivity. At best, texts bear the traces of and con-stantly refer to other texts in a parodic circle. Thus written histories are as much 'a textual labyrinth panelled with mirrors' as are filmic histories.[38] Derrida's radical vision sees the hierarchy of written and filmic histories flattened out. Neither are *forms* or *guises* of truth telling but merely language games.

Challenges to the hierarchical arrangement of written and filmic histories also run through appraisals of history and film by a number of scholars. Simon Schama, for one, has put the 'mistake that print is deep, images are shallow; that print actively argues and images passively illustrate' down to 'philistinism' born in the absence of visual education.[39] Yet even as he and other scholars try to forge a new understanding of history, they remain more or less in the sway of Derridean metaphysics. Schama, for instance, shares with Rosenstone a dislike of dismissive attitudes towards film and argues for its acceptance as a revival of an ancient 'oral and performative' tradition of history making.[40] While their moves to link film history to an ancient pedigree are admirable, the results are doubly unsatisfactory. First, despite the anti-teleological stance of current historiography, it is still all too easy to consider 'oral and performative' filmic history as a limited, primitive throwback. Second, the dichotomy of visual and written history remains unexamined. Placing it *a priori* and therefore beyond question risks leaving the hierarchy that Schama and Rosenstone seek to dismantle untouched.

Similar questions may be raised about Thomas Doherty's use of Erasmus' metaphor of 'foxes' and 'hedgehogs' to carve out a place for film.[41] Clashes and misunderstandings about film, he maintains, arise from the crossed pur-poses of print-history 'foxes', who seek to master minutiae, and 'macro-minded' filmic-history 'hedgehogs', who want to illuminate the values, morals and assumptions that shape the world. Doherty's explanation is ultimately of limited use, for equating print with 'micro'-concerns takes no account of the efforts of world historians or of historians who blend micro- and macro-methodologies and interests. Moreover, it sustains the dichotomy of print history and 'other' history, and when print is equated with 'professional', the dichotomy may be taken as hierarchical. The application of Erasmus' meta-phor to explain the efforts of world historians, for instance, has done little to draw their works in from the margins of historiography, and the same outcome might be expected when filmic histories are framed as 'other' to the efforts of print historians.

Costume, period, faction and historical films

In the writings of Schama, Rosenstone and Doherty, a historiographical dichotomy divides the efforts of filmic historians from other historians. Other scholars have contested that division, but their efforts mark not the end of dichotomy but its relocation within the field of historical film studies itself. Returning to Davis, for example, we find a distinction between films that have 'as their central plot documentable events, such as a person's life or a war or revolution' and 'those with a fictional plot but with a historical setting intrinsic to the action'.[42] On this view, we might distinguish the biographical feature about Ray Charles, *Ray* (2004), from the multiple screen adaptations of Jane Austen's novel *Pride and Prejudice* (1940, 1952, 1958, 1967, 1980, 1995, 2005). The problem with this arrangement, as Rosenstone has pointed out, is that few films are clearly one or the other. In *Gladiator* (2000), to take just one example, historical agents (e.g. Marcus Aurelius) intersect with composites of more than one historical agent (e.g. Maximus) and fictional characters (e.g. Proximus). This need not necessarily concern us, for Davis views both kinds of film to be 'historical'. However, hers is a minority view.

One feature that unites ostensibly diverse scholarship on historical films is the judgement that some films are more 'historical' than others. We again begin with Rosenstone, who in *Visions of the Past* takes great pains to disentangle 'mainstream' or 'standard' films from what he calls 'serious', 'experimental' or 'postmodern' historical films on the grounds that the former 'deliver the past in a highly developed, polished form that serves to suppress rather than raise questions', whereas the latter are 'intellectually dense' and use

> the unique capabilities of the media to create multiple meanings . . . raising questions about the very evidence on which our knowledge of the past depends, creatively interacting with its traces . . . they are forays, explorations, provocations, insights.[43]

Standard films tend to confirm what we already know about an event or person; at best they advance understanding by 'personalising, and emotionalising the past'. He makes it clear, though, that this does not mean the use of the medium at its best: that can only come from opposition to 'mainstream' conventions of realism and narrative, or in short by working to avoid the six filmic features listed above.[44] In Rosenstone's other major statement on film, *Revisioning History*, his twofold distinction remains, but the 'mainstream' is connected more specifically to 'costume dramas' and 'typical documentaries', which make use of the past 'solely as a setting for romance and adventure' or simply blend archival footage and stills with talking head interviews. Neither of these qualifies as 'new' historical film, for they are made to entertain and make profits and cannot represent the past with any density or complexity.[45]

Costume drama occupies no place in Leger Grindon's study of the historical fiction film either, because it presents a past setting detached from contemporary social and political issues. Historical fiction films may include and foreground the activities of particular historical agents or fictional characters, but there is always some link to wider political concerns. So, for example, he sees the lack of a romantic dimension in *Lawrence of Arabia* (1962) as signifying the barrenness of Western colonialism. What Grindon counts as a social and political issue is never made explicit. However, his selection and analysis of films that connect individuals to wars and revolutions would suggest a concentration on affairs of state and international relations rather than, say, power relations within and across families.[46] The 'melodramatic' films that Landy describes also lack a political dimension, but she goes further than Grindon in arguing that they use emotional appeals, the valorisation of individuals and the familiar to help viewers to manage and even avoid the complexities and crises of the present-day world. Melodramatic history, she is clear, is socially pathological because it preserves ideal past worlds instead of creating new ones: that is, it renders viewers socially and politically inactive.[47] Tashiro also connects melodrama with affect, but unlike Landy, sees it as only holding sway over viewers when the actions and values of those on screen appear to be close to our own.[48]

Our catalogue of terms that are used to suggest proximity to but ultimately distinction from 'historical films' so far includes 'costume drama' and 'melodrama'. To this we may now add at least three more: 'faction', 'heritage' and 'period'. 'Faction' is Brent Toplin's choice of term to describe the fusion of fictional characters with historical settings. Faction needs to be distinguished from 'good cinematic history' because the creators of faction tend to focus on the actions of individuals at the expense of major historical events, avoid conflicting perspectives and suggest that people in the past were motivated by values and beliefs like our own. They do so, in Toplin's view, because they believe that they will be held less to account over matters of veracity or accuracy than the makers of 'good' or 'more historically oriented films'.[49] 'Heritage' film, as Andrew Higson labels it, also denotes an absence of political engagement. In heritage, the past is no more than a look or style, or a mass of material artefacts. If faction belongs to Hollywood, then heritage belongs to 1980s Britain, for it purportedly satisfied viewer and filmmaker demands for an escape from the problematic expansion and re-articulation of British identity that was prompted by immigration from past and present parts of the Empire and now Commonwealth.[50] Where faction is 'other' to history because of its blend with fiction and heritage because of its evasion of the political, 'period' film is characterised more by happenstance. Period films are not historical films, Brian McFarlane and Stephen Crofts insist, because they just happen to be set in the past: the personal narratives they advance could just as well be set in the present or in another time. Here we gain the sense of a wasted opportunity to reconstruct and interpret historical events and even to upset viewer understandings of the present.[51]

Finally, there are those who, like Pierre Sorlin, discount films that use historical settings simply as a backdrop for romantic or comedic studies of individuals but do not give them a descriptive label. As with a number of the views described above, they are defined first and foremost by their lack of attention to affairs of state and international relations and by the supposed effect of rendering viewers politically inactive.[52] Second, they are identifiable by their lack of historiographical complexity, as measured by their presentation of a tidy and linear comedic or romantic narrative.

Taking stock of this twofold definition of the near- but still non-historical film, we might wonder how it was that the boundary was drawn around politics and open, questioning and provocative representations of past phenomena. Acts of boundary drawing are examined at a number of stages in this book, from a discussion on advertising film in the next chapter to a critical response to claims that documentary has lost its boundaries in Chapter 6. These examples will be assembled to support my conclusion that an expanded and more historical embedded notion of 'history on film' is needed. Looking at films that fall foul of the criteria for an 'historical film', it might be tempting to argue that the misogynistic nature of historical film studies has been exposed. After all, we may note that North American, British and Australian 'costume', 'melodrama', 'faction', 'heritage' and 'period' films tend to foreground the activities and experiences of women. In *Picnic at Hanging Rock* (1975), for instance, the idea of women's history as happening outside time is conveyed explicitly when the imminent disappearance of a group of schoolgirls in the Australian bush is signalled by the stopping of the school mistress's watch (Figure 1.1). And when one of the characters remarks: 'Except for those people down there, we might be the only living creatures in the whole world', the sense of the women's activities being isolated from the kinds of events historical film scholars are interested in is compounded.

However, the charge of misogyny is too simplistic, for current definitions of the 'historical film' also exclude many masculine and transgendered practices. Certain types of masculinity are repeatedly portrayed in historical films: for example, the man who leads others through state and international politics, combat or invention. Concentrating solely on the issue of gender is similarly simplistic, because prevailing definitions of 'the historical film' also mask or minimise the contributions of filmmakers who work with forms of presentation other than live action. Few animated or musical films are discussed in historical film scholarship, for instance. And once we acknowledge that some of these forms of presentation are more prevalent in some cultural and historical contexts than others, then we must acknowledge that historical film scholarship is more than gendered: it is also limited in its analysis of media and spatio-temporal contexts. In the next chapter, for example, we will highlight the neglect of Japanese historical *anime* and 'Bollywood' historical musicals, to take only two examples.

Figure 1.1 Are period films outside of time? *Picnic at Hanging Rock* (©1975, Jim McElroy and Australian Film Commission).

The democratisation of history?

Readers may see my recourse to Derrida and illumination of a limited and limiting definition of 'the historical film' as a contribution to what scholars such as Joyce Appleby, Lynn Hunt and Margaret Jacob dub 'the democratization of history'.[53] In *Telling the Truth About History*, Appleby, Hunt and Jacob frame present-day historiographical pluralism as a product of the evolution of the discipline in the mid-twentieth century towards more inclusive, democratic practices. This shift—prompted in their view by the rise of social history—not only opened the discipline up to women and other formerly excluded groups but also undercut prevailing historiographical assumptions such as the connection of 'objectivity' with neutral truths. As Parker Potter puts it, the democratisation of history does not simply mean a quota-driven expansion of the list of history makers and historical agents; rather, it entails the critical inspection of the assumptions that masked their contributions in the first place.[54] After democratisation, new and more nuanced versions of historiographical concepts emerged, as with the understanding of objectivity to be 'the result of the clash of social interests, ideologies, and social conventions within the framework of object-oriented and disciplined knowledge-seeking'.[55]

Raymond Martin sees Appleby *et al.* as promoting no more than a 'spruced up and Americanised version of [the] traditional Enlightenment values . . . [of] objectivity, realism, truth, democracy, and optimism'. He is in accord with them, though, in his belief that the fragmentation of the discipline is a recent development, and that it may be a sign of its 'maturity'.[56] More dramatically, Peter Novick has opined that history 'as a broad community of discourse, as a community of scholars united by common aims, common standards, and common purposes has ceased to exist'.[57] Moreover, countless discussions on postmodernism and the discipline have announced the 'end of History', where the use of the capital 'H' denotes a 'master' or 'meta'-narrative that legitimates some ideals and glosses over conflicting views and discontinuities. Traditionally, this has meant the adoption of a masculinist, Eurocentric position: that in this view, events and spaces are named, organised and judged in line with the hopes and ideals of white, male, Western academics.

Democratisation is seen as applying not only to the makers of histories but also to their audiences. So, as Emma Lapsansky has argued:

> No longer writing only for the uniformly educated professional, today's academic historian often seeks to speak to anyone, with any background, who wants to know about the past. . . . This democratisation has increased the number of Americans who can see themselves, their families, and their communities in the narratives they encounter.[58]

Her observations appear to be confirmed by the appearance of journals and centres for public history and heritage, as well as online discussion forums like H-Net.[59] These also seem to suggest a movement away from treating history and print media as synonymous.

While there is no doubting the pervasive presence of histories and history makers today, historiographical narratives organised by the concept of 'democratisation' strike me as ahistorical and even triumphalist. To demonstrate conclusively that history is no longer solely the province of white, Western male academics, we need to show that they dominated history making in the past. To convince ourselves that concepts such as 'objectivity' and 'truth' are now more contested, we have to show that they were unquestioned in the past. To congratulate ourselves that history has escaped the shackles of print and embraced other media, we have to show that print histories dominated in the past. Yet if we set out to confirm the opening up of history making, we would not get very far before noting how few historiographical studies there are to guide us.

My sense is that history has not *become* pluralist but has arguably never been anything *but* pluralist. Women wrote histories long before the twentieth century, African Americans wrote universal histories before and after Hegel, hundreds of thousands of people read Walter Scott's historical novels, and even more encountered the past in stage shows, dioramas, paintings, carvings and dances, magic lantern shows, photographs and silent films.[60] Nor can we say with any confidence that history today is simply *more* pluralist, because we have only begun to chart the extent of history making prior to the mid-twentieth century. The narrative of democratisation functions, rather ironically, only because historiography continues to ignore or rank as 'less serious' the histories made by all but a few writers prior to the mid-twentieth century.

That is, the narrative of the democratisation of history might well be challenged by a democratisation of historiography. For every history that is analysed, hundreds and even thousands of other histories, which may take the form of children's books, textbooks, films or theatrical productions, are passed over in silence. That silence supports a notion of history making exploding and fragmenting in the latter half of the twentieth century.

This is not to suggest that studies of history making beyond academic contexts before the mid-twentieth century do not exist. Very many do, but much remains to be done to expand and re-articulate the histories that history makers tell about themselves. Moreover, it is important to note that while we now acknowledge a great many varieties of history making, metaphysics persists in the organising concept of 'professional' history. As long as 'professionalisation' remains a dominant theme in histories of the field, and we use prefixes like *public* history or 'heritage', then a distinction and even hierarchy between history and other 'not quite history' activities persists. So too does the expectation that professional historians are the primary arbiters of historical activity. This expectation clearly underpins Toplin's warning that historians 'need to be aware of the dangers of too much tolerance', and that they must stand up for the 'ideals of scholarship' and the 'rules of traditional scholarship'.[61] On what grounds are historians the arbiters of historical activities, including film? And on what grounds do we place the communications of academic historians above those of other history makers? Is this rightful recognition of training, or as Oliver Stone and Maureen Ames would have it, 'professional arrogance'?[62]

Forms of history, history, or historical practices?

When we use the concepts 'history', 'historical' and 'historian', why do we also use qualifiers such as 'film' or 'filmmaker'? Is it because, like Paul Hirst and Michael Oakeshott, we believe that 'The domain of human knowledge can be seen to be differentiated into a number of logically distinct "forms", none of which is ultimately reducible in character to any of the others, either simply or in combination'?[63] These 'forms of knowledge' are not collections of information but rather 'complex ways of understanding experience' that may be distinguished from one another on the grounds of characteristic concepts and relations of concepts (logical structure), truth tests, and particular skills and techniques.[64] On this view, we might talk of the distinct concepts, skills and techniques of print and filmic historians. Or is it, as R.G. Collingwood would have it, that forms of history are not coordinate species equally embodying the essence of the concept but are arranged in a cumulative scale? On his view, each of the forms of history is related to the others as a greater or lesser instantiation of the concept. We might find in Collingwood's view justification for the belief in a hierarchy between professional and amateur history. But are there *forms* of history? Derrida's writings on metaphysics give us cause to think carefully about how and why we speak of 'history'. The language of forms implies that the 'historical' activities we engage in are instantiations of, are united by and can be traced back to something called 'history'. In distinction to this view, I believe that there is no 'history' apart from historical practices. Nor, in consequence, is there any logical, universal or unchanging reason to talk of one practice as 'more historical' than another. If we value some historical practices over others, it is because of historical decisions. And because our views on what history is are themselves historical, they are subject to re-evaluation and change. The remainder of this book is an invitation to reconsider our assumptions about what history is, including our expectations about the structure of its definition.

Recommended resources

Appleby, J., Hunt, J. and Jacob, M., *Telling the Truth About History*, New York: W.W. Norton, 1994.

Cannadine, D. (ed.), *History and the Media*, Basingstoke: Palgrave Macmillan, 2004.

Carnes, M.C., *Past Imperfect: History According to the Movies*, New York: Henry Holt, 1996.

Grindon, L., *Shadows on the Past: Studies in the Historical Fiction Film*, Philadelphia: Temple University Press, 1996.

Landy, M., *Cinematic Uses of the Past*, Minneapolis: University of Minnesota Press, 1996.

Landy, M. (ed.), *The Historical Film: History and Memory in Media*, New Brunswick, NJ: Rutgers University Press, 2001.

Rosen, P., *Change Mummified: Cinema, Historicity, Theory*, Minneapolis: University of Minnesota Press, 2001.

Rosenstone, R., *Revisioning History: Film and the Construction of a New Past*, Princeton, NJ: Princeton University Press, 1995.

Rosenstone, R., *Visions of the Past: The Challenge of Film to Our Understanding of History*, Cambridge, Mass.: Harvard University Press, 1995.

Sanello, F., *Reel vs Real: How Hollywood Turns Fact into Fiction*, Lanham, Md: Taylor Trade, 2003.

Toplin, B., *History by Hollywood: The Use and Abuse of the American Past*, Urbana: University of Illinois Press, 1996.

Toplin, B., *Reel History: In Defence of Hollywood*, Lawrence: Kansas University Press, 2002.

Notes

1 O. Stone, in an interview with M.C. Carnes, 'Past imperfect: history according to the movies', *Cineaste*, 1996, vol. 22(4), p. 33.
2 J. Sayles, '*Matewan*', in M.C. Carnes (ed.), *Past Imperfect: History According to the Movies*, New York: Henry Holt, 1996, p. 18.
3 *Ibid.*, pp. 18–20.
4 B. Gammage, 'Working on Gallipoli', *Australian Film and Television School Conference 2*, North Ryde, Sydney: Australian Film and Television School, 1984, pp. 67–72.

5 J. Jeffrey, '*Amistad* (1997): Steven Spielberg's "true story" ', *Historical Journal of Film, Radio and Television*, 2001, vol. 21(1), p. 4.

6 J. de Coras, 'A Memorable Decision of the High Court of Tolouse Containing the Prodigious Story of our Time of a Supposed Husband, Enriched by One Husband and Eleven Fine and Learned Annotations [1572]', trans. J.K. Ringold and J. Lewis, *Triquarterly*, 1982, spring, pp. 86–102.

7 N.Z. Davis, *The Return of Martin Guerre*, Cambridge, Mass.: Harvard University Press, 1983, p. viii.

8 R. Rosenstone, *Visions of the Past*, pp. 55–6. The definitions of romance and comedy are courtesy of H. White, *Metahistory: The Historical Imagination in Nineteenth-century Europe*, Baltimore: Johns Hopkins University Press, 1973, p. 9.

9 R. Rosenstone, *Visions of the Past*, p. 57.

10 B. Toplin, *Reel History: In Defense of Hollywood*, Lawrence: University of Kansas Press, 2002, p. 18; D. Cannadine, 'Introduction', in D. Cannadine (ed.), *Historians and the Media*, Basingstoke: Palgrave Macmillan, 2004, p. 4; and S. Harper, 'Historical pleasures: Gainsborough costume melodrama', in M. Landy (ed.), *The Historical Film: History and Memory in Media*, New Brunswick, NJ: Rutgers University Press, 2001, p. 108.

11 D. Christian, 'Scales', in M. Hughes-Warrington (ed.), *Palgrave Advances in World Histories*, Basingstoke: Palgrave Macmillan, 2005, pp. 64–89.

12 L. Althusser, 'Ideology and ideological state apparatuses (notes towards an investigation)', *Lenin and Philosophy and Other Essays*, trans. B. Brewer, London: NLB, 1971, pp. 152–6.

13 L. Althusser, 'Freud and Lacan', in *Lenin and Philosophy and Other Essays*, p. 201.

14 M. Foucault, *The Order of Things*, trans. anon., London: Tavistock, 1970, p. 387. See also p. xxiii.

15 R. Barthes, *Mythologies*, trans. A. Lavers, London: Paladin, 1973, p. 11.

16 For this criticism about microhistories, see, for example, D. North, 'Comment', *Journal of Economic History*, 1978, vol. 38(1), pp. 77–80.

17 R. Rosenstone, *Visions of the Past*, p. 59.

18 M. Landy, 'Introduction', in *The Historical Film: History and Memory in Media*, pp. 2–7; C.S. Tashiro, *Pretty Pictures: Production Design and the History Film*, Austin: University of Texas Press, 1998, p. 66; and S. Harper, 'Historical pleasures: Gainsborough costume melodrama', p. 108.

19 R. Rosenstone, *Visions of the Past*, p. 59; and M.E. Neely, 'The young Lincoln', in M. Carnes (ed.), *Past Imperfect: History According to the Movies*, New York: Henry Holt, 1996, p. 127.

20 R. Rosenstone, *Visions of the Past*, p. 60.

21 E. Olmi, as quoted in N.Z. Davis, ' "Any resemblance to persons living or dead": film and the challenge of authenticity', *The Yale Review*, 1987, vol. 76(4), p. 462.

22 M. Carnes, 'Introduction', in M. Carnes (ed.), *Past Imperfect*, p. 4. See also J. Sayles and E. Foner, 'Interview with John Sayles', in *Past Imperfect: History According to the Movies*, New York: Henry Holt, 1996, p. 13; F. Sanello, *Reel vs Real: How Hollywood Turns Fact into Fiction*, Lanham, Md: Taylor Trade, 2003, p. xiii; B. Toplin, *Reel History*, pp. 18–25; M. Landy, *The Historical Film*, p. 18; R. Rosenstone, *Visions of the Past*, pp. 57–8; and D. Cannadine, *History and the Media*, p. 4.

23 M. Arrow, ' "I want to be a TV historian when I grow up!": on being a *rewind* historian', unpublished ms., p. 2; See also M. Arrow, 'Television program yes, history no', *History Australia*, 2005, vol. 2(2), pp. 46.1–46.6.

24 O. Stone, in an interview with M.C. Carnes, 'Past imperfect', p. 33.

25 As quoted in R. Rosenstone, 'History in images', *American Historical Review*, 1988, vol. 93(5), p. 1176.

26 B. Toplin, *Reel History*, p. 18.
27 Schama offers his criticism of this view in 'Television and the trouble with history', in D. Cannadine (ed.), *History and the Media*, Basingstoke: Palgrave Macmillan, 2004, p. 24.
28 J. Derrida, 'The double session', *Dissemination*, trans. B. Johnson, London: Althone, 1981, p. 195.
29 See, for example, W. Woodward, 'History on TV a mixed blessing, say academics', *Guardian*, 21 July 2003; D. Aaronovitch, 'It's a great big Schama', *Guardian*, 22 July 2003; and C. Ashton, 'Historical Relevance', *Guardian*, 25 July 2003, all online at http://www.guardian.co.uk
30 See, for example, The Chasers' *CNNNN* series, Australian Broadcasting Corporation, 2004.
31 I.C. Jarvie, 'Seeing through the movies', *Philosophy of the Social Sciences*, 1978, vol. 8, p. 378; M. Cousins, 'Why the film so rarely beats a good book', *The Australian Financial Review*, 28 February 2003, p. R11; and K. Burns, as quoted in 'History a la Hollywood . . . hmm', *Sydney Morning Herald*, 5 October 2002, online at http://www.smh.com.au/articles/2002/10/04/1033538773406.html
32 R. Rosenstone, *Visions of the Past*, p. 49.
33 M. McLuhan, *The Interior Landscape: The Literary Criticism of Marshall McLuhan*, New York: McGraw Hill, 1969, p. 175.
34 W. Ong, 'Writing is a technology that restructures thought', in G. Baumann (ed.), *The Written Word: Literacy in Transition*, Oxford: Oxford University Press, 1986, pp. 24–6; and R. Harris, *The Origin of Writing*, La Salle, Ill.: Open Court, 1986, p. 15.
35 J. Derrida, *Limited Inc.*, ed. G. Graff, trans. S. Weber, Evanston, Ill.: Northwestern University Press, 1998, p. 236.
36 J. Derrida, *Margins of Philosophy*, trans. A. Bass, Chicago: University of Chicago Press, 1982, p. 19.
37 J. Derrida, 'The double session', p. 193.
38 *Ibid.*, p. 195. See also J. Derrida, *Of Grammatology*, trans. C. Spivak, Baltimore: Johns Hopkins University Press, 1976, pp. 14, 43.
39 S. Schama, 'Television and the trouble with history', p. 24.
40 *Ibid.*
41 T. Doherty, 'Film and history, foxes and hedgehogs', *Magazine of History*, 2002, vol. 16(4), p. 13.
42 N.Z. Davis, 'Any resemblance to persons living or dead', p. 1987.
43 R. Rosenstone, *Visions of the Past*, pp. 11, 12 and 44.
44 *Ibid.*, p. 12. See also pp. 8, 11–12, 37–44, 51–65 and 200–22.
45 R. Rosenstone, *Revisioning History: Film and the Construction of a New Past*, Princeton, NJ: Princeton University Press, 1995, pp. 3–5.
46 L. Grindon, *Shadows on the Past: Studies in the Historical Fiction Film*, Philadelphia: Temple University Press, 1994, pp. 2, 9, 10, 11, 223.
47 M. Landy, *Cinematic Uses of the Past*, Minneapolis: University of Minnesota Press, 1996, pp. 17–24, 36, 161.
48 C.S. Tashiro, *Pretty Pictures: Production Design and the History Film*, Austin: University of Texas Press, 1998, p. 66.
49 B. Toplin, *Reel History: In Defense of Hollywood*, Lawrence: Kansas University Press, 2002, pp. 92, 94, 103, 114, 118 and 131.
50 A. Higson, *Waving the Flag: Constructing a National Cinema in Britain*, Oxford: Ocford University Press, 1995, p. 113.
51 B. McFarlane, *Australian Cinema 1970–1985*, London: Secker & Warburg, 1987; and S. Crofts, 'Shifting paradigms in the Australian historical film', *East–West Film Journal*, 1991, vol. 5(2), p. 6.
52 P. Sorlin, *The Film in History*, Oxford: Blackwell, 1980, pp. 116, 144, 208.

53 J. Appleby, L. Hunt and M. Jacob, *Telling the Truth about History*, New York: W.W. Norton, 1994, p. 289. See also B. Attwood, *Telling the Truth About Aboriginal History*, Crows Nest: Allen & Unwin, 2005, pp. 35–7.

54 P.B. Potter Jr, 'Review of *Those of Little Note*', *Journal of American History*, 1995, vol. 82(2), p. 858.

55 J. Appleby, L. Hunt and M. Jacob, *Telling the Truth about History*, p. 195.

56 R. Martin, 'Forum: Raymond Martin, Joan W. Scott, and Cushing Strout on *Telling the Truth About History*', *History and Theory*, 1995, vol. 34(4), pp. 324 and 328.

57 P. Novick, *That Noble Dream: The 'Objectivity Question' and the American Historical Profession*, Cambridge: Cambridge University Press, 1988, p. 628.

58 E.J. Lapsansky, 'An honor system for historians?', *The Journal of American History*, 2004, vol. 90(4), para. 3, online at http://www.historycooperative.org/journals/jah/90.4/lapsansky.html

59 H-Net, online at http://www.h-net/org

60 See, for example, M. Spongberg, *Writing Women's History Since the Renaissance*, Basingstoke: Palgrave Macmillan, 2002; and B. Lewis, *Light and Truth: Collected from the Bible and Ancient and Modern History, Containing the Universal History of the Colored and Indian Race, from the Creation of the World to the Present Time*, Boston: published by a Committee of Colored Gentlemen, 1844; G. Cavallo and R. Chartier (eds), *A History of Reading in the West*, Cambridge: Polity Press, 1999; M.S. Phillips, *Society and Sentiment: Genres of Historical Writing in Britain, 1740–1820*, Princeton, NJ: Princeton University Press, 2000; and H. Groth, *Victorian Photography and Literary Nostalgia*, Cambridge: Cambridge University Press, 2004.

61 R.B. Toplin, *History by Hollywood: The Use and Abuse of the American Past*, Urbana: University of Illinois Press, 1996, pp. 2, 10.

62 M.O. Ames, 'letter to the editor', *Perspectives*, June 1999, online at http://www.theaha.org/perspectives/issues/1999/9909/9909let.cfm; and O. Stone, 'Past imperfect: history according to the movies', p. 33.

63 P.H. Hirst, 'The forms of knowledge re-visited', in *Knowledge and the Curriculum*, London: Routledge & Kegan Paul, 1974, p. 84; and M. Oakeshott, *Experience and its Modes*, Cambridge: Cambridge University Press, 1933.

64 P.H. Hirst, 'The forms of knowledge re-visited', p. 44.

2   Genre

Cast a look around your local movie rental shop, or print or online filmographies, and you probably will not find an 'historical' category. More likely, you will come across terms such as 'science fiction', 'comedy', 'horror' and 'romance'. Yet, as we saw in the previous chapter, a number of scholars have assumed the existence of an historical genre and worked to articulate its features and boundaries. This chapter focuses on the reasons for the disjunction in these genre classifications and on further unearthing the judgements that favour some 'historical' films over others in academic scholarship. In so doing, we will be led back to the wider historiographical question of what 'history' is and how it can be classified. This is the chief of many questions uncovered in this chapter, and as we shall see, some of these questions do not at present have solid answers.

Offering a clear, consistent and coherent account of 'the historical film' would seem to be a tall order, if not impossible, given the numerical and cultural extent of film production and reception. Scholars routinely accept that the genre does exist, however, and that it can with effort be delineated. As we saw in the previous chapter, one of the first steps that scholars commonly take to render the concept of 'the historical film' clear and manageable is to restrict their attention to a small range of works. A number of scholars dismiss 'costume', 'melodrama', 'period' and 'heritage' films in favour of 'historical' films, as if the features and distinctions between these categories are readily apparent. Others restrict their attention even further. Robert Rosenstone opens both *Revisioning History* and *Visions of the Past* by explaining that his interest lies with the 'new' or 'postmodern' history film that 'foregrounds itself as a construction'.[1] George Custen limits his study of biographical pictures or 'biopics' to those produced by Hollywood studios, and more specifically to those associated with production chief Darryl Zanuck. Guy Barefoot takes a twofold step, first identifying the sub-genre of 'gaslight melodrama' and then opting to treat works produced in the USA and UK between 1930 and 1950. Similarly, Brian Taves subdivides the 'historical' genre and selects the smaller unit of 'historical adventure' in a process clearly described in the opening chapter of *The Romance of Adventure*:

Ask six different individuals—lay person, scholar, critic, or filmmaker—
to name the first adventure film that comes to mind, and there will probably be a half-dozen widely divergent answers. One person mentions
Raiders of the Lost Ark, the second champions *Star Wars*, another replies
The Guns of Navarone, a fourth cites *Quo Vadis*, a fifth champions the
James Bond movies, and the sixth suggests *Robin Hood*. I believe that of
these examples only *Robin Hood* is truly an adventure film. The others
represent genres that are distinct in their own right. *Raiders of the Lost
Ark* is a fantasy . . . *Star Wars* is a science fiction . . . *The Guns of Navarone* is a war movie . . . *Quo Vadis* is a biblical epic . . . James Bond is a
spy. . . . *Robin Hood*, by contrast, deals with the valiant fight for freedom
and a just form of government, set in exotic locales and the historical
past. This is the central theme of adventure, a motif that is unique to the
genre. It is essential to determine what comprises an adventure film, to
analyse the genre's central tenets, and to distinguish its borders from
other forms with similar elements.[2]

Questions aside about whether *Raiders of the Lost Ark* may be excluded
by those criteria, Taves—in tune with the other scholars mentioned above—
sees boundary drawing as not only possible but also necessary in film
scholarship.

Acts of boundary drawing beg many questions. A primary problem is the
nebulous nature of the concept of genre itself: does it, for instance, denote a
form of presentation (e.g. live action or animation, widescreen or academy
ratio, black and white or colour), ontological status (truth, fiction, mythical
archetype), reception (blockbuster or independent), cultural origin or
diegetic content, or some combination of these? And who is to judge whether
a work belongs to a genre? Is it right to assume, as historical film scholars
have done, that works they label as 'historical films' will be recognised as such
by producers, distributors and viewers? Furthermore, can acts of boundary
drawing be disentangled from value judgements? Is calling a work an 'historical film' an act of approval, or might it also be used pejoratively, as with
'chick flick' or 'women's weepie'? In the drawing of boundaries, it is also
presupposed that films belong clearly and permanently to a single genre and
that the genre is immune to historical change.[3] A series of examples will
demonstrate that many of the presuppositions that historical film scholars
hold about the nature and boundaries of their subject matter should not be
taken for granted.

We begin by returning to the observation at the head of this chapter, that
perhaps not everyone uses the same labels to describe and classify films. Since
the 1960s, the number of academic publications on 'the historical film'
has grown steadily, yet the term still does not enjoy wide currency. So
while, for example, *Le Retour de Martin Guerre* (*The Return of Martin Guerre*,
1982) is to Philip Rosen and Robert Rosenstone a 'subtle' and 'well-respected,
non-Hollywood historical film', to reviewers and other film theorists it is an

'historical romance', a 'story of love and deception', a 'heritage film' and even a 'courtroom drama' in the style of *Perry Mason* (1957–66).[4] Nor is there any guarantee that theorists or reviewers will even tell viewers that a film is set in the past, as with Ken Burke's labelling of *Forrest Gump* (1994) as a 'person against the world comedy' and *Raiders of the Lost Ark* (1981) as an 'adventure'.[5] Film publicity materials make infrequent use of written generic classifications, including the term 'historical film'. Indeed, it is sometimes difficult to judge on the basis of print advertising alone whether a film has anything other than a contemporary setting, as the examples *Forrest Gump, Catch Me If You Can* (2002) and *Donnie Darko* (2001) demonstrate. Our conclusions that an advertised film is set in the past are more likely to come from visual and aural information such as costumes, sets, soundtrack and perhaps even an archaic mode of speaking. It is important to note, too, that those elements are generally combined with others that stress contemporary appeal or the presence of other genres. Advertising for *Graustark* (1925), for example, emphasises the 'modern' nature of its tale set in a time of 'gold and glory' (Figure 2.1). The only element that betrays the past setting of the film are the costumes shown in a small inset illustration.

Graustark may have an historical setting, but it was also promoted as a 'romance' and a story of 'thrills' and 'intrigue'. In this respect—the invocation of multiple genres—the advertising for *Graustark* is akin to that of many other campaigns for works that scholars might label 'historical'. Advertisements used to promote *The Lives of a Bengal Lancer* (1935) and *Pearl Harbor* (2001), for instance, promise the 'thrill of a kiss, the joy of combat' in images as well as words (Figure 2.2). Neither of these films is identified with a single genre; on the contrary, these posters suggest something for everyone, something that might bring them into the cinema. This appeal to 'something for everyone' is even clearer in an advertisement for *The Three Musketeers* (1939), with its mixture of action, comedy, romance and musical elements (Figure 2.3). This example, as with the others I have included, clearly affirms Tom Gunning, Adam Knee and Janet Staiger's observation that film publicists have little to gain from tying a work down to a single element, as film scholars do.[6]

Furthermore, as Rick Altman notes, there is little commercial advantage in employing text that can just as easily be used by competitors or, to speak more commercially, 'homebrand' or 'no name' terms (i.e. 'historical').[7] Film advertising therefore more commonly draws attention to proprietary or copyrighted elements: *Pearl Harbor* is, publicists tell us loud and clear, as much if not more about actor Ben Affleck than it is about costumes, props and a title evoking the Second World War. Sometimes advertising campaigns do imply generic grouping, as with the advertising of *The Story of Dr. Erhlich's Magic Bullet* (1940) as 'another [*Life of* Emile] Zola!' (1937). Here, the connection drawn coincides with Custen's category of biopic. In many more cases, though, the connections breach the boundaries drawn by historical film scholars. For example, a poster for *The Story of Alexander Graham Bell*

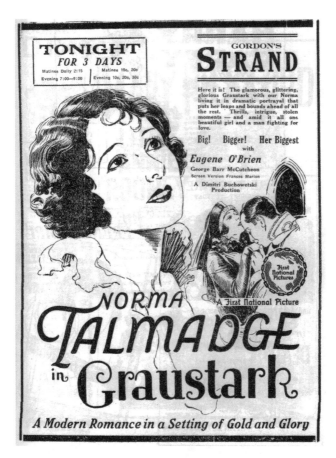

Figure 2.1 The contemporary appeal of *Graustark* (1925)

(1939) announces that it 'will rank with these never-to-be-forgotten productions *The Story of Louis Pasteur, The Citadel, The Life of Emile Zola, Anthony Adverse* [and] *The Count of Monte Cristo*!!'; *Madame Curie* (1943), which starred Greer Garson and Walter Pidgeon, is advertised as 'Mr and Mrs. Miniver ... together again!'; and *Raiders of the Lost Ark* is introduced with the tag line 'Indiana Jones—the new hero from the creators of *Jaws* and *Star Wars*'.[8] In these cases, text is used to connect a film with previous success, whether related to a genre, a star or the collaboration of a producer and director.

I will have more to say about the significance of intertextual references in film advertising in Chapter 8. For the moment, though, it suffices to note that the functions of generic classifications differ in the texts of scholars and film producers and distributors. This is hardly a surprising point, for many historical scholars have acknowledged the commercial nature of much

Figure 2.2a

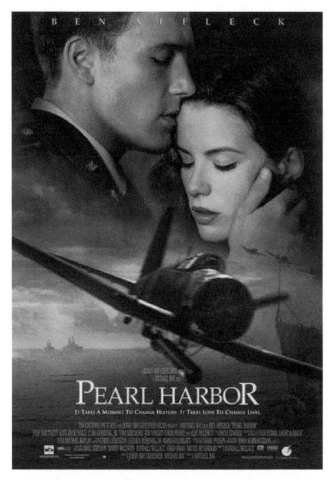

Figure 2.2b Multiple categories of viewer for *The Lives of a Bengal Lancer* (1936) and *Pearl Harbor* (© 2001, Touchstone Pictures)

film production. However, what they often neglect to do is to reflect on the functions of their own analyses. Few historical film scholars overtly style themselves as distanced from the objects they study through the use of words like 'objective' or 'scientific'. Yet their statements are laden with unexamined judgements concerning the parameters and sources for their studies. In the last chapter, I questioned the pejorative appraisal of 'costume' dramas. In this chapter, I want to reiterate the cultural stakes involved in dismissing certain works and note that scholastic writing, no less than advertising, is at least in part concerned with the promotion of certain ideals and assumptions.

Consider the preference of scholars for the analysis of films that appear to be singly and unambiguously tied to the 'historical' genre over those

Figure 2.3 Something for everyone? *The Three Musketeers* (1939)

that apparently offer a more mixed classification, that is for an historical film as distinct from an historical romance film. This preference sees not only some films chosen over others within a single national or cultural cinema but also whole cultural cinemas passed over in favour of others. The prodigious output of Indian filmmakers, for instance, is not the only reason their works are neglected by historical film scholars. Another explanation may be found in an assumed dichotomy of generic purity and impurity. Against the Western 'historical film' is Indian 'masala', a term that, as Priya Jaikumar explains:

> refers literally to a blend of Indian spices that adds flavour to food, and metaphorically to the necessary combination of filmic ingredients that best guarantees high returns on investment. Masala films were a consequence of producers and directors trying to ensure that every film had a fighting chance to reap good profits—in the absence of studio infrastructure—by incorporating something in the film for everyone. Each film had a little action and some romance with a touch of comedy, drama, tragedy, music and dance. Indian films make little sense when

viewed from the perspective of American film genres. No Indian film is a musical or action film because every mainstream Indian film is a musical and has some action sequences.[9]

This distinction along an assumed boundary of relative purity and mixing is problematic for at least two reasons. First, the accepted treatment of films as unified by the structure of a single genre—in this case the 'historical film'— masks the level of genre mixing that characterises past and present film production in Western cultures. In recent years, theorists of film genre have celebrated the 'ironic' or 'playful' hybridisation that apparently marks the movement from 'classical' to 'postclassical' or even 'postmodern' film in Western culture after the Second World War.[10] As Staiger and Altman have argued, though, film production prior to the Second World War was shaped by the perception of producers, distributors, exhibitors and viewers that films could potentially belong to several categories and that labelling films with a mix of categories was likely to broaden their appeal. Films that Custen labels 'biopics', for instance, were often given double generic classifications in the 1930s such as 'biographical drama' or 'musical biography'. In another example, 'wild west', 'western chase', 'western comedy', 'western melodrama' and 'western epic' films were codified into the 'western' genre only after 1910. Even after that date, mixing continued to be implied, as with the description of *3 Word Brand* (1921) as 'a wild west romance' and *The Prairie Wife* (1925) as 'a romance of the plains'. As we saw with the example of *Pearl Harbor* above, genre mixing continues to be stressed in promotional materials to accentuate marketing opportunities and suggest intertextual references. If there is any difference between the mixing of genres in classical and post-classical or postmodern film, Altman contends, then perhaps it is one of degree rather than kind. Publicity materials for historical films made from the 1970s onwards appear to suggest more self-conscious highlighting of genre conflict, as with the action comedy of *Raiders of the Lost Ark*, science fiction comedy and tragicomedy of the *Back to the Future* films (1985–90) and *Donnie Darko*, and the 'Holocaust comedy' of *La Vita è bella* (*Life is Beautiful*, 1997) and *Train de vie* (*Train of Life*, 1998). Further historical research on this matter is needed, and it might yet lead us to admit that the reservation of 'conscious', 'ironic' or 'playful' genre mixing to our own times stems from an underexamined assumption of progress.[11]

The apparent link between Indian and Western film on the grounds of genre mixing is worthy of further consideration by historical film scholars. Consider, for instance, the advertisement for *Aan* (*Savage Princess*, 1952; Figure 2.4) dating from the mid-1980s against the examples in Figures 2.1–2.3. Similarities across these examples suggest the circulation of transnational visual cultural elements. Scholarly treatment of the origin, circulation and adaptation of aesthetic vocabularies in historical film production has not been forthcoming, however, because of the conjunction of particular genres with political awareness and participation. In the last chapter, we saw a

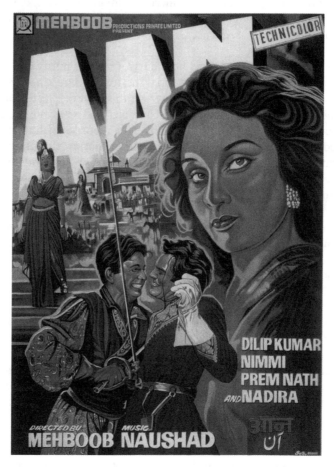

Figure 2.4 Genre mixing, Mumbai style: poster advertising for *Aan* (1952) from the 1980s

number of scholars declare their preference against the mixed offerings of historical romance or costume drama. A similar preference sees much of Indian cinema dismissed as colourful entertainment that is either at odds with, or an escape from, political engagement. Sumita Chakravarty typifies this view, writing that in Mumbai films:

> the commercial [Mumbai] cinema has sought to stay clear of controversy by converting history into pageantry and spectacle and developing a repertoire of characters . . . who are presented over and over again in forms firmly lodged in the public memory.
>   . . . colourful characters from the past reinforce themes of patriotism, and their actions are woven into narratives of romance, intrigue, conflict.

Notions of historical accuracy or attention to detail are subordinated to the larger imaginative sweep of legend and heroic sentiment.[12]

This is not a new claim, for as Ravi Vasudevan has observed, from the 1920s onwards historical films were seen as 'lower class' because of their use of spectacle.[13] Perhaps, as the director S.S. Vasan said of his own work *Chandralekha* (1948), Mumbai historical films are best summed up as 'pageantry for our peasants'.[14] But on what grounds do we distinguish entertainment and spectacle from intellectual and social engagement? Why should we assume that entertaining or even spectacular Mumbai films are less likely to foster critical social and political engagement than historical films traditionally favoured by scholars, such as *The Return of Martin Guerre*? After all, promotional materials for the film showing Nathalie Baye and Gérard Depardieu in costume and in an embrace imply 'romance' as well as 'history'. Furthermore, should film be valued for that function alone, and what should be counted as social and political participation? The answers to these questions are not at present clear; the superiority of a narrow corpus of historical films simply goes without saying. Beneath the scholarly neglect of Indian film, are there thus vestiges of the venerable antinomy between peoples with and without history, or the 'West' and the 'rest'?

Peoples with and without historical films? Animation, comedy and musical

Judgements about the relationship between particular historical films and social and political engagement do not run simply along cultural lines. This point is borne out by the paucity of attention that historical film scholars have given to a range of mixed generic offerings, particularly the combination of history with animation, comedy, musical and melodrama. In this section, we will examine each of these mixtures in turn.

Animation has until recently occupied a marginal place in Western film scholarship. This is perhaps due to critical disdain for Disney child and family entertainment, the association of animation with comedy (a topic we will explore further below) and the use of animation for well-meaning but didactic instructional and promotional films. Disdain for animation, though, is not universal: for example, experimental and *avant-garde* animations produced in Europe 'before Mickey' (1898–1930) enjoyed the critical attention of scholars at the time of their release, as they do today.[15] Furthermore, in Japan animation, or *anime* as it is usually referred to, is a pervasive cultural form and one that is increasingly seen as an intellectually demanding art.

Anime is commonly connected with the genre of science fiction. However, some *anime* focus on a recognisably historical past, such as *Hadashi no gen* (*Barefoot Gen*, 1983) and *Hotaru no Haku* (*Grave of the Fireflies*, 1988). *Barefoot Gen* relates the experiences of a boy (Gen) before and after the bombing of Hiroshima. Intercutting between shots of a calendar, a clock, the crew of the Enola Gay and Gen playing in the street with a friend, the narrative builds in suspense before the bomb that we know is coming. When it is dropped, we see Hiroshima glow before both Gen's playmate and the surrounding architecture dissolve before our eyes. The sequences depicting the destruction of Hiroshima are explicit, yet the film does not dwell on the horrific aftermath. Rather, it emphasises Gen, his mother and his adopted brother Ryotaro's resilience in the face of family deaths, food shortages and ill-health. In the final scene, viewers see both grass and Gen's hair growing again. Opening with the voiceover 'September 21, 1945 was the night I died', *Grave of the Fireflies* offers viewers far less cause for hope. Most of the story is set in Kobe near the end of the war, when Allied bombing claimed an increasingly large number of civilian casualties. Seita and Setsuko are the children of one victim, and their inability to find a supportive home with relatives leads them to make a home of their own in an abandoned bomb shelter. In that place, Setsuko experiences joy and sadness at the short life of the fireflies that Seita catches to please her, and she makes a grave for them. As the film progresses, it becomes apparent that the two children—like the fireflies—will be unable to survive for long, and in the end they succumb to malnutrition.

With their combination of animation and child protagonists (see Figure 2.5), it is tempting to read both *Barefoot Gen* and *Grave of the Fireflies* as contributions to a metaphorically 'childlike' Japanese 'victim's history', a history that sees the setting out of a 'balanced moral calculus' in which the atomic bombings cancel out Pearl Harbor and the colonisation of Korea and parts of China are forgotten.[16] This conclusion is historically and methodologically questionable: it neglects the collaborative nature of American–Japanese attempts to replace perceptions of a militaristic past with those of a new, democratic and peace-seeking society; second, it transplants the Western conflation of animation with children's entertainment; and, third, it assumes that the meaning of these films is exhausted through a single interpretation. As Susan Napier has argued, *Barefoot Gen* and *Grave of the Fireflies* can also be read as warnings about the self-inflicted postwar 'feminisation' of Japan: Seita is nurturing, sensitive and passive; Gen is active in the face of adversity and far from a passive victim.[17] It is also important to note that criticisms made about the 'avoidance' of the 'big picture' in these *anime* (i.e. causes of the war) have similarly been levelled against Edgar Reitz's account of village life in twentieth-century Germany (*Heimat*, 1984) and North American combat films set in Vietnam and Somalia. More attention will be given to this 'small picture' criticism of some combat films in Chapter 4. For the moment, I would like to make it clear that the antinomy between those 'with' and 'without' historical films that shapes film criticism does not simply coincide with notions of a divide between the 'West' and the 'rest' or the 'Occident' and the 'Orient'.

The case of comedy films further demonstrates this point. Towards the end of the film *The Name of the Rose* (1986), it becomes clear that a series of murders have been committed in a monastery in order to keep the existence

Figure 2.5 History through children's eyes? *Hadashi no Gen* (*Barefoot Gen*, © 1983, Gen Productions) and *Hotaru no Haku* (*Grave of the Fireflies*, © 1988, Akiyuki Nosaka/Shinchosha Co in Japan)

of a treatise on comedy by Aristotle secret. As T. Nelson has shown, the different views of comedy in this film and in the book of the same title—as a corrective to fanaticism, intolerance and fear or as demeaning to belief and the dignity of human life—resonate in ancient and modern writings. Comedy is often treated as if it is synonymous with laughter, but in medieval usage, as with the present-day narratological theories of Northrop Frye and Hayden White, it also denotes stories that tend towards a harmonic or resolved ending.[18] On this count, for instance, *Titanic* (1997) might be described as a comedy because it ends with the happy reunion of Rose in death with all those who perished the night the ship sank, not just because it contains a few jokes. Recognising these two elements of comedy might lead us to conclude that few historical films are not comedies. Yet only a small number of works labelled 'comedies', more particularly those associated with laughter, have enjoyed the attention of historical film scholars. Furthermore, scholars have tended to concentrate their attention on humorous works treating a small range of historical events. A great deal has been written, for instance, on the idea of 'Holocaust comedy' and whether *The Great Dictator* (1940), *The Day the Clown Cried* (1972), *Jakob Der Lügner* (1974; remade as *Jakob the Liar*, 1999), *The Producers* (1983), *Mutters Courage* (*My Mother's Courage*, 1995), *La Vita è bella* (*Life is Beautiful*, 1997) and *Train de vie* (*Train of Life*, 1998) are or even ought to be funny.

Does the constellation of horrors that crystallised into the terms 'Holocaust' or 'Shoah' permit laughter? At first sight, the answer would appear to be negative, for countless scholars have struggled against the larger question of whether it can be represented at all.[19] In historical and autobiographical works on the Holocaust, though, we do catch a glimpse of those incarcerated using humour as a survival mechanism.[20] A similar use of humour, it might be argued, runs through *Life is Beautiful, Jakob the Liar* and *Train of Life*. In the first, jokes infuse the game that Guido constructs to explain the camp he and his young son (Giosue) have been sent to. In the second, Jakob Heym's concocted radio news reports and humorous story hours bring hope to the ghetto in which he is imprisoned. And in the third, the village idiot Shlomo masquerades as a German officer to steal a train and rescue the occupants of a *shtetl* or small Jewish village in Eastern Europe. One reading of these films sees their lead characters as 'fools'—figures set apart from others on account of their social innocence or even simplicity—playing a role that defies the right or power of the Holocaust to extinguish human personalities. Another sees their use of humour as tantamount to trivialisation and a threat to the dignity and memory of those who perished. Although apparently divided, these two readings are united in crediting comedy with the ability to—as Cicero put it—mirror the manners of society, whether past (reading one) or present (reading two). Put simply, critics may doubt whether Holocaust comedy can represent the horrors of the Third Reich, but they also leave unquestioned the assumption that it can represent a current social pathology, a disease of forgetting. The assumption that comedy is a form of social diagnosis would seem to be a promising exemplar for the social and political engagement valued by film scholars. That it has not been awarded extensive critical attention beyond the bounds of the Holocaust therefore deserves reflection.

Also neglected by historical film scholars are what are commonly labelled 'musicals'. This, as Steven Cohan points out, reflects wider difficulties with an 'odd species of entertainment'. He writes:

> The plots seem not only escapist but hackneyed, recycled from film to film; the characters lack psychological depth and their passions are corny, chaste beyond belief; the Tin Pan Alley songs are out of synch with contemporary musical styles; the big production numbers are too over-the-top to be taken seriously. Most alienating of all, the convention of a character bursting into a song or breaking into dance with inexplicable orchestral accompaniment, the hallmark moments in any movie musical, occasions laughter rather than applause because it breaks with cinematic realism.[21]

Musicals are, put bluntly, an 'impossible genre' because they contain elements that appear to be in spatial, temporal or logical contradiction to understandings of historical realism.[22] Nobody, we expect, bursts into song after committing an act of murder, as Selma (Björk) does in *Dancer in the Dark* (2000). And we know that something is awry with *Moulin Rouge* (2001) when Christian inserts some lyrics from *The Sound of Music* (1965) into a stage show that is being composed around 1900. Musicals thus appear to sit firmly outside the boundary of history. Or do they? Musicals may include seemingly impossible acts, but they are not entirely constituted by them. Might their 'non-impossible' acts still justify their consideration as historical works? Unlike the early filmic practice of classifying films as '50 percent talking' or '75 percent silent', contemporary classifications do not entail numerical tallying. If there is no tally, there must be some other criteria at work for decisions of exclusion and inclusion.

A key word in relation to the judgement of musicals is 'realism'. One of the main points of this chapter and Chapter 4 is to show that the realism of canonical 'historical films' is of a certain form, a form that is not immune to change or question. This same point may be made about melodrama, which along with 'costume' has received mixed valuations. Although scholars have celebrated or expressed their disdain for melodrama as an introspective, psychological genre for women, Russell Merritt, Ben Singer and Steve Neale have pointed out that in early cinema, the term was reserved for stories of action and adventure by working-class men.[23] This difference of views extends the point just made about realism by showing us, first, that genres are not transhistorical categories that are immune to change and, second, that they are invoked for certain purposes, as with the aim of feminist film criticism to recover and rehabilitate women's activities.

Familiar paths: genre and ideology

I could go on and on, carefully cataloguing all the kinds of film that have been neglected by historical film scholars. But I hope that my selection will suffice to show that decisions of generic classification are bound up with value judgements made in a particular historical context. Genre is therefore best understood discursively, as language addressed by one party to another usually for a specific, identifiable purpose. So when on the basis of extant scholarship we build up a profile of historical films as made by Europeans or independent North American units, and as connected with serious, live-action presentation of public political events, we thus need to ask what this profile is for. What functions do the pronouncements of historical film scholars serve?

The scholarly neglect of cultural cinemas like those of India and generic mixtures involving elements of animation, comedy, music and melodrama might, as I have suggested, be explained by their purported transgression of historical reality. Perhaps, like musicals, they are 'impossible', contradicting notions of spatial, temporal and logical consistency. As we shall discover in Chapter 4, the underexamined connection of historical films with a particular concept of 'reality' has unduly limited the range of works that are accorded scholarly and educational examination. But it is worth noting that the kinds of film discussed above are not passed over simply on the basis of their *historical* diegeses. Film scholars, and not just historical film scholars, also select particular films over others. Why? This question draws us closer to assumptions about the social functions of film, the critical examination of which binds this book together. Scholars—historical and otherwise—have social and political expectations of films. As I alluded to above in my account of Mumbai historical films, these expectations are grounded in the often unspoken belief that active interpretation of a film is the hallmark of a free, participatory and even creative life.

Writing on play, Victor Turner suggests that socially transgressive, anti-realist activities can foster the creation of 'alternative models for living, from utopias to programs, which are capable of influencing the behaviour of those in mainstream social and political roles . . . in the direction of radical change, just as much as they can serve as instruments of political control'.[24] On this view, Mumbai historical films, animations, comedies, musicals and melodramas—as well as the postmodern films favoured by Rosenstone—may be liberating. The connection of transgression with the generation of awareness and action informs positive reviews of some of the films I discussed above, as with the description of *Life is Beautiful* as 'a dazzling exposition of the way in which love, tenderness and humour can sustain the human spirit under the most oppressive circumstances'.[25] 'Impossible' films might highlight social mores and cause us to reflect on whether they ought to be modified.

Far more scholarship, though, presents a contrary view, describing transgressive activity as a safety valve that defuses social pressures and preserves the established order from destruction. Thus Milan Kundera has noted how spontaneous activities can be appropriated by governments that wish to erase inconvenient memories from people's minds and keep them in a state of infancy.[26] Images of childhood and forgetting also underpin David Denby's appraisal of *Life is Beautiful*:

Comedy and art, Benigni wants us to believe, not only keep the human spirit aloft but save lives. 'Life is Beautiful' is soothing and anodyne—a hopeful fable of redemption. . . . In the end, Benigni protects the audience as much as Guido protects his son; we are all treated like children. . . . The enormous worldwide success of *Life is Beautiful* suggests that the audience is exhausted by the Holocaust, that it is sick to death of the subject's unending ability to disturb. The audience's mood is understandable, but artists are supposed to be made of sterner stuff, and surely an artist cannot transcend what he never encounters. . . . *Life is Beautiful* is a benign form of Holocaust denial. The audience comes away feeling relieved and happy and rewards Benigni for allowing it, at last, to escape.[27]

On this view, film can be an 'escapist' or 'entertaining' salve that keeps viewers in a state of arrested development. Taking their lead from Louis Althusser, a number of neo-Marxist film scholars have sketched out a similar view, seeing some or even all films as vehicles of government or industrial ideologies. Framing films in this way, particular genres or genre itself become a means of luring viewers into accepting deceptive beliefs about society and happiness that are non-solutions. Generic texts perform this function because—combining the arguments of Roland Barthes, Theodor Adorno and Frank Kermode—their *lisible* ('readerly') nature encourages 'underreading'.[28] Generic texts elicit underreading on the part of viewers through the use of familiar themes and rhetorical devices like happy endings, women in need of rescue by men, 'fools' who show us the meaning of virtue or child narrators. These devices mask and cement contemporary social and political assumptions. They do not get us to the past, and arguably, they prevent us from understanding our present. As Stephen J. Gould has complained, 'We cannot hope for even a vaguely accurate portrayal of the nub of history in film so long as movies must obey the literary conventions of ordinary plotting'.[29] 'Writerly' texts, on the other hand, draw attention to the various rhetorical techniques that produce the illusion of realism and encourage readers to participate in the construction of meaning. That is, they make it clear to us that what we are seeing is a construction, one shaped by particular assumptions about society. Literary and film theorists as well as historical film scholars favour writerly texts on the grounds that they purportedly encourage viewers to become producers rather than consumers of texts.

The divided appraisal of films as either emancipatory or stultifying remains to be challenged in later segments of this book, particularly Chapters 7 and 8. Here I would simply like to note the paradox that scholars' positioning of themselves as apart from—and able to observe—the effect of institutionally produced texts on unsuspecting subjects has led them to describe film genres in a writerly manner. Closed off from overt view are the reasons why they engage in these boundary-drawing exercises.

Images and words

In *Re-thinking History*, Keith Jenkins argues that the chief question for historians is not 'What is history?' but 'What is history *for*?' This second question captures well the shift of twentieth-century historiography towards epistemology, bringing with it an emphasis on the relationship between the content, form and function of histories. For some historians, form is ancillary to content; the narrative shape and emphases of their works are dictated by the phenomena about which they write. Without this hierarchy of content over form, it is claimed, there is little to stop the activity of writing history from merging with that of writing fiction. All but a few historians acknowledge that the accounts they offer of past events are constructions. Where opinion divides is on the historical status of those constructions. In David Carr's view, for example, life and narrative coincide. Historians thus work to draw out narrative forms that are implicit 'in the events themselves'.[30] Many more historians, of whom the best known is Hayden White, argue instead that the past does not present itself in a shape that is ready packaged for telling. Rather, historians must package it, and in this sense they are authors. Even a chronicler must decide when to begin and end an account and what details to include, exclude and emphasise. There is no necessary or absolute beginning, end or scope to any event that happened in the past: an historian may choose to write about a period in the life of one individual, as with Carlo Ginzburg's studio of the heretical miller Mennochio in *The Cheese and the Worms* or about the history of the universe from the Big Bang to the future, as with David Christian's *Maps of Time*.[31] Similarly, an historical film may represent short-term (e.g. *Thirteen Days*, 2001) or long-term events (*History of the World Part 1* (1981)). Perhaps Carla Phillips and William Phillips' evaluation of *Columbus* (1992) and *1492* (1992) can thus be applied in some degree to all written and filmed histories:

> These films treat the historical record as mere raw material, to be adapted to the needs of the screenplay. Chronology is expanded, compressed, reversed, or falsified to suit the dramatic trajectory. Historical personages are revised, deified or demonized, conflated or created from whole cloth to serve the director's will.[32]

Nor is there only one necessary or absolute way of ordering, emphasising or emplotting historical events. As E.H. Carr has argued, 'The facts speak only when the historian calls on them: it is he [*sic*] who decides to which facts to give the floor, and in what order or context'.[33] There is no logical requirement, for instance, that histories have to be in Western chronological order, as the editing techniques of flashback and cross-cutting detailed in the next chapter attest. Different meanings and significance can be bestowed on events through emphasis. Emphasis might be apparent from the proportion of space given to the representation of a phenomenon, or the favouring of particular kinds of evidence (e.g. political records) or film technique (e.g. extensive use of close-ups on a particular individual's face). Emphasis might also be signalled through the favouring of a particular perspective on events and the exclusion or minimisation of other perspectives.

In *Metahistory*, White advances the idea that histories are characterised by various conventional modes of emplotment (story or plot type). Furthermore, in line with Roland Barthes, Keith Jenkins and Paul de Mann, he notes that the nineteenth century set down the association of forms of emplotment with particular ideologies, which he classifies as:

Emplotment	Ideology
romance	anarchist
comedy	conservative
tragedy	radical
satire	liberal

In romance, the protagonists achieve release from the situations they find themselves in. Satire is the opposite of romance, conveying the message that the protagonists are ultimately captive in some way. In comedy, as was argued earlier, events tend towards to a beneficial resolution; and in tragedy, setbacks are accepted with resignation.[34] Ideologically, conservatives are the most suspicious of change to the *status quo*, fashioning history as the progressive realisation of the social and political structure that prevails in their time. Anarchists, by contrast, are the most socially transcendent, narrating the past in the hope for a better future, while liberals and radicals are located more towards the centre of White's ideological spectrum.[35] Histories, White concludes, are thus 'not only about events but also about the possible sets of relationships that those events can be demonstrated to figure'.[36]

White, along with F.R. Ankersmit, Lionel Gossman, Stephen Bann, Robert Berkhofer, Dominick La Capra, Hans Kellner, Nancy Partner, Linda Orr, Paul Ricoeur and David Harlan, stresses the importance of rhetorical conventions and linguistic form in the shaping of histories. Some writers, as we will note in more depth in Chapter 4, even invert the hierarchy of content over form and conclude that history making is primarily the stylistic fashioning of narratives, including 'reality effects', for particular readers and particular ideological purposes. Histories are thus ethically and culturally situated. The cultured, gendered and ideological positioning of language—as traditionally refracted through the viewpoints of white, male, educated Europeans—is a shaping force that cannot be ignored. Attention to the form of a history will thus tell us more about the person who made it than about the past.

We can only construct new practices of history, Foucault argues, once we expose the assumptions concealed in what we assume is the transparent view of the past delivered through narratives that are saturated with 'reality effects'. This has led to the assumption that it is better to make history in a non-narrative form or at least to break with certain narrative conventions.

Nowhere is that opinion voiced more strongly than in relation to historical film. Hence Rosenstone's favouring of the 'new' or postmodern historical film, which he sees as opposed to 'Hollywood codes of "realism" '. Postmodern films question the mainstream association of history with linear, progressive, emotional and ultimately tidy stories of individuals. Mark Carnes has also complained about the tidiness of what he calls 'Hollywood history':

> Professional historians . . . pluck from the muck of the historical record the most solid bits of evidence, mold them into meanings, and usually serve them up as books that, though encrusted with footnotes and rendolent of musty archives, can be held and cherished, pondered and disputed. Hollywood history is different. It fills irritating gaps in the historical record and polishes dulling ambiguities and complexities. The final product gleams, and it sears the imagination. . . . Hollywood history sparkles because it is so morally unambiguous, so devoid of tedious complexity, *so perfect*.[37]

To this we might add White's alignment of comedy with a conservative ideology and likewise all transgressive 'safety valves'. But on what grounds are these judgements made? White's argument about the association of modes of emplotment with various ideologies derives in part from the writings of Northrup Frye—the purposes of which White never examines—and from a small sample of nineteenth-century texts by white, male, educated Europeans. If a different collection of nineteenth-century authors had been used—for instance, writing by women or Latin American authors—might his arguments about the forms of history change? Stable boundaries are assumed for each of the forms of emplotment, and thus like many film scholars, he directs the attention of readers away from the consideration of genre mixing and changes in use. I repeat a point made earlier in this chapter: acts of boundary drawing raise many questions.

Criticisms of the attempts by White and many other film scholars to offer taxonomies of history show us that Jenkins's question 'What is history for?' should be supplemented by another: Where is history located? History is not a physical object that can be easily labelled, as with a 'cat' or a 'book'. Nor can a single book or film be used to define history. A less obvious point is that the meaning of 'history', or even 'historical film', is not exhausted by a canon of texts or a single form of emplotment (e.g. satire, as distinct from comedy). Put simply, books or films and their rhetorical devices alone do not constitute history. Nor does history reside in a process of composition, in the intentions of authors, in marketing strategies or materials or reader or viewer reception. Yet historical film scholars and historiographers routinely select one of these aspects and treat it as representative of the whole concept. Furthermore, they assume that these aspects of history can be described transparently, devoid of any reflection on the assumptions and purposes imbued in their work.

History is not a single object or even a collection of objects. Nor is it bound up simply with the activities of one group or another. Extending the argument I made in the last chapter, history is a discursive site where meaning is circulated, agreed or contested. In line with this, in the chapters that follow I will argue for the supplementation of scholars' textual concerns with insights into the promotion and reception of films.

Recommended resources

Altman, R., *Film/Genre*, London: BFI, 2000.

Barefoot, G., *Gaslight Melodrama: From Victorian London to 1940s Hollywood*, London: Continuum, 2001.

Basinger, J., *The World War II Combat Film: Anatomy of a Genre*, New York: Columbia University Press, 1986.

Bratton, J., Cook, J. and Gledhill, C. (eds), *Melodrama: Stage, Picture, Screen*, London: BFI, 1994.

Carr, D., 'Narrative and the real world: an argument for continuity', *History and Theory*, 1986, vol. 25(1), pp. 117–31.

Custen, G.F., *Bio/Pics: How Hollywood Constructed Public History*, New Brunswick, NJ: Rutgers University Press, 1992.

Dwyer, R. and Patel, D., *Cinema India: The Visual Culture of Hindi Film*, London: Reaktion Books, 2002.

Gilman, S.L., 'Is life beautiful? Can the Shoah be funny? Some thoughts on recent and older films', *Critical Inquiry*, 2000, vol. 26(2), pp. 279–308.

Gledhill, C. (ed.), *Home is Where the Heart Is: Studies in Melodrama and the Women's Film*, London: BFI, 1987.

Gunning, T., ' "Those drawn with a very fine camel's hair brush": the origins of film genres', *Iris*, 1995, no. 20, pp. 49–61.

Landy, M., *British Genres: Cinema and Society 1930–1960*, Princeton, NJ: Princeton University Press, 1991.

Lopez, D., *Films by Genre: 775 Categories, Styles, Trends and Movements Defined, with a Filmography for Each*, Jefferson, NC: McFarland, 1993.

Napier, S.J., *Anime: From Akira to Princess Mononoke*, New York: Palgrave, 2000.

Narremore, J., *More than Night: Film Noir and its Contexts*, Berkeley: University of California Press, 1998.

Taves, B., *The Romance of Adventure: The Genre of Historical Adventure Movies*, Jackson: University Press of Mississippi, 1993.

White, H., *Metahistory: The Historical Imagination in Nineteenth-century Europe*, Baltimore: Johns Hopkins University Press, 1973.

Notes

1 R. Rosenstone, *Visions of the Past: The Challenge of Film to Our Idea of History*, Cambridge, Mass.: Harvard University Press, 1995, p. 12; and R. Rosenstone (ed.), *Revisioning History: Film and the Construction of a New Past*, Princeton, NJ: Princeton University Press, 1995, p. 3.

2 B. Taves, *The Romance of Adventure: The Genre of Historical Action Movies*, Jackson: University Press of Mississippi, 1993, pp. 3–4; as quoted in R. Altman, *Film/Genre*, London: BFI, 2000, p. 18.

3 R. Altman, *Film/Genre*, pp. 11–12, 18–26.

4 P. Rosen, *Change Mummified: Cinema, Historicity, Theory*, Minneapolis: University of Minnesota Press, 2001, p. 169; and R. Rosenstone, *Visions of the Past*, p. 57. For reviews and other academic writings, see M.E. Biggs, *French Films, 1945–1993*, Jefferson, NC: McFarland, 1996, p. 232; M. Levinson, *Cineaste*, 1984, vol. 13(2), p. 47; G. Austin, *Contemporary French Cinema*, Manchester: Manchester University Press, 1993, p. 143; and C. Peachman, *TimeOut Film Guide*, 4th edn, London: Penguin, 1995, p. 609.

5 K. Burke, 'Charting relationships in American popular film, Part I', *International Journal of Instructional Media*, 1997, vol. 24(4), p. 342.

6 T. Gunning, ' "Those drawn with a very fine camel's hair brush": the origins of film genres', *Iris*, 1995, no. 20, p. 50; A. Knee, 'Generic change in the cinema', *Iris*, 1995, no. 20, p. 36; and J. Staiger, *Perverse Spectators: The Practices of Film Reception*, New York: New York University Press, 2000, p. 64.

7 R. Altman, *Film/Genre*, p. 59.

8 For reproductions of these posters, see R. Altman, *Film/Genre*, p. 59; and G. Custen, *Bio/Pics*, p. 204.

9 P. Jaikumar, 'Bollywood spectaculars', *World Literature Today*, 2003, vol. 77(3–4), pp. 25–6.

10 See, for example, J. Collins, 'Genericity in the nineties: eclectic irony and the new sincerity', in J. Collins, H. Radner and A.P. Collins (eds), *Film Theory Goes to the Movies*, New York: Routledge, 1993, pp. 242–3.

11 J. Staiger, *Perverse Spectators*, p. 71; and R. Altman, *Film/Genre*, pp. 36, 139–40, 141.

12 S. Chakravarty, *National Identity in Indian Popular Cinema, 1947–1987*, Austin: University of Texas Press, 1993, pp. 15, 158. See also T. Ganti, *Bollywood: A Guide Book to Popular Hindi Cinema*, London: Routledge, 2004, pp. 139–40. Ganti notes the pejorative division of Hindi film from Western film but seeks to address it by noting Indian examples that offer dominant or single genres.

13 R. Vasudevan, 'The politics of cultural address in a "transitional" cinema: a case study of popular Indian cinema', in C. Glenhill and L. Williams (eds), *Reinventing Film Studies*, London: Routledge, 2000, p. 133.

14 As quoted in E. Barnouw and S. Krishnaswarmy, *Indian Film*, 2nd edn, New York: Columbia University Press, 1980, p. 173.

15 See, for example, S. Cubitt, *The Cinema Effect*, Cambridge, Mass.: MIT Press, 2004, pp. 70–98; and D. Crafton, *Before Mickey: The Animated Film 1898–1928*, rev. edn, Cambridge, Mass.: MIT Press, 1993.

16 See, for example, C. Gluck, 'The past in the present', in A. Gordon (ed.), *Postwar Japan as History*, Berkeley: University of California Press, 1993, p. 83; and R. Tachibana, *Narrative as Counter-memory: A Half-century of Postwar Writings in Germany and Japan*, Albany: State University of New York, 1998.

17 S.J. Napier, *Anime: From* Akira *to* Princess Mononoke, New York: Palgrave/St Martin's Press, 2001, p. 170. See also M. Morimoto, 'The "peace dividend" in Japanese cinema: metaphors of a demilitarised nation', in W. Dissanayake (ed.), *Colonial Nationalism in Asian Cinema*, Bloomington: Indiana University Press, 1994, p. 19.

18 T.G.A. Nelson, *Comedy: An Introduction to Comedy in Literature, Drama, and Cinema*, Oxford: Oxford University Press, 1990, pp. 1–2. See also N. Frye, *Anatomy of Criticism: Four Essays*, Princeton, NJ: Princeton University Press, 1957; and H. White, *Metahistory: The Historical Imagination in Nineteenth-century Europe*, Baltimore: Johns Hopkins University Press, 1973.

19 See, for example, F. Manchel, 'A reel witness: Steven Spielberg's representation of the Holocaust in *Schindler's List*', *Journal of Modern History*, 1995, vol. 67(1), pp. 83–100; B. Lang, *Holocaust Representation: Art Within the Limits of History*

and Ethics, Baltimore: Johns Hopkins University Press, 2000; and the final section of K. Jenkins (ed.), *The Postmodern History Reader*, London: Routledge, 1997.

20 H.-J. Gamm, *Der Flusterwitz im dritten Reich*: mundliche Dokumente zur Lage der deustchen Wahrend des Nationalsocializmus, Munich: List Verlag 1973; S. Lipman, *Laughter in Hell: The Use of Humour During the Holocaust*, Northvale, NJ: Jason Aronson, 1991; and Holocaust Video Testimony 739 and 1678 of the Fortunoff Video Archive for Holocaust Testimonies, as cited in S.L. Gilman, 'Is life beautiful? Can the Shoah be funny? Some thoughts on recent and older films', *Critical Inquiry*, 2000, vol. 26(2), n. 16.

21 S. Cohan (ed.), *Hollywood Musicals, The Film Reader*, London: Routledge, 2002, p. 1.

22 M. Rubin, *Showstoppers: Busby Berkeley and the Tradition of Spectacle*, New York: Columbia University Press, 1993, p. 37.

23 R. Merritt, 'Melodrama: post-mortem for a phantom genre', *Wide Angle*, 1983, vol. 5(3), pp. 24–31; B. Singer, 'Female power in the serial-queen melodrama: the etiology of an anomaly', *Camera Obscura*, 1990, vol. 22(1), pp. 99–129; S. Neale, 'Melo talk: on the meaning and use of the term "melodrama" in the American trade press', *Velvet Light Trap*, 1993, no. 32, pp. 66–89; and S. Neale, 'Questions of genre', in B.G. Grant (ed.), *Film Genre Reader*, 2nd edn, pp. 159–83.

24 V. Turner, *From Ritual to Theatre: The Human Seriousness of Play*, New York: PAJ Publications, 1982. On the connection of comedy with the creation of new social orders, see N. Frye, *Anatomy of Criticism*.

25 D. Kotzin, 'A clown in the camps', *Jerusalem Report*, 26 October 1998, p. 40; as cited in M. Viano, '*Life is Beautiful*', *Film Quarterly*, 1999, vol. 53(1), p. 29.

26 H. White, *Metahistory*, p. 29; and M. Kundera, *The Book of Laughter and Forgetting*, New York: Harper, 1999. See also U. Eco, 'The frames of comic "freedom" ', in U. Eco, V.V. Ivanov and M. Rektor (eds), *Carnival!*, Berlin: Mouten de Grouter, 1984.

27 D. Denby, 'In the eye of the beholder', *The New Yorker*, 15 March 1999, pp. 96–9.

28 R. Barthes, *S/Z*, trans. R. Martin, New York: Hill & Wang, 1974, pp. 4–5; and F. Kermode, 'Secrets and narrative sequence', in W.J.T. Mitchell (ed.), *On Narrative*, Chicago: University of Chicago Press, 1981, pp. 79–97.

29 S.J. Gould, Review of *Jurassic Park*, in M. Carnes (ed.), *Past Imperfect: History According to the Movies*, New York: Henry Holt, 1996, p. 35.

30 D. Carr, 'Narrative and the real world: an argument for continuity', *History and Theory*, 1986, vol. 25(1), pp. 117–31.

31 C. Ginzburg, *The Cheese and the Worms: The Cosmos of a Sixteenth-century Miller*, trans. J. and A. Tedeschi, Harmondsworth: Penguin, 1980; and D. Christian, *Maps of Time: An Introduction to Big History*, Berkeley: University of California Press, 2004.

32 C. Phillips and W.D. Phillips, Review of *Columbus*, in M. Carnes (ed.), *Past Imperfect*, p. 63.

33 E.H. Carr, *What is History?*, ed. R.W. Davies, rev. edn, Harmondsworth: Penguin, 1986, p. 11.

34 *Ibid.*, p. 9.

35 *Ibid.*, p. 69.

36 H. White, *Metahistory*, p. 94.

37 M. Carnes (ed.), *Past Imperfect*, p. 9.

3 Pasts, presents, futures

Now, 1968

Opening title, *Down with Love* (2003)

What do historical films depict? For Pierre Sorlin, the answer to this question is relatively straightforward: the historical film is 'no more than a useful device to speak of the present time'.[1] History serves as a signifier of issues contemporary with filming, ranging from ethical beliefs to political aspirations. Leger Grindon, too, has written of history in the cinema as an 'address to the present', one that Frank Sanello complains has nurtured 'historical solipsism', or a belief that we can know only ourselves.[2] Across reviews of individual or groups of films we find similar sentiments echoed. To take just a few examples: Richard Slotkin sees *The Charge of the Light Brigade* (1936) as a product of contemporary debates about appeasement and rearmament; Linda Salamon contends that historical films offer an acceptable means of exploring evil in a 'contemporary popular-therapeutic culture of "closure" and "healing" '; and Arthur Lindley argues that filmic depictions of the Middle Ages are a pretext for individuals and cultures to revisit themselves 'as children'.[3]

Sorlin's view runs parallel to discussions on time and tense in cinema and wider society, views that I believe do not sufficiently recognise the temporal heterogeneity of film. Film, a number of twentieth-century writers assume, is a medium of the present tense. Exploring various forms of representation in 'The rhetoric of the image', for example, Roland Barthes distinguishes the '*having-been-there*' of photography with the '*being-there*' of film. Photographic images can appear to be identical to what they represent and thus can 'record' or capture the past existence of objects, whereas even apparently 'realistic' films transform what is represented through contemporary codes and conventions of narration, emplotment, sequencing and perspective. Barthes favours photography over film on these grounds, explaining that the latter masks or 'naturalises' the constructedness of its meaning, encouraging viewers to accept its 'reality' and to surrender an opportunity for resistance against socio-cultural mores.[4] Barthes' arguments about film, in turn, affirm contemporary pronouncements about the 'end of history' and the emergence of what Frederic Jameson calls the 'eternal present' in postmodernism.[5]

As will be clear from the chapters that follow, much can be said about whether historical films are indexical—able to attest to the past existence of objects—and socially regulatory. For present purposes, we should give further consideration to Barthes' characterisation of photography and film as temporally homogeneous. Photography is imbued with 'pastness', film with the 'presentness' of its reception, yet as Barthes admits in *Camera Lucida*, photographers commonly employ compositional devices that diminish opportunities for asocial or antisocial subjectivity. Actual—as distinct from ideal—photographs are thus temporally heterogeneous. The flip side of this admission, as Philip Rosen notes, is that temporal heterogeneity is also possible in film. Indeed, Barthes notes as much, clarifying that when he juxtaposes cinema and photography, he means 'narrative cinema'. He writes: 'the cinema participates in this domestication of Photography—at least the fictional cinema'.[6]

Barthes thus allows for temporal heterogeneity in film. Yet the range of examples through which he explores this claim is limited: his sole excursion into 'narrative' territory is a single scene in *Casanova* (directed by Federico Fellini, 1976). More expansive is Gilles Deleuze's account of the ascendancy of films of the 'time-image' after the Second World War. Across his writings on cinema, Deleuze contests the claim that film images are always 'in' the present; rather, they are groupings of various temporal relations. He writes:

> The image itself is the system of the relationships between its elements, that is, a set of relationships of time from which the variable present only flows. . . . What is specific to the image . . . is to make perceptible, to make visible, relationships of time which cannot be seen in the represented object and do not allow themselves to be reduced to the present.[7]

Films of the 'time-image' differ from those of the 'movement-image' in rendering these relations explicit to the viewer. In movement-images, linear temporal continuity is paramount and is established by character, sound, costume and camera action. For instance, characters act and react in sequence, and matches on action are used to connect shots in sometimes quite different locations. Each action and shot is the end of one and the beginning of another, producing the effect of a seamless durational whole. In films of the time-image, however, camera action is not rational or seamless but aberrant, ambiguous and disconcerting. Shots and sequences bifurcate, leaving viewers unsure as to what will come next and thus encouraging in them an increased sensitivity to time and conventions of time in the cinema. The result, as Deleuze notes, is an awareness of cinematic time as being akin to the 'dizzying net of divergent, convergent and parallel times' in the temporal labyrinth of Jorge Luis Borges' story 'The Garden of Forking Paths'.[8]

Although Deleuze's writings on films of the time-image are in some ways taxonomic, he is clear that the exposure of temporality cannot be put down to a particular technique or moment in the filming, editing, screening or reception of a work. Furthermore, his valuation of some works that are also championed by those who would readily divide cinema into 'elite' and 'popular' offerings—for example, Orson Welles' *Citizen Kane* (1941) and Alain Resnais' *Hiroshima, Mon Amour* (1959)—does not preclude the analysis of a wide range of works. This is because the relation of movement-images and time-images is not one of mutual exclusion: just as there is no one film that embodies the time-image, there may be works that are ostensibly organised by the movement-image but never fully constrained by that logic.[9] Similarly, no clear division of 'classical' (pre-1945) and 'postclassical' works can be maintained; the logic of the time-image infuses even the earliest films. In short, there is no clear dichotomy of temporal explicitness or implicitness, homogeneity or heterogeneity, that can be used to divide, classify or even rank historical films.

Temporal heterogeneity in historical films

Cinema is characterised by multiple, often conflicting, temporalities. Following Mary Ann Doane's lead, I would like to note three: the temporalities of screening technology, of reception and of diegesis.[10] We may associate screening technology with linear and irreversible viewing, but as Tom Gunning, André Gaudreault and Doane have shown, audiences of the 'cinema of attractions' at the beginning of the twentieth century were also offered film loops, works played in 'forward' and 'reverse' sequence and works that started with stills, which were then activated.[11] Video and now digital (DVD and satellite/cable) viewing technologies offer similar possibilities, with the latter also affording the viewer the chance to view and re-view isolated 'chapters' or even to play them in random order. That we typically think of this 'random shuffle' mode of viewing as aberrant perhaps reinforces Barthes' connection of images with conventions that serve to rein in socially dispersive and even disruptive subjectivity. We will look at that issue further in Chapters 4 and 7, devoted to the discussion of identity and propaganda, respectively. Here, though, it is important to note that by adopting random-shuffle mode, the viewer can transform any film—even one that in ascending chapter order is dominated by the logic of the movement-image—into a time-image.

Related to, but not necessarily identical with, technological temporalities are temporalities of reception. Many viewing settings imply a linear, irreversible temporality. The placement of the screen in relation to the seats, light levels and the location of entrances and exits fosters fixed, relentless attention to the screened work. As will be argued further in Chapters 4 and 7, though, even when we take variations in cinema design into account, such as those between a multiplex and a drive-in, there is little evidence of viewers displaying relentless attention or of them being united in recalling a linear, irreversible moviegoing experience.

Finally, there is the temporality of the diegesis: the ways in which temporal change, duration and notions of historicity, past, present and future, are invoked and implied in films. Running time is rarely the same as diegetic time.[12] *The Life and Death of Peter Sellers* (2004), for instance, may have a running time of 127 minutes, but the film purports to 'track' the final twenty years of Sellers' life. This disjunction of running time and diegetic time is present in the earliest of films, including 'actualities' that purport to capture or record current events or phenomena of interest, and is so common that that use of real time might be considered a 'special effect'. When we encounter extended sequences of real time, as with some scenes of *La Haine* (*The Hate*, 1995), for instance, we—like the young men of the Paris housing projects at the centre of the diegesis—feel that we have had too long to look and think. Conversely, real time might be utilised to impress upon viewers the approach of an imminent deadline, but it is unusual for that to be maintained for the duration of running time. In cinema, therefore, time is figurable and malleable. In the main, that shaping is achieved through the use of editing, film colour, diegetic and non-diegetic music and elements of *mise en scène*. In the following sections, I would like to focus on two of these: editing and *mise en scène*.

Editing

In simple terms, editing may be thought of as the creation of ruptures in the spatio-temporal continuity of shots through splicing and the removal of unwanted footage. Elliptical editing, for instance, allows for the elision of time, as with the use of a jump cut in the 'actuality' *Electrocution of an Elephant* (1903) to excise the 'uneventful' time in which the subject, Topsy, was secured in the executory apparatus. No attempt was made to conceal the cut, and the resulting disjunction exposes the filmmakers' coding in a time-image. Historical films also employ jump shots to explicitly suggest ellipsis, along with forms of punctuation such as fades, wipes, dissolves or irises. For instance, a series of shots connected by fades suggests the telescoping of Forrest Gump's marathon run across the United States (*Forrest Gump*, 1994). Conversely, temporal expansion can be achieved through the use of overlapping editing, as with the prolonged showering of gold coins in the coronation scene of Eisenstein's *Ivan Grozni* (*Ivan the Terrible*, 1945). Diegetic phenomena can be repeated, with or without a change in the position of the camera. In *The Story of the Kelly Gang* (1906), for instance, the ride of the Kelly gang towards the troopers in the scene depicting the siege of Glen Rowan is repeated from two slightly different points of view (Figure 3.1). Here, succession signifies its opposite, simultaneity, in order to compensate for spatial dislocation. In more recent films such as *Citizen Kane, Rashomon* (1950), *Courage Under Fire* (1996), *Donnie Darko* (2001) and *The Life and Death of Peter Sellers*, repetition is used to suggest multiple and conflicting viewpoints on the same event and to emphasise phenomena that will probably only become intelligible to viewers towards the end of the film.

Figure 3.1a

Figure 3.1b

Figure 3.1c Diegetic repetition and cross-cutting in *The Story of the Kelly Gang* (1906; © 2000, Screensound Australia)

Editing and the juxtaposition of images can also be used to suggest temporal simultaneity. One of the earliest extant examples of simultaneity can be found in *The Life of an American Fireman* (1903). In the opening shot of that film, the use of a balloon insert in the upper right of the frame allows viewers to watch a fireman sleeping and a mother putting her child to bed. These three characters later meet when the fireman rescues the mother and child from a blaze. Simultaneity might also be found in the switch between scenes in *Kelly Gang*, which show the siege at Glen Rowan and the approach of a party on horseback. This editing device of cross-cutting is often used in historical films, as the examples of *The Battle of Elderbush Gulch* (1913), *Gallipoli* (1981) and *De Tweeling* (*Twin Sisters*, 2003) attest. In the first two, rapid switches between action sequences—a cavalry troop riding to settlers in a besieged cabin in the former, and Frank running a message to stop Archie and his comrades going 'over the top' of their trench in the latter—are used to build suspense in last-minute (successful and unsuccessful) rescue attempts. The relation of shots is not simply that of addition or accumulation; it also serves to evoke anxiety and perhaps even desire.[13] In *De Tweeling*, however, cross-cutting serves a different function, tying together extended biographies of separated twins raised in the Netherlands and Germany during the Second World War. This allows the viewer access to a range of experiences wider than that of any one character or context.

Editing does not always imply temporal simultaneity, for it is not unusual for historical films to be out of chronological order or to represent phenomena in different places *and* times. Few historical films offer cross-cutting between more than two historical periods—as with D.W. Griffiths' *Intolerance* (1916)—or extended reverse-order sequences like that in Lee Chang-Dong's *Bakha Satang* (*Peppermint Candy*, 1999), a film that moves from the main character's suicide to him sitting peacefully in the same location twenty years earlier. Taken in screening order, the film emphasises the extended aftermath of conflict-related trauma. More common is the foreshadowing of the end of a film in its opening, as with the opening flashforward of *Gandhi* (1982), which is used to infuse later scenes with a sense of his death as destiny and even apotheosis. However, the editing device most commentators associate with historical films is that of flashback. As Turim defines it, a flashback is 'an image or a filmic segment that is understood as representing temporal occurrences anterior to those in the images that preceded it'.[14] In its most common form, flashback is signalled when an older character's memory of the past leads to a cut to a scene or series of scenes representing that past. Early in *Titanic* (1997), for example, a close-up of the eyes of Rose as an old woman serves as a bridge to a very wide shot of the hull of the *Titanic* just before its maiden voyage. The choice of eyes as a signal for flashback is doubly interesting: first, compared with the rest of the face, they appear to be unchanged or mummified; and, second, they are used to signify a large-scale historical event given the subjective mode of a single, fictional individual's remembered experiences. Eyes are also used to signal a return to the past in *Saving Private Ryan* (1998; Figure 3.2), and here, the conflation of subjective memory with collective memory is even more apparent: a close-up on the eyes of Private Ryan as an old man leads to a sequence showing the D-Day landings at Omaha Beach, at which he was not present.

Flashbacks are often used in historical films to 'emphasise the past as a motivational force within the psychology of character' or to signal the therapeutic address of trauma.[15] After telling their stories, Rose (*Titanic*) and Anna (*De Tweeling*) can die, Professor Borg can accept his honorary degree (*Smultronstället, Wild Strawberries*, 1957), Forrest Gump can seek out the love of his life, and Ryan can finally weep at the loss of Captain Miller (*Saving Private Ryan*). Similarly, Marty McFly (*Back to the Future*, 1985) travels to the past to assure his future existence. Connected with the ideas of trauma and therapy, it is perhaps tempting to conclude that Deleuze's description of flashback as 'a closed circuit that goes from the present to the past, and brings us back to the present' is literally and metaphorically true.[16] However, closer examination of Alain Resnais' *Hiroshima Mon Amour* (1959) and Terence Davis' *Distant Voices, Still Lives* (1988) may lead us to rethink this formulation. In *Hiroshima Mon Amour*, the link between the resolution of trauma and flashback is foregrounded and questioned, with the female character resisting the integration of a traumatic past that possesses her through flashbacks and her present life in Hiroshima, the site of a collective trauma.[17] She carries her personal trauma—the death of her German soldier lover at the liberation of Nevers—in silence, for she does not want it to inflect present, ordinary life or to risk the loss of the intensity of her flashbacks

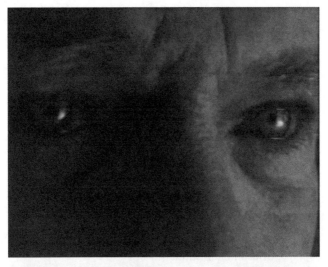

Figure 3.2 Eyes as the means of flashback in *Saving Private Ryan* (© 1998, Dreamworks SKG)

when she expresses them in a form that can be shared. Hers is the double burden of forgetting and remembering. The use of flashback in Terence Davis' diptych *Distant Voices, Still Lives* also evokes what Cathy Caruth sees as the latency of trauma: '[the trauma] is not assimilated or experienced fully at the time, but only belatedly, in its repeated *possession* of the one who experiences it. To be traumatized is precisely to be possessed by an image or event.'[18] Taking as his departure points the grouping of the main characters as if they are frozen in a photograph, Davis leads us to flashbacks that

Figure 3.3 Tableau as a departure point for flashback in *Distant Voices, Still Lives* (© 1988, British Film Institute)

sometimes return to the tableau, and sometimes not (Figure 3.3). Sometimes the use of facial close-ups and voiceover implies that a flashback is the memory of a particular character, but for other scenes, we are unsure as to whose view we share. Nor do we always know the chronological order of events. For instance, the second tableau of *Distant Voices*—arranged to mark Eileen's wedding—triggers the following sequence of shots:

1   Zoom in to close-up of Eileen, dialogue, 'I wish me Dad were here'.
2   Zoom out, right pan to close-up of Maisy, zoom in, voiceover (Maisy) 'I don't, I bleedin' hated him . . .'.
3   Jump cut to wide shot of Maisy scrubbing the cellar floor and then tilt up to her father hitting downwards with a broom (implied hitting of Maisy).
4   Jump cut back to tableau, Eileen repeats dialogue while camera pans left to close-up of Tony.
5   Jump cut to wide shot of Tony smashing a window and confronting his father in a series of sequences that will be repeated and expanded later in the film (all in wide shot).
6   Jump cut to close-up of Tony in tableau asking Eileen if she is ready; the family starts moving forward.

None of the shots is anchored to specific years or dates by narration, props displaying dates (e.g. a conspicuous calendar or newspaper front page) or explanatory titles, and shot 3 will not be repeated and expanded, as will be the case for shot 5. Furthermore, the combination of ill-matched actions and jump cuts to signal flashback enhances the viewer's sense of temporal dislocation.

In the absence of closed editing 'circuits' and sufficient temporal markers, we are unable to apply David Bordwell and Kristen Thompson's advice on making sense of a film out of chronological order:

> Such reordering does not confuse us because we mentally rearrange the events into the order in which they would logically have to occur: Childhood comes before adulthood. From the plot order, we infer the story order. If story events can be thought of as ABCD, then the plot that uses a flashback presents something like BACD.

There is no ABCD in *Distant Voices, Still Lives*. Rather, the relation of shots suggests a tissue of painful memories of physical and psychological abuse that reappear and overwhelm, defying linear management and perhaps even arresting the characters in 'still lives'.

An interesting twist on the conventional connection of flashback with psychological motivation, trauma and therapy is represented in *Donnie Darko*. Set during the 1988 presidential campaign between George Bush and Michael Dukakis, *Donnie Darko* has as its beginning and endpoint a jet engine falling on the bedroom of the title character. Bracketed between the representations of that accident, though, are 28 days, 6 hours, 42 minutes and 12 seconds of 'tangent' time made possible by a voice—later identified as Frank—that leads Donnie near the opening of the film to sleepwalk out of his room as the jet engine falls. Frank, a menacing Harvey-like figure whom we learn later is from Donnie's future, incites him to engage in more and more destructive acts, culminating in the death of his girlfriend Gretchen and his fatal shooting of Frank. Realising that these acts can be erased, Donnie works his way back to the past through a wormhole and opens up another future when he allows the jet engine to fall on him. In that past, he accepts his death with happiness. So whereas the implied past of flashback offers the potential of recovery through therapy, the flashforwards lead Donnie into behaviour which his therapist, and his community, label psychotic. In *Donnie Darko*, the future exists simultaneously with the present when Frank appears to Donnie, and although these appearances signal predetermination—as with the flashforward in *Gandhi*—they are not the end of the film. *Donnie Darko* closes not with the arresting of life with trauma or even death but with the splitting off of another temporal path.

Mise en scène and the temporal punctuation of 'spectacle'

Film theorists, Deleuze included, see the shaping of cinematic time largely in terms of editing.[19] This selection of emphasis is problematic for two reasons. First, despite the anti-teleological stance of contemporary film historiography, it fosters the perception of early, single-shot films as primitive. Second, it has meant that the relationship of *mise en scène* and cinematic time remains relatively unexamined by film theorists. Many editing devices operate in conjunction with elements of *mise en scène*. Costume, make-up, settings and props, for instance, help viewers to distinguish flashbacks from cross-cutting between simultaneous or near-simultaneous phenomena. Indeed, in films where visual differences in costuming between the implied periods are readily apparent, flashback can be signalled without other transition devices such as voiceover narration or titles. Conversely, movements between times with few differences in costuming—as with *Distant Voices, Still Lives* or *Snow Falling on Cedars* (1999)—can frustrate viewers' attempts to put actions in linear, chronological order. Furthermore, elements of *mise en scène* might suggest forward temporal movement in the diegesis with or without editing, as with the fashion changes in *Russki Kovcheg* (*Russian Ark*, 2002) and *Forrest Gump*.

There are many examples where elements of *mise en scène* support the trajectory of the diegesis. However, there are also some examples that serve to foreground temporal relations, much as editing does in films of the time-image. How they do so is through the temporal punctuation of 'spectacle'. Notions of 'spectacle' in film studies vary widely, but we can gain our bearings through Guy Debord's *Society of Spectacle*. In Debord's view, contemporary life 'presents itself as an intense accumulation of spectacles'.[20] Dominated by economic concerns, media and advertising generate an incessant stream of attention-grabbing and seductive images of plenitude and fulfilment for con-sumption by the masses. Movie stars are also embodied spectacles 'created by the need we have for them, and not by talent or absence of talent or even by the film industry or advertising. Miserable need, dismal, anonymous life that would like to expand itself to the dimensions of cinema life.' In the spectacle, everything is bigger, brighter and more detailed than daily life. Yet it also has the appearance of reality and thus is difficult to detect at work. Spectacle thus serves the economy as a tool of regulation and depoliticisation: it is a 'perma-nent opium war' that dumbfounds people and distracts them from engaging in creative activities that foster social change. A major function of spectacle is thus 'to make history forgotten within culture'.[21]

In historical film studies, spectacle is conventionally associated with the monumental sets and casts of 'epic' films set in the ancient world. As Solomon remarks, 'when cinematic frontiers were to be crossed, an ancient subject was called upon to provide the weighty narrative and a familiar, absorbing spec-tacle'.[22] In these films, as Vivian Sobchack puts it, spectacle is the '*excessive* parade and accumulation of detail and event' that '*exceeds* and *transcends* the concrete' and that 'tends to be encoded as empirically verifiable and material excess—entailing scale, quantification, and consumption in relation to money and human labor'.[23] An example cited by Rosen is that of the Tarsus sequence in DeMille's *Cleopatra* (1934), in which a final backward dolly shot reveals an enormous, detailed set and the carefully organised actions of scores of extras that, as he puts it, 'go well beyond the goals of the reality-effect'.[24] In fact, the set and cast are so extravagant that they draw attention to themselves as constructed for the entertainment of the viewer. Monumental and detailed sets and props can disrupt the temporal flow of the diegesis. Going even further, though, I think that spectacle is not restricted to demonstrations of scale and detail, and can punctuate—to a lesser or greater degree—all of the elements of *mise en scène* in historical films, even those we do not readily call 'epics'. When it does so, it generates friction with elements that are more aligned with the diegesis and thus fosters awareness of the temporal artifice of the work. This friction contributes to the unmasking of spectacle but also to the unmasking of the conventions of cinematic time in historical films. Far from being stupefied by spectacle, therefore, viewers are, as Jean-Louis Comolli puts it, 'in the position of those impatient gamblers who know the rules of the game and who one asks to remember those rules before playing: quick, the game is beginning!'[25]

Viewers know, for example, that Leonardo Di Caprio is not Jack Dawson in *Titanic*, and they probably also know that he is a spectacle that can guarantee sales. Yet they still watch on, juggling a spectacle evocative of production and post-production times with the represented time of the diegesis. More will be said about the reception of historical films in the chapters that follow. In the meantime, though, I would like to develop further the idea of spectacle in historical films as temporal punctuation through an examination of three key elements of *mise en scène*: costume and make-up; casting and the actions of figures; and setting and props.

Costume and make-up

In the Introduction and Chapter 1, we learned that the term 'costume' is often used to denote 'nearly, but not' historical films. The impression generated by this label is that of naïve or profit-driven filmmakers pouring actors and scripts into costumes and prop-filled settings in order to evoke a sense of the past. This view, as I hope to show throughout this book, underestimates the complexity of relations of temporality, representation and reception in a wide range of historical films. For the present, though, I want to note that this label has encouraged the unfortunate impression that costume is less worthy of study among historians than other filmic elements. This is ironic, given the prevalence of 'period costuming' in historical film analyses. Costumes are evidently part of what makes historical films 'historical', so what do they contribute to the figuration of time?

Costumes foreground temporal relations through the spectacle of fashion. This is because historical film costumes are never exact replications of artefacts. As Edward Maeder writes:

> To translate a painting into an exact replica of period dress, a designer must transcend the contemporary aesthetic standard, an impossible task because the designer must also create a wardrobe that will address the contemporary audience in a fashion language that they understand and that is consistent with the movie's tone. Even if there was no audience, the designer could not escape the twentieth-century aesthetic in creating period costume, as it is inherent in the way each one of us,

designer and nondesigner alike, thinks about dress. What is socially acceptable, beautiful, risqué, elegant in dress varies dramatically for different periods.[26]

As we shall see in Chapters 5 and 8, on reality and the selling of history, respectively, one of the features that characterises historical films is the publicised effort of costume and art departments to produce costumes that suggest verisimilitude. The efforts of designers, though, are always an amalgam of historiographical, moral, aesthetic, financial and pragmatic decisions, and these can be more or less explicit to viewers. Costumes, as well as make-up, may be reined in to serve other film elements such as plot or editing, as Jane Gaines and Charlotte Herzog argue; but they may also disrupt them by creating an explicit statement for viewers by the designer to be, as Stella Bruzzi puts it, 'admired or acknowledged in spite of the general trajectory of the film'.[27] In so doing, costume may foreground a dissonance of times: that of the couturier, the diegesis and viewers.

Debord would see the spectacle of historical film fashion as symptomatic of a late capitalist consumer economy, but other explanations may also be advanced. Pragmatically, for instance, designers have to adapt or even improvise materials or construction techniques because those of the represented time are unavailable. In *Dorothy Vernon of Haddon Hall* (1924), for instance, Mitchell Leisen had to substitute heavy brocaded furnishing fabrics for lighter silk brocades and velvets of the Renaissance that were no longer made, and Irene and Irene Sharaff made extensive use of rayon crêpe in *Meet Me in St. Louis* (1944)—set in 1903–4—because it was one of the few fabrics that could be obtained during the Second World War. In other works, new fabric technologies are foregrounded for aesthetic or erotic reasons, as with the use of men's tights made from Lastex and Lurex in *Bride of Vengeance* (1949), which was thought to give a more form-fitting and appealing look than the woollen hose of the Renaissance. Conversely, fashion spectacles can flow from contemporary mores about acceptable dress. The emphasis on or presentation of male genitalia or breasts, for instance, is generally evocative of the period during which a film is made. To take just two examples, Paramount and Warner Brothers did not allow the actors to wear codpieces in *Bride of Vengeance* (despite the form-fitting tights), and *Prince and the Pauper* (1937) and the various period settings of *The Robe* (1953), *The Virgin Queen* (1955), *Diane* (1955), *Land of the Pharaohs* (1955), *The Ten Commandments* (1956) and *The Buccaneer* (1958) are united by the 'lift and separate' look of 1950s bra design. Fashion spectacles may also serve as redirections to other spectacles, such as the body of a star: for example, Adrian's gowns in *Marie Antoinette* (1938) bared and emphasised Norma Shearer's shoulders; Travis Banton had Marlene Dietrich appear in trousers in *The Scarlet Empress* (1934) to accentuate her legs; and Sylvester Stallone rarely dons a shirt in *Rambo First Blood Part II* (1985). Additionally, costumes may become spectacles when they are recycled from or influenced by earlier films, as with Irene,

Howard Shoup and Gile Steele's homage to *Marie Antoinette* in *Du Barry Was a Lady* (1943) and the overtones of the television program *Xena, Warrior Princess* (1995–2001) in Keira Knightley's appearance as Guinevere in *King Arthur* (2004).[28]

Hairstyles and make-up can also contribute to the foregrounding of temporal relations in historical films. This is because, as Alicia Annas puts it, 'while period films feature sets that are routinely authentic, and costumes that are occasionally authentic, hairstyles and wigs are rarely authentic, and makeup never is'.[29] Annas' conclusion about make-up and hairstyles is a little exaggerated, but plenty of examples can be marshalled to support her claim for the influence of styles contemporary with filming. For example, Kirk Douglas sports a flat-top as the Roman slave Spartacus (*Spartacus*, 1960), Ethyl Barrymore's hair is marcelled in *Rasputin and the Empress* (1932), and Barbra Streisand appears as a nineteenth-century figure with a 'beehive' in *On a Clear Day You Can See Forever* (1970). Examples with make-up also abound: 1960s frosted lipstick is combined with costumes evoking the eighteenth century in *Tom Jones* (1963), while the style of Claudette Colbert's and Elizabeth Taylor's eye make-up and eyebrows locates *Cleopatra* (1934) and *Cleopatra* (1963) firmly in the periods during which they were filmed. Where Annas' conclusion requires refinement, though, is with cases of make-up derived from periods other than that of the diegesis or filming period, as with the use of late-antiquity woadian body painting in the thirteenth/ fourteenth-century action of *Braveheart* (1995), or where it supports other spectacles, as with the heavily promoted make-up sacrifices made by Bette Davis in *The Virgin Queen* (partly shaved head), Nicole Kidman in *The Hours* (2002, prosthetic nose), Charlize Theron in *Monster* (2003, false teeth, added weight and blotchy skin make-up) and Heath Ledger and Orlando Bloom in *Ned Kelly* (2003, unfashionable beards).

Casting and action

Actors in costume and make-up are embodied sites of temporal relations and even contestation. This is because in historical films, Jean-Louis Comolli argues, there 'are at least two bodies in competition, one body too much'.[30] On the one hand there is the body of the actor as spectacle, on the other that of a represented historical figure. That form of representation, Comolli concludes, requires a larger suspension of disbelief on the part of viewers than an actor playing a fictional character in an historical film. Ostensibly, this is right, but the dimensions of representation and thus temporality in acting are more varied than Comolli's twin poles of fictional character and historical character allow. As was noted in Chapter 1, characters in historical films may, like Maximus in *Gladiator* (2000), be composites of more than one historical figure, or they may be fictional figures inflected with actions from historical figures, as with the connection made between the Niland and Sullivan brothers and the fictional Ryans in the promotional film *Into the Breach: The Making of Saving Private Ryan* (1998). Casting decisions add another temporal dimension. Professional actors carry 'baggage'—an acting history—that may open up for some viewers a temporal path quite different to that of the diegesis: it is hard, for instance, to dissociate Robert Carlyle's performance in *Hitler: The Rise of Evil* (2003) from his role as a male stripper in *The Full Monty* (1997), or Mel Gibson's contribution to the birth of two nations in *Gallipoli* (1981) and *Braveheart* before his participation in a third in *The Patriot* (2000). Taking this baggage into account, *Hitler: The Rise of Evil* and *The Patriot* could be just as suggestive of twentieth-century discourses about the male body and performance and the intersection of war and national identity as they are of the Second World War or the American War of Independence. Alternatively, both films might be read as moments in a star's life. In either case, as we shall see throughout the remainder of this book, viewers' knowledge of an actor's previous screen credits is an important part of the 'rules of the game' of historical filmmaking.[31]

Casting non-professional actors does not prevent the opening of other time paths, for the features or activities that recommended them for casting—for example, the physical appearance of their face, or their activities as a farmer or blacksmith—are not mummified artefacts of a past time. The appearance and movements of bodies, as the historians Elias, Ariès, Foucault and Corbin have recognised, are not immune to change.[32] They too can be commodified and become spectacles. For example, many film theorists are familiar with Barthes' unmasking of sweating faces in Joseph Mankiewicz's *Julius Caesar* (1953) as a contemporary sign or code for moral torment. What Barthes neglected to note, though, is that historical films can carry the signs of multiple movement 'presents'. In *Saving Private Ryan*, to take just one example, Captain Miller's shaking hand—which clearly functions as a con-temporary sign for trauma—appears alongside the tipping of unbuckled GI helmets with forefinger and thumb, which has functioned since the 1940s as a sign for North American confidence in combat. Cinematic time, as Andrei Tarkovsky recognised, can be shaped by bodies and motion. As his examples of the use of pacing back and forth or the drumming of fingers to evoke 'time pressure' and those set out above show, cinematic time can be imprinted in the body and 'run through the shot'.[33]

Setting and props

In any one historical film, viewers may encounter multiple body and move-ment times. The same is also true of setting and props. Despite the immediately perceptible role that settings and props play in historical films, relatively little attention has been directed towards understanding the role they play in the shaping of cinematic time. Beyond Ross Gibson's and Ian Christie's historical reading of space in Australian films and Milcho Manchevski's *Before the Rain* (1994), we have very little to guide us.[34] This is due in part,

I believe, to the assimilation of props and settings with the diminutives of 'costume', 'heritage', 'melodrama' or 'period' films, evidenced in the complaint of 'accuracy in antiques' we encountered in Chapter 1. Furthermore, historiography and film and cultural studies have little to offer on the topic of space and the shaping of time in film, I believe, because despite the historicising tendencies of writers like Foucault, they continue to support the venerable dichotomy of time and space.[35] Jameson, for instance, has characterised the culture of the 'eternal present' in postmodern cinema as spatial, and Marc Augé has connected the excess of time and space in 'supermodernity' with the creation in cinema—among other sites—of pockets of '*l'espace quelconque*' or 'any space whatsoever' that are not localised in time and space.[36]

Deleuze views the use of any-space-whatsoever sets such as airport terminals, motorways and supermarket aisles as endemic in cinema and concludes that they, like the time-image, can place linear, consistent notions of character, space and plot into crisis.[37] Extending this thinking, we can say that 'any space whatsover' may also function as a temporally punctuating spectacle because it meets Sobchack's criterion of the transcendence of accuracy and specificity. Unlike her, and Rosen's examples, however, that transcendence is enabled not through the excessive parade of scale or detail but through the opposite, performative austerity. Two historical films that draw attention to the artifice of diegetic temporality through the use of any space whatsoever are Lars von Trier's *Dogville* (2003) and Steven Spielberg's *Catch Me If You Can* (2002). In the former, von Trier juxtaposes the use of titles and period costumes with the setting of a studio in which the parameters of a house are marked out with chalk lines. In the latter, Spielberg locates the activities of Frank Abagnale Jr, which titles, props and costume suggest took place between 1960 and 1969, in hotel rooms, airport lounges and a doctor's waiting room. In both, the use of generic settings jars with the temporality of the diegesis and with viewer expectations of scale and detail. As with real time, austere sets and props can be special effects in historical films.

Any space whatsoever becomes performative through its juxtaposition with the more familiar spectacle of enormous and detailed physical and digital settings and props. In these spectacles, the scale or level of detail in settings and props is so excessive to the task of convincing viewers to engage in the suspension of disbelief that it is apparent that they are constructions.[38] As Solomon has demonstrated, examples abound in the history of films representing the ancient world, from the massive Temple of Moloch in the Italian silent film *Cabiria* (1914) and Belshazzar's court in *Intolerance* (1916) to the prodigious sets representing the Circus Maximus in *Ben Hur* (1925 and 1959). The association of spectacle and ancient history continues today, with films like *Gladiator* offering viewers a surfeit of detail and scale. The first is seen in the prop-laden tent in which Maximus greets Marcus Aurelius, the second in Commodus' procession into Rome. Neither of these scenes is needed to convince viewers that the film represents a past time: in fact, they are so extravagant that they draw attention to the efforts of the property and post-production digital effects teams. Both spectacle and any space whatsoever thus work towards the same end: to encourage viewers to see the temporality of the diegesis as artifice.

Images and words

In some historical films, spectacle dominates; in others, the traces of production are not so apparent. All historical films, though, combine elements that work to convince viewers of the verisimilitude of a represented past with those that clearly signal its artifice. I have looked to editing and aspects of *mise en scène* to demonstrate that point, but I could just as easily have focused on the use of diegetic and non-diegetic film colour and sound. Griet's handling of lapis lazuli in *Girl with a Pearl Earring* (2003), for instance, throws into relief the filmic representation of the early modern world through various shades of brown, and both Fellini and Spielberg use a shift between colour and black to denote two time frames in *E La Nave Va* (*And the Ship Sails On*, 1983) and *Schindler's List* (1993). Anachronistic music is used in the final scene of *Elizabeth* (1998) and throughout *Moulin Rouge* (2001) to drive home the status of the represented actions as artifice.

My use of the word 'anachronistic' here is perhaps suggestive of the common treatment of historical films as a suspect and even embarrassing form of filmic and historical expression. Spectacle can be read as historiographical failure, a symptom of a 'weakened existential sense of connection to both the historical past and the future' in which temporal modes are muddled and 'temporal scavenging' serves nostalgia.[39] But spectacle, along with time-image editing, can also be read as a stronger understanding of the present's relationship with the past and future.[40] Between and within conflicting or dissonant relations of sound, editing, lighting and image, various time paths open up, diverge and regroup, but never in an entirely seamless way. The time paths of historical films fragment History into histories and foster awareness of their sometimes coalescing, sometimes competing, forms and functions.

This twofold reading of temporal heterogeneity in historical films also applies to written histories. Writing history entails figuring time. Even apparently simple chronicles are given shape by decisions about beginning and end dates, the division of time into units such as reigns, years or days, 'colligation'—the grouping of constellations of events under concepts such as 'Renaissance' or 'Holocaust'—and exclusion.[41] Furthermore, chroniclers are routinely uneven in the attention they give to phenomena; they compress or expand, and they may cross-cut between simultaneous phenomena. Yet the historiographical shaping of time is often characterised as 'artificial', or as Benedetto Croce puts it, 'an affair of imagination, of vocabulary, and of rhetoric, which in no way changes the substance of things'.[42] The historian's configurations of time are overlay—convenient, unavoidable or capricious—

and the cause of debates and problems rather than celebration.[43] Presupposed in these judgements is a view of time as a stream or continuous flow, apart from the historian who dips into it, removing, isolating and perhaps even misshaping phenomena. Similar images suggested by R.G. Collingwood are of histories as compilations, mosaics or webs of 'cut' and 'pasted' evidence. Collingwood finds these images of history problematic, for they all suggest that the historian puts together only preformed, date-stamped 'tiles' or 'scraps' of evidence.[44] For him, on the other hand, historians are autonomous agents who construct cohesive narratives through the active use of their minds and imaginations. He writes:

> Freed from its dependence on fixed points supplied from without, the historian's picture of the past is thus in every detail an imaginary picture. . . . Whatever goes into it, goes into it not because his imagination passively accepts it, but because it actively demands it.[45]

The historian's active thinking about and presentation of events unify a history in their present. For Collingwood, as for other writers like Fernand Braudel, Maurice Mandelbaum and Peter Munz, the figuration of time is an essential, inseparable feature of writing history.[46] The continuity of historical time is thus of less interest to them than the continuity and cohesiveness of the historian's shaping of time. However, their substitution of historiographical continuity for the temporal continuity of a stream of time is also problematic. In recent years, an increasing number of writers have argued for the recognition of multiform temporality and discontinuity in historiography. Among these writers, the works of Gaston Bachelard, Georges Canguilheim and Michel Foucault—particularly *The Archaeology of Knowledge*—are seminal.

It is difficult, Foucault writes in the introduction to *The Archaeology of Knowledge*, for historians to give thought to discontinuity: 'we feel a particular repugnance to conceiving of difference, to describing separations and dispersions, to dissociating the reassuring form of the identical'.[47] Historians are so accustomed to the discursive continuities of tradition, precursor, development and evolution that they are little aware that other approaches are possible. Foucault thus does not seek the eradication of these concepts from history writing but simply to disturb 'the tranquillity with which they are accepted'.[48] His reason for disturbing that tranquillity is to offer historians—himself included—new options. Rather than simply 'going over with bold stroke lines that have already been sketched', the historian can 'advance beyond standard territory' and create new analyses and conceptual frameworks.[49] Foucault makes it clear that he is willing to accept the risk of this creativity, but he wonders whether historians will take up that challenge, a question he leaves unanswered.

Foucault's argument for the unmasking of naturalised historiographical discourses of continuity complements Deleuze's concept of the time-image in film. Both see discontinuity as the means of exposing the artifice of histories and of encouraging those who make them to see that their works may contain linear trajectories as well as tangled gardens of 'forking paths'. Extending Deleuze's writing, I have argued that discontinuities and dissonances are to be found in a wider range of films—early and recent—than that generally valued by historical film scholars, and in both the praised techniques of editors and the derided spectacles of *mise en scène* designers. I believe that Foucault's writing requires a similar double extension, for his pronouncements about the absence of discontinuities in historiographical discourse rest upon the same small selection of historians and histories repeatedly picked over by other writers. Is discontinuity heralded only in the ruptures of periodisation favoured by Foucault in *The Birth of the Clinic, Discipline and Punish* and *Madness and Civilization*? Or may we also find it in moments of spectacle in the works of more neglected writers like Sarah Josepha Hale and Lydia Maria Child? Is discontinuity, like continuity, a masculinist, elitist discourse?

Finally, are the logic of the time-image and discourses of continuity challenges to the creativity of filmmakers and historians alone? What of the receivers of histories? Are they stupefied by spectacle, as Debord would have it? Discontinuity can foster in the receivers of history a state of uncertainty. Every edit, change in *mise en scène* or fissure in periodisation can be a 'bifurcation point'. As we shall see in the chapters that follow, histories are sites where both makers and receivers can accept the challenge of creating enabling discourses of identity and ethical possibilities. No history is a single tense, a single path. Rather, between makers and receivers, history is as Borges would have it: a garden of tangled, twisting, forking paths.

Historical films are thus never just about one time, whether that is a represented past, the filmmaker's present (as favoured by Sorlin) or the viewer's present (as favoured by Barthes). Nor do they offer a chronological continuum in which a past leads inevitably to the present and the future emerges predictably out of the present. The makers of *Down with Love* (2003) therefore have it partly right when they open with the title 'now, 1962', where the 'now' might mean any one of a number of presents of filming, post-production or reception. Whether that declaration marks the end of history in the eternal present or an enhanced understanding of the relations of past and present is a question for us to pursue in the next chapter.

Recommended resources

Affron, C. and Affron, M.J., *Sets in Motion: Art Direction and Film Narrative*, New Brunswick, NJ: Rutgers University Press, 1995.

Bogue, R., *Deleuze on Cinema*, London: Routledge, 2003.

Comolli, J.-L., 'Historical fiction: a body too much', trans. B. Brewster, *Screen*, 1978, vol. 19(2), pp. 41–53.

Deleuze, G., *Cinema 1: The Movement-image*, trans. H. Tomlinson and B. Habberjam, London: Athlone Press, 1986.

Deleuze, G., *Cinema 2: The Time-Image*, trans. H. Tomlinson and R. Galeta, London: Athlone Press, 1989.

Doane, M.A., *The Emergence of Cinematic Time*, Cambridge, Mass.: Harvard University Press, 2002.

Elsaesser, T. and Barker, A. (eds), *Early Cinema: Space, Frame, Narrative*, London: BFI, 1990.

Foucault, M., *The Archaeology of Knowledge*, trans. A.M. Sheridan Smith, New York: Pantheon Books, 1972.

Maeder, E., *Hollywood and History: Costume Design in Film*, New York: Thames & Hudson and the Los Angeles County Museum of Art, 1987.

Pallasma, J., *The Architecture of Image: Existential Space in Cinema*, Helsinki: Building Information Ltd, 2001.

Rodowick, D.N., *Gilles Deleuze's Time Machine*, London: Duke University Press, 1997.

Rosen, P., *Change Mummified: Cinema, Historicity, Theory*, Minneapolis: University of Minnesota Press, 2001.

Sobchack, V., ' "Surge and splendor": a phenomenology of the Hollywood historical epic', *Representations*, 1990, no. 29, pp. 24–49.

Tashiro, C.S., *Pretty Pictures: Production Design and the History Film*, Austin: University of Texas Press, 1998.

Turim, M., *Flashbacks in Film: Memory and History*, New York: Routledge, 1989.

Notes

1 P. Sorlin, *The Film in History*, Oxford: Blackwell, 1980, p. 208.

2 L. Grindon, *Shadows on the Past: Studies in the Historical Fiction Film*, Philadelphia: Temple University Press, 1994, p. 1; and F. Sanello, *Reel vs Real: How Hollywood Turns Fact into Fiction*, Lanham, Md: Taylor Trade, 2003, p. xiii. See also D.W. Elwood, *The Movies as History: Visions of the Twentieth Century*, Thrupp, Gloucestershire: Sutton, 1995, p. 43.

3 R. Slotkin, '*The Charge of the Light Brigade*', in M. Carnes (ed.), *Past Imperfect: History According to the Movies*, New York: Henry Holt, 1996, p. 120; L.B. Salamon, ' "Looking for Richard" in history: postmodern villainy in Richard III and Scarface', *Journal of Popular Film and Television*, 2000, vol. 28(2), p. 54; and A. Lindley, 'The ahistoricism of medieval film', *Screening the Past*, 1998, no. 3, online at www.latrobe.edu.au/screeningthepast/firstrelease/fir598/ALfr3a.htm

4 R. Barthes, 'Rhetoric of the image', in *Image Music Text*, trans. and ed. S. Heath, London: Fontana, 1977, p. 45–6; R. Barthes, *The Responsibility of Forms*, trans. R. Howard, New York: Hill & Wang, 1985, pp. 3–20, 21–62; and R. Barthes, *Camera Lucida: Reflections on Photography*, trans. R. Howard, New York: Hill & Wang, 1981, pp. 76–9, 89–90, 111. On the single (present) tense of cinema, see also G. Bluestone, 'Time in film and fiction', *Journal of Aesthetics and Art Criticism*, 1961, vol. 19, pp. 311–16; and T. Dickinson, *A Discovery of Cinema*, London: Oxford University Press, 1971, p. 111.

5 F. Jameson, *Postmodernism, or the Cultural Logic of Late Capitalism*, Durham, NC: Duke University Press, 1991.

6 P. Rosen, *Change Mummified: Cinema, Historicity, Theory*, Minneapolis: University of Minnesota Press, 2001, p. 176; and R. Barthes, *Camera Lucida*, p. 117.

7 G. Deleuze, *Cinema 2: The Time-image*, trans. H. Tomlinson and R. Galeta, London: Athlone Press, 1989, p. xii.

8 Jorge Luis Borges, 'The garden of forking paths', in *Labyrinths*, Harmondsworth: Penguin, 1998, p. 53.

9 G. Deleuze, *Cinema 2*, pp. 41, 272.

10 M.A. Doane, *The Emergence of Cinematic Time*, Cambridge, Mass.: Harvard University Press, 2002, p. 30.

11 *Ibid.*, pp. 1–32; T. Gunning, 'An aesthetic of astonishment: early film and the (in)credulous spectator', in L. Williams (ed.), *Viewing Positions: Ways of Seeing Film*, New Brunswick, NJ: Rutgers University Press, 1995, p. 118; T. Gunning, 'The cinema of attractions: early film, its spectator and the avant-garde', in T. Elsaesser (ed.), *Early Cinema: Space, Frame, Narrative*, London: BFI, 1990, pp. 56–62; and A. Gaureault, 'Showing and telling: image and word in early cinema', in T. Elsaesser (ed.), *Early Cinema*, pp. 274–81.

12 It is worth noting that films do not have single, fixed running times. Different cuts of a film may be produced for different times and cultures, and film speed can also be varied.

13 M.A. Doane, *The Emergence of Cinematic Time*, p. 193.

14 M. Turim, *Flashbacks in Film: Memory and History*, New York: Routledge, 1989, p. 1.

15 *Ibid.*, p. 48.

16 G. Deleuze, *Cinema 2*, p. 48.

17 M.S. Roth, '*Hiroshima Mon Amour*: you must remember this', in R. Rosenstone (ed.), *Revisioning History: Film and the Construction of a New Past*, Princeton, NJ: Princeton University Press, 1995, pp. 91–101.

18 C. Caruth, 'Introduction', *American Imago*, 1991, vol. 48(1), p. 3; as quoted in M.S. Roth, '*Hiroshima Mon Amour*', p. 95.

19 See, for example, G. Deleuze, *Cinema 1: The Movement-Image*, trans. H. Tomlinson and B. Habberjam, London: Athlone Press, 1986, pp. 4–7; A. Gaudreault, 'Temporality and narrativity in early cinema, 1895–1908', in J. Fell (ed.), *Film Before Griffith*, Berkeley: University of California Press, 1983, p. 314; and S. Kracauer, 'Photography', in *The Mass Ornament: Weimar Essays*, trans. and ed. T.Y. Levin, Cambridge, Mass.: Harvard University Press, 1995, pp. 62–3.

20 G. Debord, *Society of the Spectacle*, London: Rebel Press, 1987, p. 1.

21 *Ibid.*, pp. 33, 9, 44, 192.

22 J. Solomon, *The Ancient World in the Cinema*, rev. edn, New Haven, Conn.: Yale University Press, 2001, p. 14.

23 V. Sobchak, ' "Surge and splendor": a phenomenology of the Hollywood historical epic', *Representations*, 1990, no. 29, pp. 28 and 30. Author's own emphasis.

24 P. Rosen, *Change Mummified*, p. 192.

25 J.-L. Comolli, 'Historical fiction: a body too much', trans. B. Brewster, *Screen*, 1978, vol. 19(2), p. 44.

26 E. Maeder, *Hollywood and History: Costume Design in Film*, New York: Thames & Hudson and Los Angeles County Museum of Art, 1987, pp. 14, 13.

27 J. Gaines and C. Herzog (eds), *Fabrications: Costume and the Female Body*, London: Routledge, 1990, p. 196; and S. Bruzzi, *Undressing Cinema: Clothing and Identity in the Movies*, London: Routledge, 1997, p. 34.

28 E. Maeder, *Hollywood and History*, pp. 33, 36, 204, 209, 210, 231; D. Chierichetti, *Hollywood Director: The Career of Mitchell Leisen*, New York: Curtis Books, 1973, p. 275; and G.F. Custen, *BioPics: How Hollywood Constructed Public History*, New Brunswick, NJ: Rutgers University Press, 1994.

29 A. Annas, 'The photogenic formula: hairstyles and makeup in historical films', in E. Maeder (ed.), *Hollywood and History*, p. 53.

30 J.-L. Comolli, 'Historical fiction: a body too much', p. 44.

31 *Ibid.*, p. 45.

32 P. Ariès, *Centuries of Childhood*, trans. R. Baldick, London: Jonathan Cape, 1973; P. Ariès, *Hour of Our Death*, trans. H. Weaver, London: Allen Lane, 1981; M. Foucault, *Madness and Civilization: A History of Insanity in the Age of Reason*, trans. R. Howard, New York: Vintage Books, 1988; M. Foucault, *The History of*

Sexuality, trans. R. Hurley and R. McDougall, Harmondsworth: Penguin, 3 vols, 1978–86; and A. Corbin, *The Foul and the Fragrant: Odour and the Social Imagination*, trans. anon., London: Macmillan, 1986.

33 A. Tarkovsky, *Sculpting in Time: Reflections on the Cinema*, trans. K. Hunter-Blair, Houston: University of Texas Press, 1989, p. 117.

34 R. Gibson, 'Camera natura: landscape in Australian feature films', in J. Frow and M. Morris (eds), *Australian Cultural Studies: A Reader*, St Leonards, NSW: Allen & Unwin, 1993, pp. 209–21; and I. Christie, 'Landscape and "location": reading filmic space historically', *Rethinking History*, 2000, vol. 4(2), pp. 165–74.

35 M. Foucault, 'Questions on geography', in C. Gordon (ed.), *Power/Knowledge: Selected Interviews and Other Writings, 1972–1977*, New York: Pantheon Books, 1980, pp. 63–77; and M. Foucault, 'Of other spaces', *Diacritics*, 1986, vol. 16, pp. 22–7.

36 F. Jameson, *The Geopolitical Aesthetic: Cinema and Space in the World System*, London; Routledge, 1992; and M. Augé, *Non-places: Introduction to an Anthropology of Supermodernity*, trans. J. Howe, New York: Verso, 1995.

37 G. Deleuze, *Cinema 1*, pp. 108–22.

38 P. Rosen, *Change Mummified*, pp. 187–93; V. Sobchak, ' "Surge and splendor" ', p. 28.

39 *Ibid.*, p. 42.

40 L. Hutcheon, 'The politics of postmodernism: parody and history', *Cultural Critique*, 1987, vol. 5, pp. 179–207.

41 W.H. Walsh, 'Colligatory concepts in history', in P. Gardiner (ed.), *The Philosophy of History*, Oxford: Oxford University Press, 1974, pp. 127–44.

42 B. Croce, *History: Its Theory and Practice*, trans. D. Ainslie, New York: Russell and Russell, [1919] 1960, p. 110.

43 See, for example, G. Barraclough, *An Introduction to Contemporary History*, London: Watts, 1964; J. Barzun and H.F. Graff, *The Modern Researcher*, San Diego, Calif.: Harcourt Brace Jovanovich, 1985; R. Dunn, *The New World History: A Teacher's Companion*, New York; Bedford/St Martin's Press, 2000; and D. Gerhard, 'Periodization in history', *Dictionary of Historical Ideas*, [1973], vol. 3, pp. 476–81, online at: http://etext.lib.virginia.edu/cgi-local/DHI/dhi-cgi ?id=dv3–58

44 R.G. Collingwood, 'Inaugural: rough notes', in W.J. Van der Dussen and W.H. Dray (eds), *The Principles of History and Other Writings*, Oxford: Oxford University Press, 1999, p. 150.

45 R.G. Collingwood, *The Idea of History*, rev. edn ed. W.J. Van der Dussen, Oxford: Oxford University Press, 1993, p. 245.

46 F. Braudel, *On History*, trans. S. Matthews, Chicago: University of Chicago Press, 1980; M. Mandelbaum, *The Problem of Historical Knowledge: An Answer to Relativism*, New York: Harper & Row, [1938] 1967, p. 280; and P. Munz, *The Shapes of Time: A New Look at the Philosophy of History*, Middletown, Conn.: Wesleyan University Press, 1977, p. 38.

47 M. Foucault, *The Archaeology of Knowledge*, trans. A.M. Sheridan Smith, New York: Pantheon Books, 1972, p. 12.

48 *Ibid.*, p. 25.

49 *Ibid.*, pp. 38–9.

4 Identity

In a sense, this movie is a memorial to those combat veterans of the Normandy invasion, and a way for me to say thank you to my Dad and to a lot of people like him.

Steven Spielberg, 'Interview: *Saving Private Ryan*', *Rochester Democrat and Chronicle*, 24 July 1998[1]

The film is set in America. But I don't want to go to the USA. I don't want to go anywhere, let alone the USA. So we went to well, Sweden. It's rather like the USA, or so I've been told. To me, America is mythological. By not doing things where they're meant to be done, you sometimes achieve an added bonus.

Lars von Trier, *100 Eyes: The Making of Dancer in the Dark* (1998)

The concept of identity has a variety of meanings, but in historical film studies it is nearly always used to describe the processes by which individuals connect themselves with, or place themselves in, socially constructed 'national' categories. Sometimes the conjunction of nation and identity is overtly asserted, as with Jay Winter's claim that historical film has 'power in projecting national stereotypes and narratives', or Vivian Sobchack's and Roger Bell's observations that historical films are an 'inscription and interpretation' or 'refashioning' of national experience.[2] More commonly, though, the connection of nation and identity is assumed through the restriction of historical film analyses to a consideration of production, diegesis and reception in specific national communities. Thus, to take a few examples, Leger Grindon has examined changing receptions of *La Marseillaise* (1937) in France, Judith Keene has seen in the diegesis of *Il Était une Fois un Pays* (*Underground*, 1995) a questioning of assumptions about the official history of the former Yugoslavia, and Richard Howells has highlighted the differences between the British-made *A Night to Remember* (1958) and the US-made *Titanic* (1953).[3] Clearly, the concepts of national cinema and identity have currency. Yet, as I shall argue in this chapter, the conceptual frames and methodologies of current historical film scholarship present an unnecessarily limited account of the nature and quality of viewer engagements with film.

National identity

Contemporary examinations of historical films enunciate a particular view of 'nation'. A pivotal expression of that view is Benedict Anderson's *Imagined Communities*, which posits all forms of relation larger than those involving 'face-to-face' contact as imagined and invented. Imagining was the means by which nations were created, and the mainspring of that imagining was 'a half-fortuitous, but explosive, interaction between a system of production and productive relations (capitalism), a technology of communications (print), and the fatality of human linguistic diversity'.[4] Print communication takes centre-stage in his theory, and in a series of studies of postcolonial states he has identified how documents like maps articulate imagined national stories. While Anderson's theory might be seen to support the logocentric valuation of print criticised in Chapter 1, his highlighting of the importance of media in the construction of communities has prompted scholars like J. Martín-Barbero to argue that an extension of the theory to visual media is appropriate.[5]

Anderson's work appears to fit well, for instance, with explorations of the relations of 'collective' or 'social' memory and nation in historical films. These terms have been used to describe a 'body of reusable texts, images and rituals specific to each society in each epoch, whose "cultivation" serves to stabilize and convey that society's self-image'.[6] Furthermore, it has the advantage of decoupling identity from proximity to or participation in events. For instance, many scholars have noted the increase in visual representations of the Holocaust in the USA, a nation-state in which only a tiny fraction of the population has had direct experience of the events depicted.[7] Finally, Anderson's theory coheres with Michael Billig's argument for the recognition of 'banal' as well as more explicit visual representations of nationalism, a distinction explained through the example of a flag: 'The metonymic image of banal nationalism is not a flag which is being consciously waved with fervent passion; it is the flag unnoticed on the public building'.[8] Banal nationalism entails the circulation of symbols of a nation, but in a way that is so habitual that their use, as Roland Barthes would put it, 'goes without saying'.[9] Filmic examples of banal nationalism might include the JFK plate that hangs on a wall in *Dancer in the Dark* (2000) and the football pools results and shipping forecast that we hear in *Distant Voices, Still Lives* (1989).

Ostensibly, the combination of Anderson's ideas with concepts of collective memory and banal and explicit representations of nation would seem to offer us a powerful means for explaining the social and cultural significance of historical films. Yet this approach to historical film studies is undercut by at least three problems. First, we are yet to clarify the relations between individual and collective memory and imagining. Neurological, psychological and psychoanalytical methodologies used to study individuals are routinely applied without question to communities. Writing on US-made Vietnam War films, for example, D. Desser and G. Studies conclude:

Freud warned that within the context of repression and unconscious acting out, the young and childish tend to 'luxuriate their symptoms'. *Rambo* demonstrates a cultural parallel, a luxuriating in the symptoms of a desperate ideological repression manifested in the inability to speak of or remember the painful past, a cultural hysteria in which violence must substitute for understanding, victimisation for responsibility, the personal for the political.[10]

Desser and Studies' argument that US Vietnam War films from the 1980s are expressions of displacement and repression has also been extended to later productions like *We Were Soldiers* (2002) and other combat films such as *Black Hawk Down* (2001).[11] Problematically, these analyses assume that collective memory and imagining are simple cohesive aggregates of individual memories or activities of imagination. Talk of communities as remembering, visualising, suffering from trauma or being in a state of denial is at best metaphorical.[12] As Iwona Irwin-Zarecka has advised, perhaps we should 'keep psychological or psychoanalytical categories at bay and focus, rather, on the social, political, and cultural factors at work'.[13]

Second, what is represented is not necessarily the same as what is remembered or imagined. Describing the diegesis of *Rambo* or *Black Hawk Down* does not entitle me to talk about them as a particular community's understanding of past events. As we shall see more fully in Chapter 8, we cannot assume that viewers of a film form a cohesive interpretative community and that they will use a text for the same ends. Statements about collective memory and imagining require evidence of reception, regardless of whether they concern a single film, as with Howard Harper's valuation of *Saving Private Ryan* as '*our* dominant view of D-Day', or historical films in general, as with Marcia Landy's claim that the 'media's representations of the past are a barometer of the social and cultural life of the last decades of the twentieth century'.[14] Thus identity is in part the ever-shifting historical product of interactions between the producers and viewers of films.[15]

Third, Anderson's theory, and extensions of it in historical film studies, share the same limiting emphasis on the interior dimensions of a single kind of community, the nation-state. Is that community singular and cohesive? If so, how do we explain why the flag in the opening titles of *Saving Private Ryan* went unremarked in some US reviews but became the focal point for criticism in others?[16] How can the same symbol be banal and explicit within the same community? Nor does a focus on the internal dimensions of national communities help us to adequately explain *why* the Danish filmmaker Lars von Trier feels entitled—as one of the quotes that heads this chapter suggests—to imagine America. Nor again, to take other examples, does it explain why most historical films about Ireland are made outside that country, Finns and Italians make westerns, and Polish historical films tend to be set outside the borders of that state. Anderson's theory does not require proximity of identity and experience, but it does not offer us an explanation of why.[17]

To address that question, we require a better understanding of the kinds of identity on offer to film viewers. We begin by looking beyond the nation. Film scholars routinely acknowledge that film is a transnational phenomenon in their presentation of 'Hollywood history' as an extra-cultural pressure or threat to various national cinemas. However, this view of Hollywood as threat serves to cloud, first, the popular reception of Hollywood films—and those produced in 'Bollywood' and Hong Kong—around the world and, second, the transnational character and appeal of many 'national' historical films. Cinematic financing, production, distribution and reception have never fitted neatly within the analytic frame of the nation-state. From the first days of 'actuality' screenings, films have been made as co-productions, drawing together finances, resources and personnel from different nations. Filmmakers and actors have also moved to and through various locations, leaving as their legacy films that cannot be easily classified as the products of a single national culture. Is the Indian director Shekhar Kapur's *Elizabeth* (1998) a British film? Is *Girl with a Pearl Earring* (2003), made with funding from Britain, Luxembourg and the USA and featuring a North American lead, Dutch? Is the Finnish western *Villin Pohjolan salattu laakso* (*The Secret Valley of the Wild North*, 1963) a contribution to US national cinema? Many historical films are also physically altered for different export markets, whether in terms of dubbing, subtitling, re-editing or censorship. The absence of single, authoritative prints of films should alert us to the possibility that different prints can elicit different responses. There are, for instance, differences in dialogue between the versions of *Pearl Harbor* (2001) released in the USA and in Japan, and as Figure 4.1 shows us, even film posters and tag lines may be changed for export. The second poster shown, made for the North American release of *Rabbit-proof Fence* (2002), was denounced by a conservative member of the Australian government as 'sensationalising, misleading, and grossly distorting' and by more liberal intellectuals for deleting the historical agents at the centre of the film, Molly and Daisy. Both responses suggest sensitivity towards the representation of Aboriginal history outside the Australian nation-state: can a dimension of identity be a concern for the identifications of others?[18] Even when films are not altered, they may be still be viewed in ways not foreseen in the country of production: for example, the name 'Kip' in *The English Patient* (1996) might foster laughter among Dutch viewers because of its resemblance to the local word for 'chicken'. Thus a single print may still elicit multiple readings and therefore potentially multiple identifications.

It is not possible to map the imagined community of a 'nation' on to a clearly defined geopolitical space, as multiple studies of diasporas confirm.[19] Yet the idea of diasporas is also of limited explanatory power to us, for historical films are characterised in part by a complex tangle of elements in transnational circulation—ranging from editing and CGI devices to costume styles—elements that cannot be readily traced to particular national sources. Furthermore, claims to ownership over filmic elements may not result in

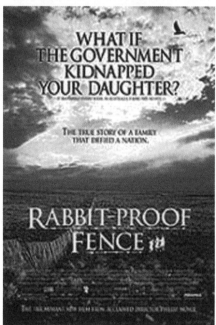

Figure 4.1 Whose *Rabbit-proof Fence*? Australian and US promotional posters
(© 2002, Australian Film Commission)

control: a 2,000-signature petition could not prevent the British rock singer Mick Jagger from playing the lead in Tony Richardson's film about an iconic Australian bushranger, *Ned Kelly* (1970); a British parliamentary motion could not stop Hollywood 'stealing' an historical example of 'British military daring' in *U-571* (2000); and film producers in the USA are increasingly complaining that the search for global profits has meant that 'Our movies no longer reflect our culture'.[20] Nor, as the case of *Rabbit-proof Fence* highlights, can the concepts of diaspora or nation drive home how heterogeneous film production, distribution and reception can be within the political boundaries of a single state. Andrew Higson and Christopher Faulkner have thus underscored that histories of national cinema are histories of contestation, resistance and negotiation.[21]

On the level of public policy, the concept of national cinema still has some meaning, for governments continue to develop defensive strategies designed to protect local cultural activities and values against imported films, which are assumed to have an imitative effect (e.g. that local linguistic idioms will be swept away by American English) and to promote nation building. Some governments, as with France and South Korea, have placed quotas on imported films at different times.[22] However, government and film institute policies also consistently suggest an interest in sponsoring domestic projects that are both commercially viable (often implying international distribution) and that 'express and sustain' a national culture, language and identity. Judgements vary about what counts as an expression of national culture. As Mette Hjort and Eric Rentschler have shown, for example, Danish and German politicians, film organisations and filmmakers themselves have repeatedly emphasised their delivery of national films that are deemed to mirror contemporary social and material 'banal' culture. In the United Kingdom, on the other hand, nation is more frequently conveyed through a choice of past settings and stories.[23] In the case of Australian filmmaking in the late 1970s, too, more support was given for historical film projects after questions were raised about the use of government funds to support the production of the commercially successful risqué or crude 'Ocker' comedies *Alvin Purple* (1973), *Stork* (1971) and *The Adventures of Barry Mckenzie* (1972). As these examples demonstrate, perceptions of 'nation' do not come readily packaged with an obvious historical dimension.

Where nation is conjoined with history in film, Marcia Landy believes that a combination of Friedrich Nietzsche's, Michel Foucault's and Antonio Gramsci's views on the uses of history is of explanatory value. Through the use of discontinuous and fragmented narration, historical filmmakers can draw attention to the use of history to shore up prevailing 'mythical' notions of the nation-state. Through the use of emotional representations (affect) and continuity editing, however, they cement inconsistent, illogical and discrete discourses together and render a past that is worthy of unquestioned respect, imitation and preservation. This form of history is at best moribund and at worst socially crippling, for it 'knows only how to *preserve* life, not how to engender it; it always undervalues that which is becoming . . . it hinders any resolve to attempt something new'.[24] Landy's explanation has the appeal of fitting in with the generally pejorative appraisals of the social functions of film canvassed in the last chapter. Like them, though, it remains a rhetorical venture if it is not backed up by evidence from specific contexts. In the last chapter, I drew upon a range of examples to suggest a counterview: that all historical films are, to a greater or lesser extent, discontinuous or punctuated. Furthermore, as we shall see later in this chapter, Landy's view rests upon the unquestioned condemnation of affect.

As is perhaps now clear, my call for the investigation of the uses of history in different cultural contexts should not be read as an invitation to engage solely in the exploration of national cinemas. To focus on only 'nation' and identity is to ignore the fact that communication networks operate on an increasingly transnational basis and that cultural expressions are widely exchanged across national borders. Indeed, as was noted in Chapter 1, scholars of historical films routinely overlook popular local cinematic cultures in favour of 'art' productions that are distributed internationally. Yet augmenting our analysis of historical films to encompass their transnational dimensions will still not bear the fruit of a comprehensive account of their social and cultural significance. It is simply not the case that audiences will more readily identify with historical films that enjoy international distribution than with other kinds of historical film. Why?

Identities

The simple answer to this question is that national, transnational and even global communities are not the only communities that can be 'imagined'. The various discourses we encounter day to day—including those in historical films—offer us opportunities to imagine, 'inhabit' or fashion multiple identities.[25] Moral, religious, public political, professional, family and gender discourses, to name a few, may foster competing notions of 'self'. Historical films may therefore generate multiple and even divergent positions for identity. Mia Mask, for instance, has argued that reviewers of *Eve's Bayou* (1997) were reluctant to call it an African-American film lest that frighten off viewers who were otherwise attracted to the more 'universally appealing' representation of 1960s family life it offered.[26] One discourse was thought to conflict and repel another. However, discourses may also intertwine and elide. In the Polish film *Ogniem i mieczem* (*With Fire and Sword*, 1999), for instance, the non-Christian Tatars of the seventeenth century are portrayed as decadent, effeminate and only able to win battles through sheer strength of numbers and dirty tricks. Conversely, the Poles and Ukrainian Cossacks are united in the Catholic faith, a faith that marks their civilisation. Discourses of Catholicism and masculinity, Mazierska argues, are what offer Poles a link to the historical stories of other nation-states.[27] To take another example, oedipal and homosexual 'panic' have been suggested as the framework for

Oliver Stone's representations of US political events in *JFK* (1992) and *Nixon* (1995).[28] And most of the approximately 180 historical films made in Australia show men experiencing death and defeat. This has led Katherine Biber to argue that death and defeat are diegetic devices that support a view of Australian national identity predicated upon heterosexual hegemony and homosocial collectivity.[29] These examples show that historical films offer judgements of inclusion and exclusion.[30] Following on from this, we can say that historical film discourses are relational: they are delineated and refined by the process of looking both inward and outward, of asserting sameness, difference and otherness. The three examples I have cited, from Poland, the USA and Australia, support Godard's observation that cinema is a masculinist discourse that depersonalises and erases women and competing notions of masculinity. This relational dimension of identity also allows us to gain some understanding of Lars von Trier's decision to imagine the USA in *Dancer in the Dark*; his film is at base a statement that the use of capital punishment in the USA is different or 'other' to his own ethical beliefs. What is asserted as 'different' and 'other' varies from discourse to discourse, but again, discourses may combine, as with the representation of the Vietnamese women Phuong in *The Quiet American* (2002) as a silent, exotic object of colonial fantasy.

The commonplace mixing, fusion and creolisation of discourses in historical films might explain why—as suggested in the quote that heads this chapter—Steven Spielberg sees *Saving Private Ryan* as both a public memorial to those who participated in the D-Day landings *and* a personal thank you to his father. In theorising historical film, though, scholars have assumed that public national discourses are of greater historiographical significance than familial or more local ones. We recall from Chapter 1 the persistent dismissal of 'melodramas' as ahistorical or even anti-historical: as C.S. Tashiro explains, 'melodramas must appear to happen here and now to create an emotional response'. The historical film, on the other hand, 'is fundamentally concerned with the association of the individual and the state and the relationship between personal experience and the extrapersonal forces shaping history'.[31] On this estimation, melodramas are, like *Rambo* and *Black Hawk Down*, expressions of displacement and repression, and they point to audiences who are unable or unwilling to face up to historical differences or national 'myths'. I have already questioned the appropriateness of psychological and psychoanalytical assessments of film representation, but I would now like to explore whether identity of emotions is possible in film viewing and whether it can contribute to historical understanding.

First, I would like to draw out a point I made earlier about methodology. Tashiro posits the existence of spectators addressed or constructed by films, spectators that he assumes are insularly focused on the personal and lured by anti-historical affect. These hypothetical spectators, let us be clear, are not to be confused with actual persons who go to cinemas and watch films. Scholars who write on hypothetical or 'implied' viewers look to cues within films—like point-of-view shots, that are thought to encourage viewers to 'guess ahead', 'identify' or 'take sides'.[32] Tashiro's construction of hypothetical spectators confirms a preference for text-centred analysis in historical film studies: inquiry focused on films and their author-directors. Ironically, it means that historical films are analysed as if they were not consumed in particular times and places.

Tashiro's division of text from context weakens the analytical potential of historical film studies. Consider as an example these two statements of reception concerning *Titanic* (1997) and *Atlantic* (1929). The first is from Martin Barker's study of 'implied' viewers; the second is from Annette Kuhn's ethnographic study of British people's memories of going to the cinema:

> Many young women will have gone to see *Titanic* because of the promise of screens-full of Leonardo diCaprio . . . the more such young women (a) wanted to fantasise Leo as *their* potential lover, and (b) saw him as quintessentially a 'modern' boy/man, the more they would be disappointed by *Titanic*, and decline the role that the film proffered.[33]

> My earliest recollection is of a silent film *Atlantic*. The pianist played . . . as the water rose eventually to cover the sinking passengers as the [Titanic] sank. I can still visualise the scene. Everyone cried.[34]

In isolation, these statements are problematic sources for historical film scholars. The first might be proved wrong by interviews with film viewers and does not allow for changes in reception over time. The second is subject to the vicissitudes of memory and perhaps even reduces *Atlantic* to an epiphenomenon, a symptom of some other social discourse rather than a discourse in its own right. A way beyond the division of text and context, as Janet Staiger has argued, lies with the recognition of film texts as entangled in and shaping contexts, and vice versa. However, Staiger's treatment of 'context' as equivalent to the views of contemporary reviewers means that her studies stop short of offering us an account of the 'non-authoritative' audiences that reception scholars have tried to reclaim. Many of the nineteen reviews of *Le Retour de Martin Guerre* (1982) that she has analysed, for instance, equate authenticity and 'realism' with the correspondence of props, setting, lighting and costumes to contemporary representations such as Brueghel's paintings. This might lead us to affirm the judgement expressed in Chapter 1 that the 'history' of many historical films is no more than 'accuracy in antiques'.[35] If that were the case, though, why did the detailed Civil War and post-Second World War settings of the US remakes of *Martin Guerre*—*Sommersby* (1993) and *The Majestic* (2001)—not guarantee healthy sales? Staiger's analysis is also at odds with the results of non-authoritative reception studies, like Alberto Angelini and Elio Pasquali's study of eye movement during film watching, which suggests that faces, and more specifically eyes and mouths, are the focal points for viewers. Furthermore, it does not appear to sit well with Ien

Ang's much cited study of the Dutch reception of the 1970s soap opera *Dallas*, which saw viewers connecting 'authenticity' with depicted emotions.[36] In turn, however, the results of these two studies cannot be applied with much confidence to historical film studies, because neither has these films as their focus, and neither considers the possibility of changes in reception over time.

Where can we turn to for information on viewer activities of identification? Ironically, few historical film scholars have considered historical reception contexts. Notable exceptions are Annette Kuhn, Sue Harper and Mary Ann Doane, who have used structured interviews and questionnaires to understand audience interactions with films in Britain and the USA at particular times. Using a 1943 Ministry of Information survey on cinema audiences, for example, Harper notes that while male viewers of the Gainsborough historical melodramas *The Man in Grey* (1943) and *Madonna of the Seven Moons* (1944) berated their salaciousness or cited nostalgia for sexual inequality as excuses for viewing, female viewers responded more favourably for reasons of star identification, revelling in 'seeing bold bad men', emotional sincerity and the pleasure of looking at costumes, hairstyles and sets. One respondent saw herself after screening as 'the lovely heroine in a beautiful blue crinoline with a feather in her hair', but most female respondents were quite choosy about the costume elements they chose to make into clothes they would wear.[37] Star identification and selective appropriation and refashioning also emerges as a major theme in Annette Kuhn's interviews with female film viewers in the 1930s.[38]

Kuhn's research on the historical reception of *Maytime* (1937), an MGM musical set at the turn of the twentieth century, is particularly fruitful. The first day of May has political connotations in Britain, but in *Maytime*, the focus is the 'tender romance of two souls [Marcia and Paul, played by Jeanette MacDonald and Nelson Eddy] that become one as their voices blend in love-swept song', their separation and reunion in death.[39] Kuhn's interviews with viewers Vee Entwistle and Dorris Braithwaite about the film in 1995 also suggest the importance of interpersonal connections:

VE: . . . our Hilda used to sit there absolutely gone and think he [Nelson Eddy] was just singing to her!

DB: Well you did!

VE: And you know, he was.

DB: Yeah, yeah.

VE: I used to keep watching her, you know. And when he was smiling she was, as though he was . . . actually smiling at her. Any minute he would come off the screen and she would. . . .

DB: . . . Well my friend and I used to act them out. We used to act the films out. . . . And she was Nelson Eddy because she was blonde and she had a deep wave. And she used to deepen it and draw her hair back. I wish I could find that photo. I took a photo of her once. And she's doing, like that [*demonstrates friend deepening wave*]. She's looking like him on it.

Drew her hair back. And she was Nelson Eddy, see. And I acted Cesar Romero [*laughter*]. . . .

DB: Now Nelson is gone and so is my husband. But I play records and videos and they are both with me again and I feel just as young and in love as I was all those years ago.[40]

A number of personal connections are hinted at in the interviews, from the viewers' substitution of Jeanette MacDonald for themselves (Hilda, and Dorris and her friend acting out) and watching a friend connect with a film character (Vee watching Hilda), to the alignment of the end of the film—in which a youthful Marcia and Paul are reunited in death—to viewer memories that overcome ageing and death. Importantly, these reminiscences show viewers being drawn into the film *and* drawing the film into their lives. *Maytime* helps to articulate and secure memories of lost friends, lovers and youth. This is a pattern that Kuhn detects across interviews with 1930s cinemagoers: for 'the majority', she writes, 'going to the pictures is remembered as being less about films and stars than about daily and weekly routines, neighbourhood comings and goings and organising spare time. Cinemagoing is remembered, that is, as part of the fabric of everyday life . . . .'[41] Kuhn's observation is borne out by other studies of filmgoers' experiences, who note with her that male viewers tend to focus on childhood experiences and female viewers on experiences during adolescence.[42]

Historical film watching may thus be 'historical' in two senses. First, films may—via their representations—engage viewers in an exploration of past activities. Second, films may be embedded in, and used to delineate and secure, viewers' understandings of their past imagined communities. The remembered and imagined communities of cinemagoers tend to be local, familiar and 'everyday'. As such, they appear to be a long way from the national, public and political communities generally selected for analysis by historical film scholars. Clearly, a combination of textual and reception analysis offers us the widest view of the identities connected with films. So why have viewer discourses—and the imagined communities they construct—been so neglected? One word stands out in scholars' dismissals of viewers' responses to historical films: 'affect'.

Affect and identification

Affect, we recall from earlier in this chapter, has been presented as the 'cement' for monumental, preserving and mythical history (Landy) or as the means for avoiding history (Tashiro). A number of the historical film theories canvassed in Chapter 1 offer a similarly pejorative view of emotional engagement as an obstacle to historical understanding, an obstacle encountered in costume dramas and most commercially successful historical films. These views might also be considered in the wider context of film theory, which has until recently neglected the study of emotional response.

Carl Plantinga has offered a threefold explanation of this neglect. First, film theory usually constructs or implies emotional responses on the basis of textual analysis alone.[43] This is problematic, as I have already argued, because it posits a necessary connection between filmic devices and inherent, universal effects. Landy's association of discontinuity with critical thinking, for example, may not be borne out by studies of actual, rather than implied, reception. Furthermore, the automatic valuation of discontinuity and its supposed effects of rationality and reflexivity must be subject to question. As was made clear in Chapter 2, for example, Michel Foucault—whom Landy draws upon—sees a place for continuity as well as discontinuity in historical discourses. Second, film theory has carried over from cultural critics as far back as Plato the assumption that emotional engagement is detrimental to the development of critical judgement and political participation. And, third, film theorists commonly view emotional engagement through the psychoanalytical lenses of desire and pleasure and assume that like them, it is conjoined with perverse or regressive psychic states such as sadistic voyeurism, fetishistic scopophilia, regressive narcissism, transvestism, masochism or any combination of these.[44]

Both cultural critics and psychoanalytical theorists clearly distrust the emotions and profess their support for distanced and alienated responses, which they assume foster critical and rational thought. This dualism of emotion and rationality, Plantinga makes clear, does not withstand scrutiny, because it rests upon the erroneous view of emotions as private mental events that are beyond interpersonal—and thus historical—understanding. Contrary to this, Plantinga, echoing Aristotle, John Wilson and Anthony Kenny, argues that emotions are cognitive. Emotions have objects: for example, we are scared *of* a snake, upset *with* an examiner or afraid *that* we left the iron on. Furthermore, emotions involve concepts, judgements and beliefs: for example, an awareness of a broken social more can lead to embarrassment or a loss to sadness. Emotions are intentional because they must be about something or directed to an object.[45] That is, intentionality furnishes the 'content' of emotions. That content may not be connected with any physiological state or behavioural expression; for example, there is no characteristic behavioural expression of jealousy as there is for anger. Thus my emotions are not defined by my clenched teeth but rather by my concepts, judgements and beliefs about my situation. On this cognitive view, an emotion is a particular way of viewing and responding to the world and may or may not be expressed in certain forms of behaviour. Furthermore, as Ronald de Sousa argues, an emotion can be rational because it may guide our reasoning and our identification of courses of action.[46] Therefore, as emotions consist in part of cognition, they are open to the same processes of historical inquiry that are used to understand thoughts and beliefs.

Emotions are, in principle, open to historical understanding. So how might that understanding arise from film watching? As we recall from the results of the 'Presence of the Past' and 'Australians and the Past' projects described in the Introduction, many people report a stronger connection with the past when they watch films or television than when they study history or read books.[47] For many of Kuhn's informants, too, cinema is attractive because it offers the opportunity of entering, being 'immersed' in or 'lost' in another world.[48] When viewers are 'connected' with a filmic representation of the past, emotions may be involved, as with Vee's report of Hilda's smile during a serenade by Nelson Eddy. This has led some critics to describe the process of 'entering' the world of a film as a form of identification that entails identity of thought and emotion *and* the loss of a viewer's separate selfhood. However, this view is not borne out by empirical observations of viewer responses. Without an awareness of the screened events as representations, for instance, viewers would have a hard time staying in their seats during combat scenes. And without an awareness of the process of identification, these comments by filmgoer Doreen Lyell would not make any sense:

> Well I really was immersed in the cinema. . . . Because, eh, that was part of your dreams, you know. You didn't expect them to come true.

Nor would any of the other comments that Kuhn reports, which display the knowledge that the world that films offer is not of the actual present and lasts only a little while.[49] Like actors, it seems, viewers may experience the same emotions as those of screen characters, but in the process they do not relinquish their sense of themselves. In sum, therefore, neither the involvement of emotions nor reports of viewers being 'lost' in historical films is logically sufficient to support the dismissal of viewer identification as contrary to rational, socially empowering thought. This is a conclusion that I will reaffirm, through a different angle of inquiry, in Chapter 8.

Images and words

The study of identification and emotional response has received more attention in historiography than in film studies, though, as we shall see, the conventional orientation towards these concepts is also one of distrust and suspicion. In historiography, the term 'identity' is connected with a varied collection of cognates whose popularity has waxed and waned at various times. In the eighteenth century, for instance, writers like David Hume and Adam Smith argued that identification achieved through 'sympathy' was indispensable to moral and social activities. Hume saw sympathy as made possible through the overlapping beliefs and sentiments of people, but he noted that it could not be sustained for long before being eroded by jealousy and selfish tendencies. We can look to the experiences of others via sympathy, but ultimately only out of concern for what we can learn about ourselves. Similarly, Smith saw sympathy as working most easily when we consider feelings that we approve of, look to the experiences of people we know well or consider pain caused by external sources like a blow. Conversely, we may need to know the causes of and even tone down the feelings of others—as with anger that repulses us—or work harder to contemplate the experiences of strangers. Pain due to internal causes, like migraine, generates little possibility for sympathy, because it is private to the sufferer.[50] The term 'sympathy' continued to be used in historical writings through to the twentieth century, as seen in A.B. Hart's declaration that 'a little imagination helps one to sympathise with the great men of the past'[51] or Harold Ritter's conclusion that sympathetic, and emotional, alignment is necessary in historical understanding:

> Unlike *explanation, understanding* is not a *logical* process but a largely emotional and intuitive experience through which the practitioner of the human sciences establishes a 'psychological rapport' with the object of his study. . . . Through this process he 'internalises' the past by 'imagining what emotions may have been aroused by the impact of a given situation or event'. . . . By steeping himself in the records of the past, the historian may intuitively enter into a sympathetic relationship with the past and can to some degree reexperience the past and 'rethink' the thoughts of historical personalities.[52]

Whereas modern English writers organised their discussions on identification under the concept of 'sympathy', German writers generally opted for the terms *einfühlen, Einfühlung* or *mitfühlen*, meaning literally 'in-feeling' or 'with feeling'. In *Yet Another Philosophy of History*, for example, Johann Herder exhorted his readers to 'enter the century, the region, the entire history— empathise with or "feel oneself into" [*sich einfühlen*] every part of it'.[53] In distinction, Wilhelm Dilthey declared a preference for the terms *nachfühlen* and *nacherleben*, meaning 're-feel' and 're-live', respectively. The use of the prefix *nach-* is important here, suggesting critical distance on the part of the person contemplating the experience of others. *Einfühlen*, on the other hand, implies emotional and ethical engagement.[54] To German writers, the prefixes *ein-, mit-* and *nach-* signalled some important conceptual distinctions, distinctions that were not carried over into English after Vernon Lee's coining of the term 'empathy' in 1904. After that time, a number of writers also dissolved the boundaries between 'sympathy' and 'empathy' by using them interchangeably.[55]

The task of disentangling the terms 'sympathy' and 're-live' was taken up in the first half of the twentieth century by R.G. Collingwood. Across a variety of writings, Collingwood elucidated a theory of historical 're-enactment' underpinned by a social view of language. An historian and an historical agent, he argues, may share 'the same' thoughts, by which he means an identity of mental concepts. Re-enactment is conceptual identity but not *numerical, spatial* or *temporal* identity. Collingwood demonstrates the distinction between these different kinds of identity by citing the examples of a person who thinks 'the angles are equal' for five seconds and a person who thinks 'the angles are equal', wanders off that thought and returns to it after three seconds. Do we not talk of these two individuals thinking the same thought, even though there was a break and revival in the second case and there may be two or more 'numerically different but specifically identical' thoughts in the first case? Given this, why not talk of the same thought held by different people at different times?[56] Collingwood reinforces this point when he asks:

> If the objector says that *no* kind of re-enactment is possible, merely because nothing can happen twice, we shall treat his objection with less courtesy: pointing out that he would himself not hesitate to speak of dining twice in the same inn, or bathing twice in the same river, or reading twice out of the same book, or hearing the same symphony twice. Is the binomial theorem as known to him, we should ask, the same theorem that Newton invented, or not? If he says yes, he has admitted all we want. If he says no, we can easily convict him of self-contradiction: for he is assuming that in our mutual discourse we have ideas in common, and this is inconsistent with his thesis.[57]

Through re-enactment, we share the same concepts as historical agents, including emotional ones. Again, though, that 'enactment' is conceptual and does not presuppose numerical, spatial or temporal identity. As with the example of thinking a theorem and then returning to it, or returning to a bath, inn or book, so it is with emotions. If I feel anger, then the feeling subsides and then I feel anger again, it is still anger. If you close this book on your thumb and I do the same then it is perfectly reasonable for us to say that we have the same pain. If emotions are private, common statements like 'Are you happy?' or 'That looks painful' would make no sense at all. Furthermore, if I learn the meaning of the concept of joy from my own experience, then a person who has never experienced joy would not be able to use the concept, just as a blind person would never be able to use the word 'see'. All of this tells us that emotions like 'joy' are not private sensations; they are concepts in language, the use of which requires us to know grammar. Thus a concept is not merely formed by experiencing a sensation. To have a concept means to know how a word is used, to be able to follow the rules that govern the use of the word. That requires shared or public language.[58] Public language is the means by which we can share the 'same' thoughts and emotions as others, past and present.

Conceptual identity allows for the possibility of awareness and critical distance and reflection—we are not taken over or subsumed by the person we identify with—hence Collingwood's use of the prefix 're-' before 'enactment'. In his view, though, that awareness and critical distance is absent from 'sympathy'; we are simplify satisfied with sharing another's emotion. In Collingwood's view, re-enactment belongs to historical inquiry, whereas sympathy belongs to biography, which is also built out of malice and materials chosen for gossip and snobbery value. A feminist critique could well take Collingwood's coupling of sympathy and biography as akin to the conventional dismissal of costume dramas in historical film studies and read both as a masculinist response to emotions and interpersonal relations that are denigrated as feminine. That is, underlying dismissals of biography and costume drama is a common distinction between reason and emotion, and the alignment of rationality with masculinity and emotion and irrationality with femininity. In this chapter, I have questioned the dichotomy of thought and emotion, and I want to reiterate a point made in Chapter 1, that the alignment of any genre and form of identification with a gender may support rather than question stereotypes and serve to obscure other reasons for critics' responses to genres.

A good demonstrative case is Eric Hobsbawm's writing on identity and historical studies. In 'Identity history is not enough', Hobsbawm makes clear his preference for a scholastic stance of detached 'universalism', arguing that the identification of an historian with a community may lead to the production of scholarship that supports national myths or ends up as 'some version of the opium of the people' or 'dangerous ... sentences of death'.[59] His criticisms are not couched in terms of a gendered dichotomy of reason and emotion but are a response to two 'threats': the public use of history to support political programs and even acts of violence, and postmodernism. Hobsbawm's essay was written during the disintegration of the former Yugoslavia through armed combat, and it expresses his assumption that too close an engagement between the historian and the materials they study can hinder critical reflection. This is a reasonably commonplace historiographical assumption, echoed across journals and monographs. Like Lars von Trier, historians hold that being an 'outsider' can help you to see that which passes by unnoticed 'inside' a community. Like some other historians, Hobsbawm sees in being an 'insider' the increased risk of deleterious political and ethical outcomes. It was primarily for that reason, for example, that Theodore Moody, D.B. Quinn and R. Dudley Edwards argued for the 'scientific' and detached writing of Irish history.[60] This argument for a detached stance invites two criticisms. First, it presupposes a necessary and universal connection between historiographical identification and deleterious social outcomes. We cannot assume that all identity histories are politically divisive and thus unethical. The converse might be true, as with Brendan Bradshaw's complaint that a detached treatment of the Irish Famine has served to obscure the scale of the tragedy involved.[61] Second, there is the question of whether a detached stance can be achieved. One of the criticisms of postmodern scholars—the second source of threat in Hobsbawm's article—is that 'detached', 'scientific' and 'universal' stances are really the principles, beliefs and hopes of Western, European, male scholars writ large. Unlike Hobsbawm, postmodern historians do not see it as possible to turn off or step outside one's community allegiances. It might be argued, on their view, that the professed identity historian is more honest than those claiming more universal stances. To postmodernists, there is no single, detached, 'meta' or god's eye view of historical events. Every historical discourse shapes and is shaped by other discourses that imagine a panoply of communities: political, religious, gender, class, ethnicity, and so on. As with film viewers, therefore, an historian's sense of connection with a community may be complex and ambiguous and may change over the course of a narrative. Therefore, while we should be aware of the uses of identity histories—a claim I will follow up in Chapter 7—it makes little sense to condemn identification outright.

There is no agreed, neatly packaged concept of identity in historiography and historical film studies. While it has been most often connected with 'imagined' nations, it can also be used to refer to a potentially unlimited number of other communities. In this chapter, we have caught sight of the concept in the ways that viewers and historians talk about their connections with communities via discourses like historical films and written texts. We have also questioned the grounds upon which identification has been dismissed as a historiographical process, pointing out that thoughts and emotions are united in being cognitive, that it is possible to share 'the same' thoughts and emotions as others and that identification does not guarantee unethical social outcomes. Furthermore, we have seen that discussion about identity in historical film studies is strengthened through the consideration of viewer responses as well as discourse analysis. All these points raise a crucial issue that remains unresolved at the end of this chapter and in historiography more generally: is there a self or single identity that binds together our encounters with the various imagined communities described? That is a question that we now know demands historical as well as discursive investigation.

Recommended resources

Anderson, B., *Imagined Communities: Reflections on the Origin and Spread of Nationalism*, rev. edn, London: Verso, 1991.

Barefoot, G., *Gaslight Melodrama: From Victorian London to 1940s Hollywood*, London: Continuum, 2001.

Billig, M., *Banal Nationalism*, London: Sage, 1995.

Bourdieu, P., *Distinction: A Social Critique of the Judgement of Taste*, trans. R. Nice, Cambridge, Mass.: Harvard University Press, 1987.

Hansen, M., *Babel and Babylon: Spectatorship in American Silent Film*, Cambridge, Mass.: Harvard University Press, 1991.

Harper, S., *Home is Where the Heart Is: Melodrama and the Women's Film*, London: BFI, 1987.

Hjort, M. and Mackenzie, S. (eds), *Cinema and Nation*, London: Routledge, 2000.

Hobsbawm, E., 'Identity history is not enough', in *On History*, New York: Free Press, 1997, pp. 266–77.

Hobsbawm, E. and Ranger, T., *The Invention of Tradition*, Cambridge: Cambridge University Press, 1983.

Kansteiner, W., 'Finding meaning in memory: a methodological critique of collective memory studies', *History and Theory*, 2002, vol. 41(2), pp. 179–97.

Kuhn, A., *Dreaming of Fred and Ginger: Cinema and Cultural Memory*, New York: New York University Press, 2002.

Plantinga, C., 'Notes on spectator emotion and ideological film criticism', in R. Allen and M. Smith (eds), *Film Theory and Philosophy*, Oxford: Oxford University Press, 1997, pp. 372–93.

Notes

1 Available online at http://www.rochestergoesout.com/mov/s/savsid.html

2 J. Winter, 'Film and the matrix of memory', *American Historical Review*, 2001, vol. 106(3), pp. 857–64; V. Sobchack, 'Beyond visual aids: American film as American culture', *American Quarterly*, 1980, vol. 32(3), p. 293; and R. Bell, 'Review of Robert Borgoyne, *Film Nation: Hollywood looks at US History*', *Screening the Past*, 2001, no. 12, online at www.latrobe.edu.au/screeningthepast/reviews/rev0301/rbbr12a.htm

3 L. Grindon, *Shadows on the Past: Studies in the Historical Fiction Film*, Philadelphia: Temple University Press, 1994, pp. 63–8; 'The filmmaker as historian, above and below ground', *Rethinking History*, 2001, vol. 5(2), pp. 233–53; and R. Howells, 'Atlantic Crossings: Nation, Class and Identity in *Titanic* (1953) and *A Night to Remember* (1958)', *Historical Journal of Film, Radio and Television*, 1999, vol. 19(4), pp. 421–38.

4 B. Anderson, *Imagined Communities: Reflections on the Origin and Spread of Nationalism*, rev. edn, London: Verso, 1991, p. 46.

5 J. Martín-Barbero, *Communication, Culture and Hegemony: From the Media to Mediations*, London: Sage, 1993.

6 E. Hobsbawm and T. Ranger (eds), *The Invention of Tradition*, Cambridge: Cambridge University Press, 1983; and J. Assman, 'Collective memory and cultural identity', *New German Critique*, 1995, no. 65, p. 132. See also R. Rosenzweig and D. Thelen, *The Presence of the Past: Popular Uses of History in American Life*, New York: Columbia University Press, 1998, p. 3.

7 See, for example, H. Flanzebaum (ed.), *The Americanization of the Holocaust*, Baltimore: Johns Hopkins University Press, 1999; and Y. Loshitzsky (ed.), *Spielberg's Holocaust: Critical Perspectives on 'Schindler's List'*, Bloomington: Indiana University Press, 1997.

8 M. Billig, *Banal Nationalism*, London: Sage, 1995, p. 8.

9 See also Pierre Bourdieu's idea of 'habitus', as explained in *Distinction: A Social Critique of the Judgement of Taste*, trans. R. Nice, Cambridge, Mass.: Harvard University Press, 1987.

10 D. Desser and G. Studies, 'Never having to say you're sorry: Rambo's rewriting of the Vietnam War', *Film Quarterly*, 1988, vol. 42(1), pp. 9–16.

11 M.R. Young, 'In the combat zone', *Radical History Review*, 2003, no. 85, pp. 253–64.

12 On criticisms of collective memory and trauma, see W. Kansteiner, 'Finding meaning in memory: a methodological critique of collective memory studies', *History and Theory*, 2002, vol. 41(2), pp. 179–97; J. Winter, 'Film and the matrix of memory', p. 860; J. Olick, 'Collective memory: the two cultures', *Sociological Theory*, 1999, vol. 17(3), pp. 333–48; and D. LaCapra, *Representing the Holocaust: History, Theory, Trauma*, Ithaca, NJ: Cornell University Press, 1994.

13 I. Irwin-Zarecka, *Frames of Remembrance: The Dynamics of Collective Memory*, New Brunswick, NY: Transaction, 1994, p. 116.

14 H. Harper, 'The military and society: reaching and reflecting audiences in fiction and film', *Armed Forces and Society*, 2001, vol. 27(2), p. 231, emphasis added;

and M. Landy (ed.), *The Historical Film: History and Memory in Media*, New Brunswick, NJ: Rutgers University Press, 2001, p. 1.

15 W. Kansteiner, 'Finding meaning in memory', pp. 192–3.

16 For a critical review, see T. Doherty, 'Saving Private Ryan', *Cineaste*, 1998, vol. 24(1), pp. 68–71.

17 K. Rockett, 'Emmet on Film', *History Ireland*, 2003, vol. 11(3), pp. 46–9; M. McLoone, 'Reimagining the nation: themes and issues in Irish cinema', *Cineaste*, 1999, vol. 24(2–3), pp. 28–34; S. Hannu, 'The Indians of the north: western traditions and Finnish indians', *Film and History*, 1993, vol. 23(1–4), pp. 27–43; and E. Mazierska, 'In the land of noble knights and mute princesses: Polish heritage cinema', *Historical Journal of Film, Radio and Television*, 2001, vol. 21(2), pp. 167–77.

18 T. Hughes-D'Aeth, 'Which rabbit-proof fence? Empathy, assimilation, Hollywood', *Australian Humanities Review*, 2002, available online at http://www.lib.Latrobe.edu.au/AHR

19 E. Gellner, *Nationalism*, London: Weidenfeld & Nicolson, 1997, pp. 102–8.

20 M. Griffin, 'Sex, drugs and posting bail', *Sydney Morning Herald*, Metropolitan section, 16 August 2003, p. 1; D. Puttnam, 'Has Hollywood stolen our history?', in D. Cannadine (ed.), *History and the Media*, Basingstoke: Palgrave Macmillan, 2004, pp. 160–6; and L. Hirschberg, 'Losing America', *The Weekend Australian Review*, 27–28 November 2004, p. R5.

21 A. Higson, 'The concept of national cinema', *Screen*, 1989, vol. 30(4), pp. 39–47; and C. Faulkner, 'Affective identities: French national cinema and the 1930s', *Canadian Journal of Film Studies*, 1994, vol. 3(2), pp. 3–24.

22 J. Ulff-Moller, 'The origin of the French film quota policy controlling the import of American films', *Historical Journal of Film, Radio and Television*, 1998, vol. 18(2), pp. 167–83.

23 M. Hjort, 'Themes of nation' and E. Rentschler, 'From new German cinema to the post-Wall cinema of consensus', in *Cinema and Nation*, London: Routledge, 2000, pp. 103–17, 260–77; J. Tusa, 'A deep and continuing use of history', in D. Cannadine (ed.), *History and the Media*, pp. 124–40; and A. Higson, *Waving the Flag: Constructing a National Cinema in Britain*, Oxford: Oxford University Press, 1995, p. 113.

24 F. Nietszche, 'The uses and disadvantages of history for life', in J.O. Stern (ed.), *Untimely Meditations*, trans. R.J. Hollingdale, Cambridge: Cambridge University Press, 1991, pp. 63–75, quote at p. 75; M. Foucault, 'Nietzsche, genealogy, history', in D.F. Bouchard (ed.), *Logic, Counter-Memory, Practice: Selected Essays and Interviews*, Ithaca, NY: Cornell University Press, 1988, pp. 139–65; A. Gramsci, *Selections from the Prison Notebooks*, ed. and trans. Q. Hoare and G.N. Smith, New York: International Publishers, 1978, pp. 323–33, 419–25. All discussed in M. Landy, 'Introduction', in *The Historical Film: History and Memory in Media*, New Brunswick, NJ: Rutgers University Press, 2000, pp. 2–7.

25 On 'inhabiting' identities, see M. Foucault, *The Order of Things: An Archaeology of the Human Sciences*, trans. anon., London: Tavistock, 1970; and P. Bourdieu, *Distinction*.

26 M. Mask, '*Eve's Bayou*: too good to be a black film?', *Cineaste*, 1998, vol. 23(4), pp. 26–7.

27 E. Mazierska, 'In the land of noble knights and mute princesses', p. 169.

28 M. Rogin, '*AHR* forum: *JFK* the movie', *American Historical Review*, 1992, vol. 97(2), pp. 500–5; and C. Sharrett, 'The belly of the beast: Oliver Stone's *Nixon* and the American nightmare', *Cineaste*, 1996, vol. 22(1), pp. 4–10.

29 K. Biber, ' "Turned out real nice after all": death and masculinity in Australian cinema', in K. Biber, T. Sear and D. Trudinger (eds), *Playing the Man: New Approaches to Masculinity*, Annandale, NSW: Pluto Press, 1999, pp. 27–37.

30 Z. Bauman, 'Modernity and ambivalence', in M. Featherstone (ed.), *Global Culture: Nationalism, Globalization and Modernity*, London: Sage, 1990, p. 145.

31 C.S. Tashiro, *Pretty Pictures: Production Design and the History Film*, Austin: University of Texas Press, 1998, p. 66; and G. Lindon, *Shadows on the Past*, p. 223.

32 M. Baker with T. Austin, *From Antz to Titanic: Reinventing Film Analysis*, London: Pluto Press, 2000, p. 48. See, for example, M. Hansen, *From Babel to Babylon: Spectatorship in American Silent Film*, Cambridge, Mass.: Harvard University Press, 1991.

33 M. Barker with T. Austin, *From Antz to Titanic*, p. 187.

34 Recollection of Oliver Dewar, in A. Kuhn, *Dreaming of Fred and Ginger: Cinema and Cultural Memory*, New York: New York University Press, 2002, pp. 39–40.

35 J. Staiger, 'Securing the fictional narrative as a tale of the historical real: *The Return of Martin Guerre*', in *Perverse Spectators: The Practices of Film Reception*, New York: New York University Press, 2000, pp. 191–209. A similar limitation may be seen in Ulf Hedetoft's consideration of the European reception of *Saving Private Ryan* in 'Contemporary cinema: between cultural globalisation and national interpretation', in M. Hjort and S. Mackenzie (eds), *Cinema and Nation*, pp. 278–97.

36 A. Angelini and E. Pasquali, 'Movimenti oculari e percezione di sequenze filmiche', *Bianco e Nero*, 1983, vol. 44(1), pp. 76–87, as cited in J. Simmons, 'The ontology of perception in cinema', *Film and Philosophy*, 1997, vol. 4, pp. 74–84; and I. Ang, *Watching Dallas: Soap Opera and Melodramatic Imagination*, London: Methuen, 1985.

37 S. Harper, 'Historical pleasures: Gainsborough costume drama', in M. Landy (ed.), *The Historical Film*, p. 116. This is an excerpt from her larger study, *Home is Where the Heart Is: Studies in Melodrama and Women's Film*, London: BFI, 1987.

38 See also M.A. Doane, *The Desire to Desire: The Women's Films of the 1940s*, Bloomington: Indiana University Press, 1987. For more general accounts of early cinema audiences in the USA, see R. Rosensweig, *Eight Hours for What We Will: Workers and Leisure in an Industrial City 1870–1920*, New York: Cambridge University Press, 1983; K. Peiss, *Cheap Amusements: Working Women and Leisure in Turn-of-the-century New York*, Philadelphia: Temple University Press, 1986; and E. Ewen, 'City lights: immigrant women and the rise of the movies', *Signs*, 1980, vol. 5(3), pp. 45–66.

39 *Maytime* publicity poster, as reproduced in A. Kuhn, *Dreaming of Fred and Ginger*, p. 199.

40 *Ibid.*, pp. 205, 206, 211.

41 *Ibid.*, p. 100.

42 *Ibid.*; see, for example, S. Harper, *Home is Where the Heart Is* and L. Spigel, 'Same bat channel, different bat times: mass culture and popular memory', in R.A. Pearson and W. Uricchio (eds), *The Many Lives of the Batman*, London: Routledge and BFI, 1991, pp. 117–44.

43 C. Plantinga, 'Notes on spectator emotion and ideological film criticism', in R. Allen and M. Smith (eds), *Film Theory and Philosophy*, Oxford: Oxford University Press, 1997, pp. 372–7.

44 B. Gaut, 'On cinema and perversion', *Film and Philosophy*, 1994, vol. 1, pp. 3–17. See also the response to this by Michael Levine, 'Depraved spectators and impossible audiences', *Film and Philosophy*, special issue on horror, 2001, pp. 63–71.

45 Aristotle, *On Rhetoric*, trans. G.A. Kennedy, Oxford: Oxford University Press, 1991, p. 139; A. Kenny, *The Metaphysics of Mind*, Oxford: Oxford University Press, 1989, p. 52. See also A. Kenny, *Action, Emotion and Will*, London: Routledge & Kegan Paul, 1963, ch. 9 and J.R.S. Wilson, *Emotion and Object*, Cambridge: Cambridge University Press, 1972, ch. 15.

46 R. de Sousa, *The Rationality of Emotions*, Cambridge, Mass.: MIT Press, 1987, ch. 7. See also P. Greenspan, *Emotions and Reasons*, New York: Routledge, 1988;

and R.C. Solomon, *The Passions: Emotions and the Meaning of Life*, Indianapolis: Hackett Publishing, 1993.

47 R. Rosenzweig and D. Thelen, *The Presence of the Past: Popular Uses of History in American Life*, New York: Columbia University Press, 1998. Survey results are also available online at http://chnm.gmu.edu/survey/; and P. Ashton and P. Hamilton, 'At home with the past: initial findings from the survey', *Australian Cultural History*, 2003, vol. 23, pp. 5–30. Some survey results are also available online at http://www.austpast.uts.edu.au

48 A. Kuhn, *Dreaming of Fred and Ginger*, pp. 215–33.

49 *Ibid.*, p. 232.

50 D. Hume, *A Treatise on Human Nature* [1739], ed. D. and M. Norton, Oxford: Oxford University Press, 2000, §§3.2.2, 2.2.5; D. Hume, *Enquiry Concerning the Principles of Morals* [1772], ed. L.A. Selby-Bigge, Oxford: Oxford University Press, 1975, §6.1; and A. Smith, *The Theory of Moral Sentiments* [1759], Indianapolis: Liberty, 1969, §§1.1.1–1.1.4, 1.2.1, 1.2.3, 1.3.1, 7.3.1.

51 A.B. Hart, 'Imagination in history', in *American Historical Review*, 1910, vol. 15, p. 240.

52 H. Ritter, 'Understanding', in *Dictionary of Concepts in History*, Westport, Conn.: Greenwood Press, p. 436. See also H. Butterfield, *History and Human Relations*, London: Collins, 1951.

53 J.G. Herder, 'Yet another philosophy of history' [1774], *Against Pure Reason: Writings on Religion, Language and History*, trans. and ed. M. Bunge, Minneapolis: Augsburg Fortress, 1993, p. 39. The translation has been slightly modified to recall the sense that readers might have got before Lee's coining of the English term 'empathy' in 1904.

54 A. Harrington, 'Dilthey, empathy and *Verstehen*: a contemporary reappraisal', *European Journal of Social Theory*, 2001, vol. 4(3), pp. 311–29.

55 V. Lee and C. Anstruther Thomson, *Beauty and Ugliness and Other Studies in Psychological Aesthetics*, New York: Browne, 1904.

56 R.G. Collingwood, *The Idea of History*, p. 286; see R.G. Collingwood, *Religion and Philosophy* [1916], Bristol: Thoemmes, 1994, p. 116.

57 R.G. Collingwood, 'Outlines of a philosophy of history', *The Idea of History*, rev. edn ed. W.J. van der Dussen, Oxford: Oxford University Press, 1995, p. 446.

58 For an expanded treatment of 're-enactment', see my *'How Good an Historian Shall I Be?': R.G. Collingwood, the Historical Imagination and Education*, Thorveton, Exeter: Imprint Academic, 2003, ch. 2.

59 E. Hobsbawm, 'Identity history is not enough', in *On History*, New York: Free Press, 1997, pp. 266–77.

60 C. Brady, ' "Constructive and instrumental": the dilemma of Ireland's first "new historians" ', in C. Brady (ed.), *Interpreting Irish History: The Debate on Historical Revisionism 1938–1994*, Blackrock, Co. Dublin: Irish Academic Press, 1994, pp. 1–31.

61 B. Bradshaw, 'Nationalism and historical scholarship in modern Ireland', *Irish Historical Studies*, 1988–9, vol. 26, pp. 329–51; reprinted in C. Brady (ed.), *Interpreting Irish History*, pp. 191–216. A similar claim is made about Keith Windschuttle's lack of 'sympathy' and 'empathy' in writing Australian Aboriginal history. See H. Reynolds, 'Terra nullius reborn', in R. Manne (ed.), *Whitewash*, Melbourne: Black Agenda Inc., 2003, p. 133.

5   Reality

> To the best of our knowledge, there was no violation of historical truth. We have a great responsibility. Whatever we make will become the truth, the visual reality that a generation will accept.
>
> James Cameron, *'Titanic'*, *Newsweek*, 15 December 1997, p. 65

In the short, stop-motion clay animation *Harvie Krumpet* (2003), ten inter-titles display some of the 'fakts' the protagonist has collected over the course of his twentieth-century life:

> Fakt 48: Fakts still exist even when they are ignored; Fakt 116: Certain frogs can come back to life when thawed. Humans do not; Fakt 142: A cigarette is a substitute for your mothers [*sic*] nipple; Fakt 268: There are three times more chickens in the world than humans; Fakt 372: The trouble with nude dancing is that not everything stops when the music does; Fakt 586: Love does not conquer all; Fakt 698: The average person uses nineteen miles of dental floss in their lifetime; Fakt 804: 42 percent of the population can't remember their PIN number; Fakt 914: Alcohol can cause drunkenness and nudity; and Fakt 1034: Life is like a cigarette. Smoke it to the butt.

Collated in this way, apart from their explanatory contexts, they appear trivial and amusing. They might evoke a response similar to that of Michel Foucault on reading a quote from 'a certain Chinese encyclopedia' in Juan Luis Borges' writing: laughter that shatters

> all the familiar landmarks of thought—*our* thought, the thought that bears the stamp of our age and our geography—breaking up all the ordered surfaces and all the planes with which we are accustomed to tame the wild profusion of existing things and continuing long after-wards to disturb and threaten with collapse our age-old distinction between the Same and the Other. . . . In the wonderment of this taxonomy,

the thing we apprehend . . . is the limitation of our own [system of thought], the stark impossibility of [us] thinking *that*.[1]

We may laugh at *Harvie Krumpet*, but does our laughter veil the uncomfortable recognition of the arbitrary constructedness and insularity of his world, and perhaps our own? The aim of this chapter is to navigate between the common scholastic construction of viewers as enthralled by a 'hyperreal' filmic world that renders them passive consumers and the idea of individual viewers constructing filmic reality in idiosyncratic ways. The view advanced here is rather that of reality as constructed by historical communities of viewers, communities in need of further investigation.

To what extent, if at all, can historical films capture historical reality? Or is reality something made and controlled by filmmakers, as James Cameron claims in the quote that opens this chapter? The connection of historical reality with film is commonly assumed and rarely discussed. Scholars routinely presume that there is some form of relationship between represented and real times, whether those real times correspond to those of the diegesis or of production. Only a few writers have explicitly articulated an account of realism, and they too presuppose some form of connection between representation and reality. In 'Any resemblance to persons living or dead', for example, Natalie Zemon Davis takes as a given a 'dialogue between present and past' and therefore sees her writing as a contribution to the discussion on how reality and the related notion of 'authenticity' can be 'best achieved'. Reality is to be found, she concludes

> When films represent values, relations and issues in a period; when they animate props and locations by their connections with historical people . . . when they let the past have its distinctiveness before remaking it to resemble the present . . . suggesting the possibility that there may be a very different way of reporting what happened, and giving some indication of their own truth status, an indication of where knowledge of the past comes from and our relation to it.[2]

Those outcomes are challenging, but they are achievable. The interrelation of reality and representation is also assumed by Robert Rosenstone, who sees in his own scholarship on historical films the admission that he believes 'in the reality of the signified—which is to say, the world . . . that empirical facts exist and insist[s] that if we let go of that belief then we are no longer historians'.[3] Marc Ferro and Pierre Sorlin are more sceptical, but they too believe that historical films are able to offer viewers access to the times in which they are made.[4]

Hyperreality

The belief that cinema is in some way a realistic medium jars against one of the major tenets of postmodernist and poststructuralist film theory, that representation has no stable or reflective relationship with the phenomenal world. Film images are suggestive not of reality but of what Jean Baudrillard calls 'hyperreality'. According to Baudrillard, 'hyperreality' denotes a step in the historical process whereby images have become unshackled from the real. There are four successive phases in societal apprehensions of the image: 'It is the reflection of a basic reality. It masks and perverts a basic reality. It marks the absence of a basic reality. It bears no relation to reality whatever: it is its own pure simulacrum.'[5] The last of these is the hyperreal, a state whereby films are not maps, doubles or mirrors of any domain regarded as 'the real' but visions of a world that appears more legitimate, more believable and more valuable than the real. In short, the hyperreal is 'more real than real'.[6] Baudrillard is not merely suggesting that images are artificial, because the concept of artificiality implies some reality against which to judge the artifice. His argument is rather that we have lost our ability to make sense of the distinction between reality and artifice. Hyperreality limits our participation in the world to the role of consumers or responders rather than producers or initiators. We no longer acquire goods because of real needs or because we want to use them to achieve social transformation but because of desires that are increasingly defined by commercial images, which keep us one step removed from the reality of our bodies and of the physical and socio-political world. Capital thus defines what we are.

Various media make possible the 'mutation' of the real into the hyperreal.[7] In film, ironically, this is played out through the heavily promoted aim of perfection of representation, for 'absolute realistic verisimilitude' and the elimination of overtly symbolic content.[8] Baudrillard is therefore highly critical of historical films such as *Chinatown* (1974), *Barry Lyndon* (1975) and *1900* (1976), which claim to offer only visual historical correspondence 'whose very perfection is disquieting'.[9] Many more recent examples of 'disquieting perfection' might be cited: for example, *Titanic* (1997), the film's production designer Peter Lamont argues, offers viewers:

> a Titanic as close as possible to the real thing, down to the exact shade of green on the leather chairs in the smoking lounge. The sumptuous sets have made-to-order replicas of the lighting fixtures, the china, the stained-glass windows. . . .[10]

James Cameron, as the quote that opens this chapter suggests, saw his role as director as one of making a reality that 'a generation will accept'. Reviewers of *Saving Private Ryan* (1998), too, lauded the 'fanatical' realism of its opening sequence and, like most viewers who saw the film in the United States, I had that impression strengthened by the print and on-screen announcements for a hotline that veterans could call if they found the movie upsetting.[11] Steven Spielberg was no stranger to this adulatory reception, as *Schindler's List* (1993) received presidential endorsements and attracted sponsorship for subsidised, mandatory and commercial free broadcasts in cinemas and on television.[12] Visual hyperrealism is also apparent in the promotional materials for *Gladiator* (2000), from the 30,000 handmade mud bricks of a North African amphitheatre set to Colin Capon's food art:

> The honeyed butterflies were too fragile; the scorpions didn't look right. But Colin Capon's locusts and cicadas were a triumph. Made of powdered sugar and gelatin, packed in cotton and flown from London to Morocco, where *Gladiator* was being shot, they appear on the table at Proximo's desert training camp. In costume dramas, the clothes receive the attention. But getting the food right—or at least plausible—is important too. . . . 'There's nothing worse in a historical film', says the Royal Air Force Chef . . . 'than having fruit straight from the supermarket'.[13]

Even light can be 'got right', as the cinematographer for *Eliza Fraser* (1976) explains: 'We were dealing with the 1830 period and it had to look totally genuine. . . . Overall, we were trying very hard to get the actual light that would have existed at the time.'[14] All these examples and many more appear to be underpinned by the belief that the truth of an historical phenomenon can be realised through the sheer accumulation of contemporary signs of the real. Spielberg's concentrated compilation in the ghetto-clearing scene of *Schindler's List* of signs of the Holocaust—known to viewers through multiple other films on the Holocaust—epitomises the trajectory towards the hyperreal. Actions, costumes, props and dialogue circulate, impressing upon us through their sheer numbers that we are witnessing the real.[15] But what we see is better than the real, a 'hyperreality' that breaks from the real and in which the extermination of memory is achieved:

> One no longer makes the Jews pass through the crematorium or the gas chamber, but through the sound track and image track, through the universal screen and microprocessor. Forgetting, annihilation, finally achieves its aesthetic dimension in this way. . . .[16]

Visual hyperreality thus offers us nothing 'except the empty figure of resemblance'.[17] The interrelation of visual hyperfidelity and film promotion will be explored in more depth in Chapter 8.

Digital images

Visual hyperreality is advanced not only through the use of detailed props and sets; digital technologies are more often the focus of film theorists' explorations of cinema as a hyperreal medium. Digital technologies are now commonly used to add to, remove from, substitute for or enhance elements of filmic images. In *Forrest Gump* (1994), digital processes made it possible to show Gary Sinise as an amputee without having to conceal his limbs through binding or loose costuming. Similar processes are used to delete wires in choreographed fight sequences, as in *Wo Hu Zang Long* (*Crouching Tiger, Hidden Dragon*, 2000), and anachronistic architectural elements, like those in the South Carolina location shot for *The Patriot* (2000) reproduced in Figure 5.1. Compared with a 'before shot', it is apparent just how extensively an image can be changed. Anachronistic architecture has been removed (left) to make way for a harbour, but so too has a tree (foreground, right), for which no justification was offered on the part of the effects company Centropolis. Similarly, no explanation is offered for the addition of 'synthespians' (digitally generated extras or actors) or the substitution of a blue sky dotted with cumulus clouds for a grey one.[18] Were all these changes made for historical reasons? Are there historical grounds for favouring a blue sky over a grey one? Not always, as is clear from Lars von Trier's suggestion that he added blue skies to *Dancer in the Dark* (2000) simply because it was raining during shooting, and post-production digital technologies 'work just fine'.[19] We might raise similar questions about the pink hue to the buildings in the digital images of Rome in *Gladiator* or the addition of synthespians on deck in *Titanic*.

Digital technologies may 'work just fine' for directors, but their reception among film scholars has not been so warm. Thomas Doherty and J. Robert Craig, for instance, have warned of the ethical problems that might arise from

Figure 5.1 'Before' and 'after': digital alteration of location in *The Patriot* (© 2000 Centropolis Effects)

the use of screen technologies that have outpaced the ability of viewers to detect them. These technologies, Craig argues, 'could be dangerous in the hands of demagogues working with supposedly "non fiction" material or those addressing naïve audiences of any sort'.[20] Can changing the colour of the sky, or changing the mouth movements and utterances of a person in a newsreel, be dangerous? Will all changes be unacceptable, or are some benign? Is viewer naïvety assumed in the judgement of images? Sean Cubitt does not see the viewers of digital images as necessarily naïve but as accepting consumers. Writing of the 'neobaroque technological film', he complains:

> Digital technologies promise to elevate fantasy worlds above the trouble-some everyday world. Beauty there will be more intense, emotions more powerful, the adrenalin indistinguishable from the real rush. . . . Rather than invite to the voyage or the ascent, they cajole us to step inward, into miniaturised infinities bracketed off from the world . . . the artificial worlds of the neobaroque offer us a stronger sense of being than we experience outside, among the wreckage of modernity, betrayed by the reality of the world, deprived of truth and justice.[21]

In digital historical films, we can achieve satisfaction and deny the exploit-ation, poverty and ecological deterioration that mark our consumerist world. Baudrillard has nothing to say directly on digital images, but his attitude to this means of achieving hyperreality is not difficult to discern because his comments on hyperfidelity of detail apply here too. The hyper-clean, hyper-smooth, perfectly executed digital image ends the quest of film for the real and moves us away from the particular and discomforting phenomena of history.

Baudrillard paints a bleak picture of film: our escapist enjoyment enslaves us in a world like that of the Wachowski brothers' *The Matrix* (1999), in which nothing appears as it seems. Ironically, the film *The Matrix* is itself an object of consumption. We want Neo to prevail, but we also want to buy the glasses and the video game. Considered through the lens of hyperreality, *Bill and Ted's Excellent Adventure* (1988) also serves as an indictment of our times. At the end of history comes shopping for historical figures and histor-ies that will help us to satisfy our desires, such as being part of a rock band. I do not dispute that contemporary cultures of film viewing and appreciation are consumerist. However, what I do question is, first, whether the social and cultural significance of historical films is exhaustively explained by consumer-ism; second, whether consumption undercuts agency; and, third, whether films are consistently hyperreal.

Unquestionably, historical filmmakers modify all sorts of phenomena—objects, settings, sound and bodies—through the use of various technologies and processes. Digital technologies belong to a long and varied lineage of special effects that includes make-up, lighting, camera lenses, editing, miniatures and stop-motion photography. Yet modification may be applied by degrees, and thus the relation between the 'before' and 'after' shots of Figure 5.1 is not one of simple mutual exclusion. Some filmic elements are manipulated and enhanced more than others. Sound, for instance, often has a closer link to analogue sources than other film effects, as one of the sound team for *Terminator 2: Judgment Day* (1991) wryly observes: 'What's amazing to me is ... Industrial Light and Magic [the special effects company] using millions of dollars of high-tech digital equipment and computers to come up with the visuals, and meanwhile I'm inverting a dog food can'.[22] This differential treatment of sound and vision is evident, for example, in the 'making of' featurette that comes bundled with the DVD version of *Troy* (2004). Whereas the discussion on visual effects focuses on the 'magic' of computer programming and digital effects, the chief sound artist makes it clear that all of his materials originated in a dumpster. And this difference of treatment is also apparent in Lars von Trier's commentary on *Dancer in the Dark*: the digital alteration of skies is something to be pleased about, but the substitution of the 'real sound' of filming by studio-recorded songs is a 'problem'. Sound, he complains, 'should be ugly every now and again'.[23] Moreover, different sounds may be subject to different treatments. For example, the digitally 'sweetened' bullet fire of the opening sequence of *Saving Private Ryan*, which includes some raw sonic material, appears together with dialogue that has not been subject to the same level of manipulation and layering. It is clear that phenomena with varying relationships to analogue sources commonly appear together; for example, an analogue sound may accompany an extreme wide shot of a set that has been digitally created. We recall from the last chapter, too, that efforts to achieve fidelity are not uniform for all filmic elements. The mark of a designer may be more apparent in make-up than in props. The hyperreality of historical films is not monolithic and thus, unlike *The Matrix*, may not present a seamless, persuasive artifice.

Historical realities

Baudrillard's theory assumes the wholesale substitution of reality by a hyperreal world that shapes and is shaped by consumerist economies. I have questioned whether that substitution is wholesale, and now I want to consider whether there is any substitution at all. For a small group of theorists, including Jean-Luc Godard and Walter Benjamin, cinema is characterised not by the erasure of the real by the hyperreal but by the persistence of a reality anterior to our world. In *Histoire(s) du cinéma*, for instance, Godard advances the idea that cinema is shaped by the 'dream' and logic of a prior world, the nineteenth century. That world is one that enshrines the autonomous and self-constituting subject described in Hegel's *Phenomenology of Spirit*.[24] The subject, as Hegel sees it, exists only by being recognised by another subject. This is intolerable, because we also want to be independent and self-made. This tug between wanting and not wanting recognition results in a mutual struggle that ends with one subject as master and the other as slave, a relation of inequality in which the former depersonalises the latter.[25] Mainstream North American cinema, Godard holds, enshrines a master–slave relation through the imposition of an emphatically masculine identity on its version of the autonomous and self-constituting subject. In so doing it depersonalises and erases women, and indeed all those that do not fit the vision of masculinity offered. All film will remain for him historical—suspended in the dream of the nineteenth century—until its logic is exposed or denaturalised through the use of dialectical images: juxtaposed or super-imposed images from different genres (e.g. documentary and fiction film) and from different times or places.[26] Historical films that spring to mind as meeting that dialectical aim are dual- or multi-setting films such as Vincent Ward's *The Navigator: A Medieval Odyssey* (1988), in which a medieval boy's vision of a cathedral in a celestial city leads him and five other Cumbrian villagers to tunnel through to that city—twentieth-century Auckland—and to restore the cathedral spire in the hope that it will save his village from the encroaching plague. When the boy reaches Auckland, his visions are revisited and revealed as flashforwards, and together with the other phenomena that the Cumbrians view as wondrous and monstrous are historicised and thus denaturalised to the spectator. *The Navigator* provides a route to historical awareness through the recasting of the familiar as the sublime. Looking on from a position of relative safety, we become aware of phenomena as confus-ing, dangerous and uncontrollable, and we see the time- and culture-bound nature of our own ways of experiencing the world.[27]

It is understandable that Ward's work has been celebrated as 'revision-ary'.[28] However, any one of the editing devices and spectacles of *mise en scène* described in the last chapter might also perform the same function of reveal-ing the logic of the nineteenth century. This more positive appraisal of the reality-revealing potential of film—including commercial works produced in North America—characterises the writings of Walter Benjamin, who looms as a major influence in Godard's *Histoire(s)* project.[29] For Godard, the dream of the nineteenth century is the sovereignty of the autonomous and self-constituting subject; for Benjamin, it is commodification. In his view, the nineteenth century saw the shift from a culture of production to a culture of consumption. Cinema is implicated in that shift yet still able to expose it, for culture is in a mutual relationship with economy.[30] Film can be received absentmindedly or be a means of slowing down or even suspending time to avoid the shock effects of urban existence. We may, like Captain Millar in *Saving Private Ryan* or Maximus in *Gladiator* (Figure 5.2), seek to slow time in order to protect ourselves from the embodied senses of fear, pain, anger or disgust that result from our interactions with phenomena.

We may seek solace in historical films to protect us from the sublime, but shock can and must be worked through, and in Benjamin's view, film offers the best route for searching out and facing up to our consumerist milieu.[31] As with Godard, Benjamin favours the use of montage and juxtaposition rather than a systematic presentation of evidence in support of a clearly stated

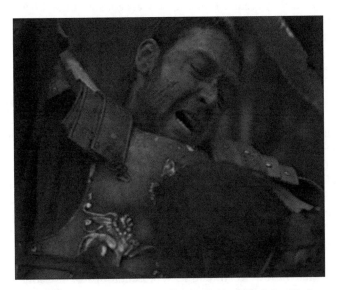

Figure 5.2 The slowing of time as a protection against shock in *Gladiator* (© 2000, Dreamworks SKG)

thesis.[32] He is suspicious of works that claim to show things 'as they really are', for he sees them as a form of narcotic that dulls our awareness of the logic of commodification that gives them form. Thus films about one of the great shocks of the twentieth century—the Holocaust—may render it safe through continuity editing or, as was suggested above, contemporary signs of the real. As Godard affirms, 'Suffering is not a star, nor is it a burned church, nor a devastated landscape'.[33] But again, as was shown in Chapter 3, historical films are never entirely cohesive, and in their ruptures and inconsistencies we may find awareness and the impetus for social transformation. We might cite here *24 Hour Party People* (2002), where the lead, Tony Wilson, appears as a character and a direct-address narrator who repeatedly undercuts viewer belief in the diegesis as a coherent or accurate account of the British music scene from the 1970s. For instance, after we are shown Wilson's wife Lindsay discovering him in the back of a van with a prostitute and her seeking revenge sex with singer Howard Devoto, Wilson summons the real Howard Devoto, who claims that the incident never happened. Later, freeze-frame is used by Wilson to identify the Manchester musicians who are playing cameos, including one who will be left on the cutting room floor but will probably be included in the DVD. The foregrounded use of multiple and conflicting accounts of phenomena in *Rashomon* (1950) and *Courage Under Fire* (1996) and anachronism in *Moulin Rouge* (2001) and *Walker* (1987) also offers the opportunity for one history to interrogate another.[34]

Baudrillard, Godard and Benjamin are united in the belief that film is a form of illusion that deceives viewers. For André Bazin, however, spectators know that what they see is a film and actively construct the illusion of filmic reality. In Bazin's view, film offers better access to history than any other art form because it 'mummifies' and transforms reality, yet it is never apart from subjects who seek meaning in it.[35] Historical reality apart from the intentionality of subjects is not available to us. He writes:

> The same event, the same object, can be represented in various ways. Each representation discards or retains various of the qualities that permit us to recognise the object on the screen. Each introduces, for didactic or aesthetic reasons, abstractions that operate more or less corrosively and thus do not permit the original to subsist in its entirety. At the conclusion of this inevitable and necessary 'chemical' action, for the initial reality there has been substituted an illusion of reality composed of a complex of abstraction (black and white, plane surface), of conventions (the rule of montage, for example), and of authentic reality. It is a necessary illusion.[36]

There are thus various abstractions, representations or illusions of reality, and reality will never be fully grasped in its concreteness. Photography and cinema simply 'satisfy once and for all and in its very essence, our obsession with realism'.[37] Thus realism is to be found in the satisfaction of a viewer's fixation with it, never apart from it. That obsession, Bazin believes, need not be satisfied only in spatial likeness or cohesiveness, so a film like *Harvie Krumpet* can be considered more realistic by some viewers than other films that use human actors and historical locations. The same may be true of films that make extensive use of digital technologies. Nor is temporal likeness or cohesiveness required. A film need not be made in real time to be real for viewers.

Rather, satisfaction may be attained through any one or many indexical markers that are taken by viewers as suggestive of phenomena in the world, as for instance a kite attests to the existence of wind. Some indexical markers are traces because they are suggestive of an historical relationship with phenomena. For example, an empty shoe next to a wrecked car, a pile of suitcases at Auschwitz or lipstick on a collar are evocative of events that happened before the present. As Philip Rosen explains: 'The spectator is supposed to read pastness in the image, not only a past as a signified (as in, say, an historical painting), but also a past of the signifier, which is in turn that of a signifier–referent relation as a production'.[38] Bazin does not explain how viewers, individually and collectively, come to regard some elements of films as indexical traces. Furthermore, he reduces all expressions of our cinematic obsession with realism to a defence against death: it is simply the 'last word in the argument with death by means of the form that endures'.[39] Thus his notion of cinema as the locus of an obsession to mummify, embalm and preserve is open to the charge of being acultural and ahistorical. Importantly, though, his theory does allow for viewer agency and for various admixtures and degrees of reality satisfaction in film. Reality is not simply a matter to be decided at the level of the whole film: viewers may find some elements of a film more persuasive than others. Any search for the reality of historical films is thus a search for viewer responses. In Chapters 7 and 8, on propaganda and selling history, respectively, I will explore the ways in which viewers have engaged with films and film technologies as agents and question whether they are to be viewed solely through the lens of consumerism.

Cinematic engagement, perception and imaging

On Bazin's view, filmic reality should not be considered apart from viewer engagement. What is the epistemological nature of that engagement? One view promoted by analytical philosophers of film—as distinct from the continental theories considered so far in this chapter—is that cinematic engagement is an act of imagination. Gregory Currie, for instance, argues that the attitude we take towards feature films is that of imagination, as in the attribution of attitudes to other people by simulating their hopes and beliefs.[40] Unfortunately, Currie's view shifts us away from the more traditional association of imagination with imaging, which can be illuminating in this context. Writing in the mid-twentieth century, Jean-Paul Sartre, Gilbert Ryle and Ludwig Wittgenstein sketched out what they saw as the key differences between perceptions and images. First, we can be mistaken about sensory perceptions in ways that do not apply to images: for example, I cannot mistake an image of a bird for an image of a leaf as I might mistake seeing a leaf as a bird. Second, images can manifest temporal and spatial characteristics we are unused to with perception: moving images may be slowed down or accelerated at will, repeated or considered in reverse sequence, and we might 'see' the front and back of an object at the same time.[41] Third, in comparison with perceptions, images are impoverished because we cannot learn anything new from them. For instance, when I look at a building, I can locate a certain feature such as a gargoyle, but if, on the other hand, I was to entertain an image of the same building and I do not know the location of a certain gargoyle, then my image will not provide me with this new information.[42] Similarly, when I have a mental image, I cannot crane my head or adjust the way that I look at it to see it more clearly.[43] Fourth, the entertainment of images is always accompanied by our awareness of such.[44] Fifth, images are always images of something; they are 'intentional'. Sixth, I can be requested to entertain an image but not to see ordinarily.[45] Finally, and most importantly, images are a form of consciousness, not objects of consciousness or pictures 'in the mind'.[46]

When we watch films, are we imaging? If so, is this imaging, as Sartre, Wittgenstein and Ryle would have it, an impoverished form of consciousness? A useful example for exploring the intersections of reality, perception and imaging is, as Psathas has demonstrated, Woody Allen's *The Purple Rose of Cairo* (1985).[47] Allen's film opens with a cinema audience watching a black and white film with the same title as Allen's film. Not long after, the screen character Tom Baxter pauses, shakes his head and says to Cecilia, who is watching the film, 'you must really *love* this picture'. Cecilia, incredulous, repeatedly responds 'Me?', while another audience member complains to the similarly startled screen characters 'What's the point of the film if they don't do what they did before?' Then, not heeding the complaints of the other screen characters—'you're on the wrong side', 'we're in the middle of the story' and 'we can't continue with the story'—Tom steps out of the screen and into a series of interactions with Cecilia's world. In those interactions, it soon becomes apparent that Tom is unable to age, change or have a future, unlike the actor who plays him on screen (Gil Shepherd), who is concerned that his career will be adversely affected by Tom's actions. Furthermore, it is apparent that Tom knows nothing beyond what he knows in the film: Cecilia has to tell him about money, cars, prostitution, taxes and religion. Cecilia fares better when she later steps through the screen and joins Tom in 'filmic reality' because her repeated viewings have furnished her with knowledge of what will happen in the diegesis. Ultimately, however, she cannot reside there, because as an unscripted character she threatens the plot and the continuing realisation of what the characters do at each screening. She has also been tricked by stagecraft: the screen champagne is only ginger ale, and there is no place for her character to grow in such artifice.

Allen's film highlights the impoverished nature of our perceptual engagement with film. When we look at a film in a cinema, we can identify and locate phenomena, stand further from or closer to the screen and put our glasses on and take them off. But we cannot see anything more than is depicted: if a film offers only close-ups of a character's head, for instance, repeated viewings, putting on my glasses or moving closer to the screen will not tell me what kind of shoes that character is wearing. Similarly, if a phenomenon is filmed out of focus, I cannot do anything to see it more clearly. These points are demonstrated in Tom Baxter's lack of familiarity with many of the features of our world: his knowledge is limited to the diegesis. Like Tom, what we see on screen is not as open to alteration as our perceptions can be. With perception, if I see something far away, I can move closer to it; if I want to see someone's shoes, I look down. I do not have the same control when I watch a film. In this way, film watching is akin to imaging. Unlike imaging, though, we cannot control the temporal and spatial characteristics of what we see in a film: it is the filmmaker who slows down, accelerates or reverses time, not us. Nor can we change the ending of a film while we are watching it, no matter how much we would like to and how many screenings we have attended. Cecilia's plight within the diegesis of *Purple Rose of Cairo* conveys this point. On the other hand, our engagement with film is a conscious one. We are aware that we are watching a film and not looking out of a window perceiving phenomena. As with Sartre's experiment in which he altered a window view to match a woman's hallucinations, or Tom Baxter's greeting to Cecilia, we would be shocked if diegetic phenomena moved into our viewing space.

Furthermore, as Chapter 8 will show us, we may alter the spatial, temporal and diegetic features of a film after we have seen it through mental images and memories or viewing technologies such as DVD players. It is clear that our engagement with film cannot be readily assimilated to the activities of either perception or imaging. What we see is neither entirely beyond our control nor completely within it. Film viewing, like diegeses themselves, is heterogeneous: part perceptual, part idiosyncratic, part social in construction.

Images and words

As with historical film scholars, many historians take as 'an article of faith' that history is a description, analysis or explanation that more or less corresponds to a real past that is no longer present.[48] Classic expressions of this position date from nineteenth-century Germany, such as Wilhelm von Humboldt's declaration that

> The historian's past is to present what actually happened. The more purely and completely he achieves this, the more perfectly has he solved his problem. A simple presentation is at the same time the primary, indispensable condition of his work and the highest achievement he will be able to attain.[49]

More infamously, realism is often reduced to a single quotation from Leopold von Ranke, that history should be an account of the past '*wie es eigentlich gewesen*'. This phrase has often been translated as 'what actually happened' and thus taken as an endorsement of the view that historians should endeavour to be transparent ciphers of the past 'as it really was'. However, this treatment of Ranke, and to a lesser extent Humboldt ignores the idealist inflection of their views. While they desired factual representations of the past, they also held that events could only be understood by gleaning the general truths or ideas that gave them shape. Georg Iggers thus translates Ranke's phrase as '[history] wants to show how, *essentially*, things happened'.[50] Idealism, along with historicism, relativism and constructivism, fostered the emergence of minimal or 'perspectival' realism at the end of the nineteenth century. In this modified view, it is held that the historian cannot gain unmediated access to the past: the survival of only fragments of evidence—most the products of humans who always see the world through 'lenses of their own grinding'—and their consideration by an historian who also sees the world through lenses of their own grinding rules that out. Nor is unmediated access seen as totally desirable: no historian, R.G. Collingwood argues, should be subject to the omissions and fabrications of historical agents, and W.H. Walsh sees colligation as necessary for helping people in the present to better understand the past.[51] Nevertheless, as Edward Cheyney puts it, historians should still aim to offer a 'plain, unvarnished tale of real life'.[52]

In the latter half of the twentieth century, challenges to the prevailing belief in a relationship between past and present in history gained momentum. To Roland Barthes, for example, history was no more than a discourse of sobriety riddled with reality conventions, 'an inscription on the past pretending to be a likeness of it, a parade of signifiers masquerading as a collection of facts'. Histories are 'readerly' texts: they elicit a more or less passive response on the part of readers through the use of familiar themes and rhetorical devices like footnotes, the citation of details, quotations or an omniscient narrator. They disguise their status as time-bound cultural products and encourage readers to treat them as timeless, transparent windows on to reality. They do so in the service of bourgeois ideology, which seeks to naturalise or render ahistorical the historical. Simply put, written history is one form of expression among many, but its proponents—the white bourgeois Europeans whose interests it most serves—have managed to convince us that it occupies a privileged relationship with reality. 'Writerly' texts, on the other hand, draw attention to the various rhetorical techniques they employ to produce the illusion of realism and encourage readers to participate in the construction of meaning. They may also be polysemic, that is, capable of being read in multiple ways. Barthes clearly favoured writerly texts, insisting that 'the goal of literary work (of literature as work) is to make the reader no longer a consumer, but a producer of the text'.[53]

Jacques Derrida, too, sees that historians have only been able to claim a privileged status for their writings by denying the unstable qualities of language. Their works, as was suggested in Chapter 1, are characterised by a logocentric obsession: the desire to identify origins, fix points of reference or certify truths. Historians enshrine a distinction between what is imitated and what imitates, and they assert that the former is anterior and superior. What Derrida questions is whether any mode of representation—books or images—refers to some real meaning external to language, whether it be a transcendental truth or human subjectivity. Like other post- or neostructuralists, he challenges the view of linguistic structures such as signifiers (sounds or scriptive symbols or words) as stable and reflective of the mind and reality. For instance, there is nothing more logical or inherently superior about calling something a 'chicken' rather than a '*Huhn*', 'fowl' or 'chook'. At best, texts bear the traces of and constantly refer to other texts in an endless chain of signification that he calls *différance*. We enter here, as was argued in Chapter 1, a maze of mirrors.[54] Without beginnings and ends, historical texts are without pasts, without authors, without even readers. Thus poststructuralist history entails not the substitution of the study of historians for history, as Keith Jenkins would have it, but the recognition that we are left only with multiple and shifting readings.[55]

In the wake of Barthes' and Derrida's challenges to history, there arises a concern to focus on and lay bare the rhetorical strategies that foster a 'reality effect'. Historians do not capture reality; they only give the appearance of doing so. In this age of 'reality effects', historical films might be seen to have more of an honest air about them than written histories. After all, many Western historical films end with a statement to this effect:

> The characters and incidents portrayed and the names used herein are fictitious, and any resemblance to the names, character or history of any person is coincidental and unintentional.

Historical film scholars like Davis see statements of this sort simply as disclaimers used to minimise the risk of legal action.[56] This singular reading, though, falls prey to logocentrism and thus fails to recognise other readings. The statement could also be read as a gesture of self-reflexivity or as an attempt to undercut the power of conspiracy theories. Furthermore, as was noted in Chapters 2 and 3, historical films are punctuated by temporal and emplotment devices that may serve to remind viewers that what they are seeing is not an unmediated view of the past.

Before we rush to invert the hierarchical relation of words and images identified in Chapter 1, though, it is important to note that varying degrees of self-reflexivity and 'reality effect' are found across historical films. Many films end with disclaimers, but many also open or are promoted with phrases like these:

> Everything you are about to see is true (*The Last Days*, 1998)
>
> Never let the truth get in the way of a good story (*Chopper*, 2000)
>
> Based on a true story (*Boys Don't Cry*, 1999)
>
> Inspired by true events (*Windtalkers*, 2002)
>
> Recent archaeological evidence makes statements about the true identity of King Arthur possible (*King Arthur*, 2004)
>
> This is a pure and true story (*Le Retour de Martin Guerre*, 1982)

You might find some of these more suggestive of reality than others. Similarly, combinations of genres in historical films might be more or less suggestive of reality. Which is more realistic: the combat film *Saving Private Ryan*, the Holocaust comedy *La Vita è Bella* (*Life is Beautiful*, 1997), the melodrama *Pearl Harbor* (2001) or the animation *Harvie Krumpet*? How and why particular histories come to be seen as more realistic than others requires, as Barthes, Derrida and Bazin recognise, an exploration of the changing contours of the relationships between history makers and their audiences.

Our arrival at a view of historical reality as relational and as subject to historical change is bound to generate dismay among some readers, for the challenge of poststructuralism to history is commonly seen as a stark choice between realism and relativism. If we acknowledge the tenets of poststructuralists, Lawrence Stone has opined, 'then history as we have known it collapses altogether, and fact and fiction become indistinguishable from one another'.[57] In his *Companion to Historical Studies*, too, Alan Munslow presents the choice as clear: the alternative to realism is 'to adopt Ludwig Wittgenstein's position that language is a set of games each possessing its own rules for constituting truth (see Relativism)'.[58] In disagreement with Stone and Munslow, though, I do not see the admission of poststructuralist arguments as tantamount to the embrace of relativism and the beginning of a slippery slope towards nihilism. Another option neglected by these two writers, and many others, is objective foundationalism, which finds support in the writings of E.H. Carr, R.G. Collingwood, Richard Evans and, contrary to Munslow's judgement, Ludwig Wittgenstein.

It is often held that without a foundation, historical inquiry collapses or is rendered impossible. Traditionally, as we have seen, historians have sought to secure such a firm foundation by arguing that their writings mirror or correspond to an independent, true past. Consequently, the possibility of historical understanding rests on a correspondence between thought and reality or truth. As a result of postmodernist and poststructuralist challenges, though, a consideration of foundations has come to be seen as an outmoded or ideological activity. Furthermore, as I suggested above, a number of commentators, like Munslow, Stone and Richard Rorty, have equated the rejection of realism with an anti-foundationalist stance.[59] It is clear that many historians hold that their works rest upon foundational assumptions about what a history is. At the same time, though, they are aware that understandings of 'history' have changed over time. Collingwood, Carr, Evans and Wittgenstein recognise the combination of these two claims in their transformation of 'foundationalism' into what I will call objective foundationalism.

For Collingwood, constellations of presuppositions provide the foundations for human activities, including those of historians. These constellations of presuppositions may vary across cultures, but also across times.[60] Any constellation is perpetually subject to strains and conflicts, and when the strains become too great it collapses and is replaced by another.[61] They are neither subject only to rapid change due to whim or fashion nor permanent. The imagery of Wittgenstein's later works suggests a similar view: in *Philosophical Investigations*, for instance, he writes of the 'forms of life' that ground language and meaning.[62] As he argues in *On Certainty*, though, the ground is not bedrock, but a river bed:

> It might be imagined that some propositions, of the form of empirical propositions, were hardened and functioned as channels for such empirical propositions as were not hardened but fluid; and that this relation altered with time, in that fluid propositions hardened, and hard ones became fluid. The mythology may change back into a state of flux, the

river-bed of thoughts may shift. But I distinguish between the movement of the waters and the shift of the bed itself; though there is not a sharp distinction of the one from the other.[63]

The bed of the river is made partly of hard rock, which appears as unalterable or as subject only to minor alterations, and partly of sand, which does shift, washing away, being redeposited or carried in the river flow. In this image of our world we see that while some presuppositions are subject to great historical and cultural variation, others hardly move at all. This is a promising image, for poststructuralism and realism need not imply the acceptance of all or only rapidly changing assumptions or immutable ones. As Fernand Braudel recognised, the phenomena of our world evidence different rates of change.[64] That is as much true of the presuppositions that historians hold as those of the historical agents they study.

The writings of Collingwood and Wittgenstein point to 'objectivism' rather than to absolutism or extreme relativism.[65] Absolutism posits absolute or permanent, unchanging standards, principles, presuppositions and concepts. Objectivism, on the other hand, allows for objective principles of judgement, standards and concepts that are not decided solely by personal preference or the whim of individuals. A similar view is at work in the writings of E.H. Carr when he argues that calling a history 'objective' means not that it mirrors the past but that it conforms to socially acceptable ways of viewing the past. What counts as socially acceptable and thus as objective is that which puts into words the will and goals of the historian's age. If the will and goals of a society change, then what is counted as objective will also change.[66] Similarly, Richard Evans has noted that what counts as a history and what counts as evidence 'is not determined solely by one historian's perspective, but is subject to a wide measure of agreement which transcends the individual'.[67]

Nothing in the writings of Barthes and Derrida suggests an immediate incompatibility with the view of objective foundationalism I have just sketched. The difference between their views and those of Collingwood, Wittgenstein, Carr and Evans turns on whether we consider the conventional nature of histories and their 'reality effects' to be problematic or not. To Derrida and Barthes as well as to Baudrillard, Godard and Benjamin, the suspension of the flow of our 'forms of life'—whether through conscious agreement or unconscious acceptance—results in our enslavement in the matrices of consumerism and masculinity. Laughing at *Harvie Krumpet*, or watching any historical film, signals our complicity in the perpetuation of a world in which we know little of ourselves, let alone paths of social transformation. Yet all the writers canvassed in this chapter promote the view that awareness and transformation can be achieved through historicisation. Taking that advice seriously, how can we know whether history is an instrument of consumerism or masculinity until we, like Bazin, give thought to the engagements of actual rather than hypothetical viewers with films? That question will be at the forefront of our thinking in the rest of this book.

Recommended resources

Ankersmit, F. and Kellner, H. (eds), *A New Philosophy of History*, Chicago: University of Chicago Press, 1995.

Barthes, R., 'Le discours de l'histoire', in *Comparative Criticism: A Yearbook*, vol. 3, trans. S. Bann, University Park: Pennsylvania University Press, [1967], 1981, pp. 65–75.

Baudrillard, J., *Simulations*, trans. P. Foss, P. Patton and P. Beitchman, New York: Semiotext(e), 1983.

Baudrillard, J., 'History: a retro scenario', in *Simulcra and Simulations*, trans. S.F. Glaser, Ann Arbor: University of Michigan Press, 1994, pp. 43–8.

Bazin, A., *What is Cinema?*, trans. H. Gray, 2 vols, Berkeley: University of California Press, pp. 196–7.

Benjamin, W., *The Arcades Project*, trans. H. Eiland and K. McLaughlin, Cambridge, Mass.: Harvard University Press, 1999.

Benjamin, W., *Iluminations*, trans. H. Zohn, ed. H. Arendt, New York: Schocken, 1969.

Cubitt, S., *The Cinema Effect*, Cambridge, Mass.: MIT Press, 2004.

Godard, J.-L., *Histoire(s) du cinéma: introduction à une veritable historie du cinéma, la seule, la vraie*, producer M. Eicher, Munich: ECM Records, 1999.

Lipkin, S.N., *Real Emotional Logic: Film and Television Docudrama as Persuasive Practice*, Carbondale: Southern Illinois University Press, 2002.

Pierson, M., *Special Effects: Still in Search of Wonder*, New York: Columbia University Press, 2002.

Rosen, P., *Change Mummified: Cinema, Historicity, Theory*, Minneapolis: University of Minnesota Press, 2001.

Notes

1 M. Foucault, *The Order of Things: An Archaeology of the Human Sciences*, trans. anon., New York: Vintage Books, 1970, p. xv.

2 N.Z. Davis, ' "Any resemblance to persons living or dead": film and the challenge of authenticity', *The Yale Review*, 1987, vol. 76(4), p. 476.

3 R. Rosenstone, *Visions of the Past: The Challenge of Film to Our Idea of History*, Cambridge, Mass.: Harvard University Press, 1995, p. 246.

4 P. Sorlin, *The Film in History*, Oxford: Blackwell, 1980, p. 208; and M. Ferro, *Cinema and History*, trans. N. Greene, Detroit: Wayne State University Press, 1988, p. 47.

5 J. Baudrillard, 'History: a retro scenario', in *Simulcra and Simulations*, trans. S.F. Glaser, Ann Arbor: University of Michigan Press, [1981] 1994, p. 6.

6 J. Baudrillard, *Simulations*, trans. P. Foss, P. Patton and P. Beitchman, New York: Semiotext(e), 1983, p. 2.

7 *Ibid.*, p. 55.

8 *Ibid.*, pp. 46–7.

9 *Ibid.*, p. 45.

10 Anon., '*Titanic*', *Newsweek*, 15 December 1997, vol. 130(24), p. 65.

11 Anon., '*Saving Private Ryan*', *Time*, 27 July 1998, vol. 152(4), p. 56; see also

E. Cohen, 'What combat does to man: *Private Ryan* and its critics', *The National Interest*, 1998, no. 54, pp. 82–8.

12 See, for example, F. Manchel, 'A reel witness: Steven Spielberg's representation of the Holocaust in *Schindler's List*', *Journal of Modern History*, 1995, vol. 67(1), pp. 83–100.

13 Anon., 'Horror d'oeuvre', *People Weekly*, 3 July 2000, vol. 54(1), p. 103.

14 Anon, 'Eliza Frazer', *Cinema Papers*, 13 July 1977, no. 13, centrespread.

15 J. Baudrillard, 'History: a retro scenario', p. 47. On *Schindler's List*, see M. Brantu Hansen, '*Schindler's List* is not *Shoah*: the second commandment, popular modernism, and public memory', reproduced in M. Landy (ed.), *The Historical Film: History and Memory in Media*, New Brunswick, NJ: Rutgers University Press, 2001, pp. 201–17.

16 J. Baudrillard, 'Holocaust', in *Simulcra and Simulation*, p. 49.

17 J. Baudrillard, *Simulations*, p. 45.

18 Centropolis Effects Showcase, at http://www.thepatriot.com; and B. Logan, 'Things to do in Hollywood when you're dead', *Guardian*, 17 September 1999, G2, pp. 16–17.

19 L. von Trier, 'Director's commentary', *Dancer in the Dark* [DVD], 1998, ch. 5.

20 J.R. Craig, 'Establishing new boundaries for special effects: Robert Zemeckis's *Contact* and computer-generated imagery', *Journal of Popular Film and Television*, 2001, vol. 28(4), p. 162; T. Doherty, 'Seamless matching: film, history and *JFK*', *Phi Kappa Journal*, 1997, vol. 77(3), p. 39.

21 S. Cubitt, *The Cinema Effect*, Cambridge, Mass.: MIT Press, 2004, p. 247.

22 T. Kenny, '*T2*: behind the scenes with the terminator 2 sound team', *Mix: Professional Recording and Sound and Music Production*, 9 September 1991, no. 15, p. 64; as cited in S. Cubitt, *The Cinema Effect*, p. 266.

23 L. von Trier, 'Director's commentary', *Dancer in the Dark* [DVD], 1998, ch. 5.

24 J.-L. Godard, *Histoire(s) du cinéma: Introduction à une veritable historie du cinéma, la seule, la vraie*, producer M. Eicher, Munich: ECM Records, 1999, esp. 3A.

25 G.W.F. Hegel, *The Phenomenology of Spirit*, trans. A.V. Miller, Oxford: Oxford University Press, 1970.

26 J.-L. Godard, *Histoire(s) du cinéma*, part 3A.

27 On the sublime, see I. Kant, *The Critique of Judgement*, trans. J.C. Meredith, Oxford: Oxford University Press, 1973; and H. White, 'The politics of historical interpretation: discipline and de-sublimation', in *The Content of the Form: Narrative Discourse and Historical Interpretation*, Baltimore: Johns Hopkins University Press, 1989, pp. 58–82.

28 S. Cubitt, *The Cinema Effect*, pp. 322–30.

29 W. Benjamin, 'The work of art in the age of mechanical reproduction', in *Illuminations*, ed. H. Arendt, trans. H. Zohn, New York, 1969, p. 464.

30 W. Benjamin, *The Arcades Project*, trans. H. Eiland and K. McLaughlin, Cambridge, Mass.: Harvard University Press, 1999, p. 463.

31 W. Benjamin, 'On some motifs in Baudelaire', in *Illuminations*, pp. 163, 174–5.

32 W. Benjamin, *The Arcades Project*, p. 4; 'Theses on philosophy of history', in *Illuminations*, pp. 254, 261.

33 J.-L. Godard, *Histoire(s) du cinéma*, part 1A.

34 V. Sobchack, ' "Surge and splendor": a phenomenology of the Hollywood historical epic', *Representations*, 1990, no. 29, p. 44.

35 A. Bazin, *What is Cinema?*, trans. H. Gray, vol. 2, Berkeley: University of California Press, 1967, pp. 9–16, 97. See also J. Aumont, *Amnésies: fictions du cinema d'après Jean-Luc Godard*, Paris: P.O.L., 1999, p. 162.

36 *Ibid.*, p. 27.

37 A. Bazin, *What is Cinema?*, trans. H. Gray, vol. 1, Berkeley: University of California Press, 1967, p. 12.

38 P. Rosen, *Change Mummified*, p. 20.

39 A. Bazin, *What is Cinema?*, vol. 1, p. 10.

40 G. Currie, *Image and Mind: Film Philosophy and Cognitive Science*, Cambridge: Cambridge University Press, ch. 6.

41 J.-P. Sartre, *The Psychology of Imagination*, trans. anon., New York: Citadel, 1972, pp. 103, 105; and L. Wittgenstein, *Remarks on the Psychology of Philosophy*, vol. 2, ed. G.E.M. Anscombe and G.H. von Wright, Oxford: Blackwell, 1992, §§100–4.

42 J.-P. Sartre, *The Psychology of Imagination*, pp. 12–13.

43 *Ibid.*, p. 87; G. Ryle, *The Concept of Mind*, Harmondsworth: Penguin, 1949, p. 256; and L. Wittgenstein, *Remarks on the Psychology of Philosophy*, vol. 2, §§63–104.

44 J.-P. Sartre, *The Psychology of Imagination*, p. 13.

45 *Ibid.*, pp. 1–3, 181–243; L. Wittgenstein, *Remarks on the Psychology of Philosophy*, vol. 1, §§314, 400, 653, 663, 759–60, 1052, 1132; vol. 2, §§89, 121, 725–7; L. Wittgenstein, *Philosophical Investigations*, trans. G.E.M. Anscombe, ed. G.E.M. Anscombe, R. Rhees and G.H. von Wright, Oxford: Blackwell, 1953, §344; and G. Ryle, *The Concept of Mind*, p. 248.

46 J.-P. Sartre, *The Psychology of Imagination*, pp. 5, 44, 59, 138, 157, 212–19; G. Ryle, *The Concept of Mind*, p. 232.

47 G. Psanthas, 'On multiple realities and the world of film', in L. Embree (ed.), *Alfred Schulz's 'Sociological Aspect of Literature'*, Amsterdam: Kluwer, 1998, pp. 219–35.

48 D. Fischer, *Historians' Fallacies: Toward a Logic of Historical Thought*, London: Routledge & Kegan Paul, 1971, p. 70; see also P.H. Nowell-Smith, *What Actually Happened*, Lawrence: University of Kansas Press, 1971, p. 3.

49 W. von Humboldt, 'On the historian's task' [1821], *History and Theory*, 1967, vol. 6(1), p. 57.

50 G.G. Iggers, 'Introduction', in G.G. Iggers and K. von Moltke (eds), *The Theory and Practice of History*, Indianapolis: Bobbs-Merrill, 1973, pp. xli–xlii.

51 R.G. Collingwood, *The Idea of History*, rev. edn, ed. W.J. van der Dussen, Oxford: Oxford University Press, 1993, pp. 234–5; W.H. Walsh, 'Colligatory concepts in history', in P. Gardiner (ed.), *The Philosophy of History*, Oxford: Oxford University Press, 1974, pp. 127–44.

52 E. Cheyney, *Law in History and Other Essays*, New York: A.A. Kopf, 1927, p. 166.

53 R. Barthes, 'Le discours de l'histoire', in *Comparative Criticism: A Yearbook*, vol. 3, trans. S. Bann, University Park: Pennsylvania University Press, [1967], 1981, pp. 65–75; and R. Barthes, *S/Z*, trans. R. Miller, New York: Hill & Wang, 1974, pp. 4–5.

54 J. Derrida, 'The double session', *Dissemination*, trans. B. Johnson, London: Athlone Press, 1981, p. 195; on this point in relation to histories, see F. Ankersmit, *History and Tropology: The Rise and Fall of Metaphor*, Berkeley: University of California Press, 1994, pp. 167–8.

55 K. Jenkins, *Re-thinking History*, London: Routledge, 1991, p. 34.

56 N.Z. Davis, ' "Any resemblance to persons living or dead" ', p. 476.

57 L. Stone, 'History and postmodernism: II', *Past and Present*, 1992, no. 131, p. 194.

58 A. Munslow, 'Linguistic turn', in *The Routledge Companion to Historical Studies*, London: Routledge, 2000, p. 151.

59 R. Rorty, *Philosophy and the Mirror of Nature*, Oxford: Blackwell, 1980, p. 5.

60 R.G. Collingwood, *An Essay on Metaphysics*, rev. edn, ed. R. Martin, Oxford: Oxford University Press, 1999, p. 60.

61 *Ibid.*, p. 48n.

62 L. Wittgenstein, *Philosophical Investigations*, §§19, 23, 241, II, pp. 174, 226.

63 L. Wittgenstein, *On Certainty*, ed. G.E.M. Anscombe and G.H. von Wright, Oxford: Blackwell, 1969, §§96–7.

64 F. Braudel, 'The situation of history in 1950', in *On History*, trans. S. Matthews, Chicago: University of Chicago Press, 1989, pp. 10–11.

65 For a more extended discussion on Collingwood's and Wittgenstein's objectivism, see my *'How Good an Historian Shall I Be?': R.G. Collingwood, the Historical Imagination and Education*, Thorveton, Exeter: Imprint Academic, 2003, ch. 3.

66 E.H. Carr, *What is History?*, rev. edn, ed. R.W. Davies, Harmondsworth: Penguin, 1986, p. 26.

67 R.J. Evans, *In Defence of History*, London: Granta, 1997, p. 128.

6 Documentary

When I was a child, the only television programs I was permitted to watch were documentaries. In the microcosm of that childhood spent watching *Civilisation* (1969) and *The World at War* (1974), my parents endorsed the conventional view of documentary as one of the more realistic forms of filmic expression. Furthermore, they trusted that I would learn something about history from the documentaries I watched. Building on the relational and historical view of reality proposed in the previous chapter, the aim of this chapter is to understand how and why historical documentaries elicit such trust.

Our starting point will be with the concept of 'documentary', for approaches to its definition vary considerably across film and historical film studies. When John Grierson first argued that Robert Flaherty's *Moana* (1926) had 'documentary' value, for example, he recognised that films, like written 'documents', could be a means of education and of proof.[1] But not all films, for the 'speedy snip-snap' of newsreels or works that simply recorded events were of a 'lower' category than 'documentary proper'. Wanting to exclude works that did not make 'any considerable contribution to the fuller art of documentary', he specified that his interest lay with those works that offered 'the creative treatment of actuality', a treatment that could reveal truths 'more real in the philosophic sense' than those offered in either mimetic records or dramatic features.[2] As Aitken has pointed out, Grierson's connection of documentary with reality in the 'philosophic sense' reflects the idealist project of wanting to reveal the presuppositions that give shape to human activities.[3] Presuppositions shape past and present activities, but Grierson's interest was in those connected with present-day social problems. Thus although Grierson considered Robert Flaherty to be the 'father of documentary', he complained that he wasted his talents on making films about the past.[4] Grierson's interest in the filmic addressing of present-day problems appears to leave historical topics outside the definition of documentary. Similarly, we might ask what room there is for history in Paul Rotha and Lewis Jacob's definition of documentary as the expression of 'social purpose' or Comolli's contrasting account of it as the 'transparent' treatment of actuality, for unmediated representations of the past are neither possible nor, arguably, desirable.[5]

The problem of defining documentary, as Carl Plantinga and Bill Nichols have pointed out, is due in part to conventional practices of definition that focus on the identification of essential characteristics. Documentaries do not all share the same qualities; rather, as Plantinga puts it, 'the concept has no essence, but rather a braid of family resemblances'.[6] That is, just as there may be no one feature or set of features common to all the members of a family, there may still be a collection of facial characteristics among them that allows a person to be recognised as a member of it nonetheless.[7] This more open, Wittgensteinian view of the concept of documentary better allows for the inclusion of works focusing on historical topics. Furthermore, the organising idea of a 'family resemblance' draws attention to practices and contexts of production, distribution and reception. Put simply, a family likeness is a family likeness *to someone*.

Seeing a film as a documentary depends in part on 'situational cues' or 'indexes' advanced in advertisements, websites, reviews, synopses, labels, shelving decisions and programming.[8] The advertisement for *The Last Days* (1998; Figure 6.1), for example, invites us to view the work as a documentary through both the direct endorsement of it as such by the Academy of Motion Picture Arts and Sciences and indirectly through the tagline—introduced in the last chapter—'Everything you are about to see is true'. This sets up a different expectation to the one we might form in response to advertising for

Figure 6.1 Advertisement for *The Last Days* (© 1998, USC Shoah Foundation)

Chopper (2000), which bears the tagline 'Never let the truth get in the way of a good story'. Similarly, the regular programming of documentaries on Saturday and Sunday evenings in Australia no doubt helped my parents to decide what I was permitted to watch. However, these situational cues alone may not be enough to convince an audience that what they are seeing is a documentary or—as we shall see—may be used to promote a 'mock-documentary', 'promo-documentary' or 'docudrama'. Indexing thus also occurs within documentaries.[9]

Modes and voices: wherein lies history?

No single, unified body of filmic techniques signals that a work is a documentary. Rather, as Nichols has argued, an analysis of the history of documentary making reveals a cumulative scale of six constellations of practices or 'modes': poetic, expository, observational, participatory, reflexive and performative. Documentary cinema is often associated with indexing or preserving phenomena and its origins traced to actuality making in the late nineteenth century. It is only with the addition of visual narrative conventions, the cinematic shaping of time and space and *avant-garde* interests and techniques that filmic document becomes documentary in Grierson's sense of the 'creative treatment of actuality'.

Poetic documentary

Working to disrupt or to draw attention to cinematic conventions designed to build temporal and spatial continuity and specificity—such as matches on action and a focus on named individuals—poetic documentary makers highlight the aesthetic dimensions of images of past and present phenomena.[10] In poetic film, the aim is, as Dziga Vertov puts it, to create a 'fresh perception of the world', including the historical world.[11] Similarly, Slajov Zizek sees poetic film as turning over social problems that go without saying: 'what emerges via distortions of the accurate representation of reality is the real—that is, the trauma around which social reality is structured'.[12] Poetic fascination with montage as a source for social awareness aligns with Walter Benjamin's remedy for the 'dream' of the nineteenth century outlined in the previous chapter. In *Sans Soleil* (*Sunless*, 1982), for example, Chris Marker uses fragmentary images and personal comments couched in the third person to disturb conventional understandings of both recent political events and the use of memory, history and film itself to understand them. Similarly, Péter Forgác's arrangement and aural and visual manipulation of amateur footage by Nandor Andrasovits—captain of the ship the *Queen Elizabeth*—of the exodus of Jews to Palestine and the exodus of Bessarabian Germans to Poland in *A dunai exodus* (*The Danube Exodus*, 1999) draws us away from conventional historiography and towards moods and minute actions.

Poetic films predate *Moana*, and they, like Flaherty, were criticised by

Grierson for offering escapist, backward-looking and impractical works that would do little to orient citizens in a nation-state. Russian directors, he complained

> are too bound up—too aesthetically vain—in what they call their 'play films' to contribute to Russia's instructional cinema. They have, indeed, suffered greatly from the freedom given to artists in a first uncritical moment of revolutionary enthusiasm, for they have tended to isolate themselves more and more in private impression and private perform-ance. . . . One's impression is that when some of the art and all of the bohemian self-indulgence have been knocked out of them, the Russian cinema will fulfil its high promise of the late twenties.[13]

In a position parallel to that of new idealists such as R.G. Collingwood, Grierson saw art alone as not up to the task of drawing people to social and political consciousness and action.[14] Grierson thus set in train the association of documentary with what Nichols calls the 'expository mode'.

Expository documentary

Anecdotally, expository works would appear to align most with conven-tional situational and textual cues and indices for 'documentary'. Expository documentaries are characterised by a heavy dependence on commentary delivered by inter- and subtitles, 'talking heads' and voiceover narration. Those commentaries—usually taking the form of older male voices—deliver what appear to be expert and authoritative arguments and conclusions that are above or at least distinct from the visual and material evidence that is used. Interviews with expert 'talking heads', for instance, take place in offices, and institutional pedigrees are displayed in subtitles; they are rarely shown touching or even looking at the images, materials and places shown to viewers. Nor are viewers told who the interviewer is or even what questions prompted the recorded comments. 'Voice of God' narrators generate the impression of seeing and translating images for viewers, but they too are often detached from what is presented by virtue of their training and previous film credits.[15] Lawrence Olivier (*The World at War*), Sean Barrett (*People's Century*, 1995, UK version) and John Forsythe (*People's Century*, 1995, US version), to take just three examples, were not professional historians; their training consisted of performances as Shakespeare's kings and the con-trolling voice of 'Charlie' in *Charlie's Angels* (1976, 2000, 2003). On what grounds is the professional actor chosen over the historian, and what does this say about the purposes of documentary?

Lauded and trusted documentaries are often dominated by expository conventions. A good case in point is the critically celebrated and popular television series *The Civil War* (1990), directed by Ken Burns. In filmic terms, Burns' work is a sequence of close-up shots of photographs (6–12 seconds' duration without camera movement, 12–15 with camera movement) interspersed with colour landscape scans (12–15 seconds) and 'talking head' segments (12–15 seconds). These elements are cemented together by the narration of actor David McCullough. The narration and commentary by identified and professionally affiliated talking heads (e.g. 'writer', 'historian') work like super-, sub- or even inter-titles, translating and explaining the succession of images. The images we see are not presented as artefacts that can be held, engaged with or debated; rather, they float by, waiting to be anchored and unlocked by the spoken word. For example, photos of unnamed individuals captured in formal poses and after death in unspecified contexts are harnessed to this 'translation' at the beginning of episode 1:

> Americans slaughtered one another wholesale here in America. In their own cornfields and peach orchards. Along familiar roads and by waters with old American names. . . . Men who had never strayed twenty miles from their own front doors found themselves soldiers in great armies fighting epic battles hundreds of miles from home. They knew they were making history.

Poses and deaths that might have come about for a host of reasons are swept together in a single epic war, one in which the participants knew its significance. Did those who fought know that they were making history? Did they see their battle as one of 'American' against 'American'? Were the battles 'epic' for them? Did their poses—in life and death—function as signs of the real at the time they were captured on film? Or did they signify other things? These questions, like the literal questions put to the talking heads, remain outside the narrative frame.

On the basis of examples like *The Civil War*, we might be tempted to conclude that in expository documentary, the past is, as Lowenstahl puts it, 'a foreign country' that requires translation by a detached, authoritative commentator.[16] There is, though, another form of expository historical documentary in which the interaction between commentary and images is more fluid: that characterised by the use of an on-screen historian commentator. In the 1960s and 1970s, historians such as A.J.P. Taylor (*Men of Our Time: Mussolini*, 1970; *Peacemaking 1919*, 1971), Theodore Moody (*The Course of Irish History*, 1966) and J.M. Roberts (*The Triumph of the West*, 1985) offered what we might call on-screen lectures. While their demeanour and accoutrements—consider Colin Hughes' pipe in *Mister Prime Minister* (1966; Figure 6.2)—have been lampooned in television comedies such as *Monty Python's Flying Circus* (1969) and *We Are History* (2000), this form of presentation has nonetheless undergone a revival. Today we have the choice of Michael Wood walking in the footsteps of Alexander the Great and the Conquistadors (*In the Footsteps of Alexander the Great*, 1998; *Conquistadors*, 2000),[17] Simon Schama, David Starkey and Niall Ferguson guiding us through the history of Britain and its empire (*A History of Britain*, 2000; *The Monarchy*

Figure 6.2 Colin Hughes lectures in *Mister Prime Minister* (© 1966, Australian Broadcasting Corporation)

of England, 2004; *Empire*, 2003), and Richard Holmes taking us into past battlefields (*War Walks* 1996, 1997). A former lampooner, Terry Jones, has also been drawn into the expository form to bring medieval history to the small screen (*Crusades*, 1995; *Medieval Lives*, 2004). Part travelogue and part lecture, recent presenter-led historical documentaries offer the expert commentary of the expository form, but one that is embodied and that makes contact with the material dimensions of the past on the viewer's behalf. Whether they are less detached or even aloof than off-screen narrators and earlier contributors to the presenter form is an open question. In some ways, the description of recent presenters as 'telly dons' is appropriate, for their mannerisms, patterns of speech and approaches to history were shaped in part by their experiences as students at Cambridge or in the case of Jones and Ferguson, Oxford. History thus appears to be embodied in the middle-aged, Oxbridge-educated male authority figure who translates the past for us. Bettany Hughes' *The Spartans* (2002) and *Seven Ages of Britain* (2003) show us that the translator of history does not have to be male, but her departure from the norm is not as radical as it might first appear, for she too was educated at Oxford, and she offers many of the same mannerisms and patterns of speech as her male counterparts.

Ostensibly, an 'everyman' alternative to British 'telly dons' may be found in the figure of Mike Moore, particularly in his examination of explanations for the Columbine High School shootings in *Bowling for Columbine* (2002). Moore's dress, mannerisms and modes of address suggest anything but a polished, university-endorsed take on the past. Yet he too functions as an authoritative translator, clearly encouraging us to trust his connection between political and economic practices with many of North America's political, social and economic woes. The opening sequence of *Bowling for Columbine*, to take just one example, shares 'expository' features in common with *The Civil War*. A sequence of eight, 5–9-second stills and movie images of (in the main) unnamed individuals in unspecified contexts is united by Moore's words:

> It was the morning of April 20th 1999 and it was pretty much like any other morning in America. The farmer did his chores, the milkman made his deliveries and the President bombed another country whose name we couldn't pronounce. . . . And out in a little town in Colorado, two boys went bowling at 6am. It was a typical day in the United States of America.

As with *The Civil War*, the varying activities, motivations and achievements of the individuals captured on film—and possibilities for debate about them— are leached out, replaced by Moore's belief in a United States in which violence is systemic and even mundane.

Observational documentary

In Nichols' view, the shaping force of expository documentaries is spoken or written text. Images generally play an ancillary role, distinct from but ultimately confirming and sustaining the arguments presented, and those arguments do not need to be presented by a professional historian.[18] Consequently, the rendering of many of the expository documentaries listed above as either radio serials or audio books would not present too many technical difficulties, and 'companion' books accompany many. In the observational mode of documentary, by comparison, the controlling logic of the spoken or written word gives way to the recording of phenomena as they happen, with little or no commentary. Elements of 'reality' television history programs such as *The Edwardian Country House* (2002) or *Outback House* (2005), for example, generate the impression of 'fly on the wall' observations of historical re-enactments. This impression masks the interventions of the film production team, including requests for repeated actions, editing and sequencing. As Forgác's *A dunai exodus* and Alain Resnais' meditation on the Holocaust in *Nuit et brouillard* (*Night and Fog*, 1955) highlight, the re-editing of observational footage can lead to the reconstruction of historical events. It reminds us of the constructedness of even the most trusted of 'expository' works.

Participatory documentary

Observational documentaries foster the impression that past phenomena can be captured and understood through detached contemplation. Participatory documentaries, by contrast, put filmmakers before the lens and show them interacting with and shaping our understanding of objects, places and people. We expect, as Nichols argues, that our understanding of past phenomena will depend at least in part on the nature of the filmmaker's relationship with the traces of the past. In *The Trouble with Merle* (2002), for example, Marée Delofski takes us on a filmic journey in which Tasmanian beliefs about a local girl of mixed parentage, Mumbai school tales of 'Queenie' Thompson and painful memories of an unknown stepsister coalesce in the figure of Merle Oberon. Born Estelle Merle O'Brien Thompson, Oberon became a legend through her appearance in over forty films and her fashioning as a tragically orphaned Tasmanian. Inserting herself in the film as an inquirer rather than as a translator and commentator, Delofski is a model for all her viewers and encourages them to unravel the many conflicting claims about Oberon's life and identity. Biography opens out to local, national and transnational discourse on race and class, and viewers are tugged between identities that have been marginalised and desired. At the end of the film, we realise that the 'trouble' with Merle probably lies with us as viewers wanting to reconcile conflicting truths and beliefs.

Claude Lanzmann also acts as a mentor and *provocateur* in *Shoah* (1985). Over the course of nine and a half hours, Lanzmann steadfastly refuses to provide us with the visual exposition on the Holocaust that filmic—particularly expository—convention has led us to expect. Eschewing the use of historical file and photographic footage, Lanzmann instead shows us that our recognition of the banality, scale and incomprehensibility of the Holocaust must be achieved through an engagement with the present. The Holocaust cannot be completed, closed and moved on from. He writes:

> The worst crime, simultaneously moral and artistic, that can be committed when it is a question of realising a work dedicated to the Holocaust is to consider the latter as past. The Holocaust is either legend or present. It is no case of the order of memory. A film consecrated to the Holocaust can only be a countermyth, that is, an inquiry to the present of the Holocaust or at the very least into a past whose scars are still so freshly and vividly inscribed in places and consciences that it gives itself to be seen in an hallucinatory intemporality.[19]

But *Shoah* is not simply about the past; like Chapter 3 it shows us that past, present and future cannot be disentangled. Questions too have been raised about the nature of Lanzmann's relationship with the people—and more specifically survivors—whom he interviews. In Dominick LaCapra's view, Lanzmann's engagement with the present slips into identification:

> The question is whether Lanzmann in his more absolutist gestures tends to confine performativity to acting-out and tends even to give way to a displaced, secular religiosity in which authenticity becomes tantamount

to a movement beyond secondary witnessing to a full identification with the victim. This full identification would allow one not only to act out trauma vicariously in the self as surrogate victim but cause one to insist on having the victim relive traumatising events, thus concealing one's own intrusiveness in asking questions that prod the victim to the point of breakdown.[20]

LaCapra's argument for Lanzmann being fully immersed in and vicariously acting out the trauma of Holocaust survivors is out of tune with the conceptual view of identification that was advanced in the previous chapter. Furthermore, Gelley sees Lanzmann's tenacious questioning as generating a clear division between interviewer and interviewee. Indeed, Gelley even wonders if Lanzmann's tenacity has the effect of making his interviewees victims twice over.[21] Consider, for example, this excerpt from Lanzmann's interview with Mordechaï Podchlebnik, one of two known survivors of gassings at Chelmno in Poland:

CL: What died in him at Chelmno?

MP: Everything died. But I'm only human, and I want to live. So I must forget. I thank God for what remains, and that I can forget. And let's not talk about that.

CL: Does he think it is good to think about it?

MP: For me it's not good.

CL: Then why is he talking about it?

MP: Because you're insisting on it. I was sent books on Eichmann's trial. I was a witness, and I didn't even read them. At the time I felt as if I were dead, because I never thought I'd survive, but I'm alive.

CL: Why does he smile all the time?

MP: What do you want me to do, cry? Sometimes you smile, sometimes you cry. And if you're alive, it's better to smile.[22]

Lifted out of context, Lanzmann's question to Podchlebnik about his smile might be read as a self-righteous condemnation and an act of victimisation. Surely Podchlebnik has suffered enough, we might think. But in combination, all four of Lanzmann's questions reinforce the main point of the film: that the Holocaust is not a closed, completed past but something that is lived with. Podchlebnik's attempts to forget, to ignore, and his smiles cannot be disentangled from the past experiences he relays to us. They are all a part of Holocaust history. It is also not evident that Lanzmann is always the focus of, or even directs, the interviews conducted with survivors. Additionally, not all of Lanzmann's interviews are with survivors, and LaCapra offers no comment on whether identification and victimisation are the end result of interviews with participants in or witnesses to practices of removal and murder. The nature of the interviewer–subject relationship varies within *Shoah* as it does in other participatory documentaries. In combination, these variations may serve as 'alienation effects' or *ostranenie* that make the routine use of interviews in expository documentaries strange to us and deserving of critical attention.

Reflexive documentary

In participatory documentaries, the attention of viewers is directed towards the relationship between an on-screen inquirer and traces of past phenomena. In reflexive documentaries, attention is also directed to the relationship between on-screen inquirers, informants and historical traces and the audience itself. These documentaries are thus as much concerned with the problems and limits of representation as they are about historical phenomena themselves.[23] For example, the combined use of interviews and unannounced performances of interviews by actors—sometimes with ostensibly the same historical agent—in Jean Godmilow's *Far From Poland* (1984) and Trinh T. Minh-ha's *Surname Viet Given Name Nam* (1989) gives us cause to think about conventional filmic cues that connote authenticity.[24] Suspicion also falls upon the ability of documentary to provide direct access to the past or to provide persuasive proof that is educative or edifying. Documentary is recognised as representation, and representation is recognised as political positioning. Politically reflexive documentaries foster social and political awareness and open up, Nichols argues:

> a gap between knowledge and desire, between what is and what might be. Politically reflexive documentaries point to *us* as viewers and social actors, not to films, as the agents who can bridge this gap between what exists and the new forms we can make from it.[25]

Performative documentaries

Knowledge is situated: the same historical trace can prompt different responses among historians and viewers. Performative documentaries use the experiences of individuals, including their emotional responses, to illuminate the concrete and embodied nature of knowledge. In so doing, they remind us of the subjective qualities of the assumptions that shape society. The actual and the imagined are also mixed. This is the case in films like Marlon Fuentes' *Bontoc Eulogy* (1995), in which the filmmaker stages a fantasy where his grandfather escapes from being an item on display in the 1904 World's Fair. This serves the aim of highlighting the elision of race and empire at the end of the nineteenth century.

Nichols' typology is a cumulative scale of modes. That is, the idea of 'documentary' appeared in the 1910s with a response to 'Hollywood fiction', 'fictional narratives of imaginary worlds' and an 'absence of "reality"'. New modes were then added in the 1920s (expository and poetic), the 1960s (observational and participatory) and finally the 1980s (reflexive and performative). All of the modes are united in being 'documentaries', but Nichols sees in their chronological unfolding both changing social contexts and the overcoming of technological, technical and intellectual limitations. However, later modes do include aspects of earlier ones. Thus the concept of documentary is a cumulative collection of conventions.[26] While Nichols' later writings steer away from the direct admission that the typology 'gives the impression of . . . an evolution toward greater complexity and self-awareness', it is still possible to see in it a teleology that favours the reflexive and performative modes over earlier ones.[27] Put more plainly, each of the modes represents the best embodiment of the concept of documentary until it is revealed as inadequate. When that inadequacy is exposed, a new mode of documentary is adopted. It follows from this that modes are not only distinct from one another, as one specification from another, but also in some part opposed to one another, as a higher specification to a lower, a more to a less adequate embodiment. Nichols' teleological formulation of the concept of documentary, as Plantinga has argued, rests upon the problematic assumption that particular film practices can be connected to particular intellectual, social and political outcomes, and that some outcomes ought to be valued above others.[28] In the previous chapter, for example, it was seen that for theorists like Benjamin, the use of montage—and thus the poetic mode of documentary making—was the best means of achieving the desired outcome of awareness of commodification. Grierson, on the other hand, showed a preference for expository works. In the next chapter, we will question the attachment of any mode of filmmaking with a determined social or political outcome.

Plantinga's response to Nichols takes the form of another typology, one in which the degree or absence of 'narrational authority' is used to identify the functions or purposes of 'nonfiction' film. His three filmic 'voices'—formal, open and poetic—'speak' with 'epistemic authority, hesitance or aestheticism', respectively. None of the voices is socially preferable, and all avow or take the stance that what is represented 'occurs in the actual world'.[29] The definition of nonfiction film thus turns not on a correspondence between reality and representation but on the presence of textual and situational cues that are read by viewers as assertions that the work is about phenomena that 'occur(red) or exist(ed) in the actual world'. Nonfiction films share the criterion of a worldly assertion. However, some fuzziness accompanies the concept as a result of historical and cultural variations in situational and textual cues.[30] Opening the concept of nonfiction or even documentary film to variations in historical and cultural readings renders the task of analysing examples pragmatically difficult. Plantinga's response to this problem is to focus on films whose membership of the concept is more certain.[31] While practical, the difficulty with this solution is that it does little to examine why it is that some cues are more readily recognised as indexical than others. The social and political assumptions that shape readings of a film as a marginal documentary, for example, may be just as instructive to us as those for a canonical work. It is also important to establish just who it is that judges a work to be a clear or a marginal documentary.

Post-documentary: the appropriation of documentary aesthetics and diversion

If recent commentators are to be believed, filmmaking has moved into a 'post-documentary' age.[32] Underlying this claim is the belief that the movement of new technologies, filmic techniques and situational and textual cues both in and out of documentary making have blurred its boundaries and undermined its status. Put bluntly, documentary is no longer a trusted form of filmmaking. As Jane Roscoe and Craig Hight see it, for instance, textual and situational cues often associated with documentary, including advertising, are increasingly being used in the fictional realm. This observation appears to be well supported by the apparent proliferation of 'making of' television specials and promotional documentaries or 'promo-docs', which often come bundled with DVDs. The 'Into the Breach' promo-doc that accompanies *Saving Private Ryan*, to take just one example, is characterised by a mixture of 'talking head' interviews with the cast, Stephen Spielberg and the historian Stephen Ambrose—complete with text titles indicating character or professional affiliation—which all support the conclusion that the film gets its history of the D-Day landings 'just right'.[33] This film, like 'mock documentaries', makes 'a partial or concerted effort to appropriate documentary elements and conventions in order to represent a fictional subject'.[34] These elements include interviews but also photographic stills, archival footage and 'naturalisatic' sound, lighting and make-up techniques. Thus defined, 'documentary' may include works ranging from *Making of Gladiator* (HBO First Look, 2000) to the parodic treatment of the Beatles in *The Rutles* (1978).

Furthermore, it appears to draw in feature films such as *Schindler's List* (1995), *Saving Private Ryan* (1995) and *Band of Brothers* (2001). As Yosefa Loshitzky sees it, *Schindler's List* provides a 'master narrative' about the Holocaust in no small part through its appropriation of documentary conventions and practices.[35] These include the use of minimal or no lighting, handheld shots, black and white film and titles identifying locations, dates and primary documents. The handheld shots and desaturated colour used in the opening thirty minutes of *Saving Private Ryan* and throughout *Band of Brothers* also have 'the look' of a documentary. Add contextual cues such as the cinema codes of conduct for screenings of *Schindler's List* recommending—among other things—that popcorn should not be consumed at screenings, and it is hard to resist the impression that Spielberg's works 'document' historical phenomena.[36] The use of desaturated colour in Terence Davis' *Distant Voices, Still Lives* (1989) might be enough to suggest that it is also 'documentary-like', and the boundaries of the concept might be stretched still further by noting the use of archival footage in features like *Forrest Gump* (1994) and *JFK* (1995). In *Forrest Gump*, the protagonist is often seen in archival film footage that is spliced with colour reconstructions. *Forrest Gump* thus presents itself not as a reconstruction of the past but as the archived past remade. Archival footage and reconstruction also merge in *JFK*, most notably in the splicing of the colour Zapruder home movie of Kennedy's assassination with black and white simulations of it.

From this ever-widening assortment of works, it might be argued that documentary is really nothing more than a constellation of 'reality effects', one that (as the last chapter suggested) brings with it the fear that belief in film as historically indexical might be lost to an incoming tide of relativism. Plantinga, Roscoe and Hight and Michael Renov, among others, therefore seek to rein in the boundaries of the genre by arguing that an integral part of a documentary is its encouragement of audience awareness of the work as fictional or as a representation.[37] As Renov writes:

> The bottom line is that the artwork should encourage inquiry, offer space for judgement, and provide the tools for evaluation and further action—in short, encourage an active response. The film or videotape that considers its own processes rather than seals over every gap of a never-seamless discourse is more likely to engender the healthy scepticism that begets knowledge, offering itself as a model.[38]

'Docudrama' and 'reality TV' are excluded or denoted as 'marginal forms' on the grounds that their stance towards the phenomena they represent is assertive rather than parodic, critical or deconstructive.

Reflexivity could be the mark of a documentary, including an historical documentary. However, not all commentators agree that it is a quality worthy of focus and praise. Jon Dovey for one holds that we can no longer trust works that employ textual and situational cues that were comfortably associated with documentary in times past, and that the combined use of reflexivity, humour and simulated game play in present-day works 'threaten'

> to float the whole . . . documentary tradition off into some Disneyfied pleasure garden of primary colour delights, in which our hearts, our minds or our souls are hardly ever touched by anything more demanding than the fate of the latest evictee from the *Big Brother* house or *Survivor's* tribal council.[39]

In his view, reflexivity must mean more than simply the pleasure of knowing that documentaries are representations or even games. If not, documentary serves the 'hyperreal' rather than the 'real' and, as was described in the last chapter, reduces viewers from creators to consumers. Dovey's complaint echoes John Corner's evaluation that diversion is emerging as a 'documentary imperative'. Diversion documentaries borrow fictional formats, particularly from soap operas and gameshows, in order to entertain their audiences. This comes at the price of critical political engagement on the part of viewers and the loss of documentary authority, 'sobriety' and any claims to a direct relationship between filmic images and their historical referents.[40] Conversely, documentary has been drawn into fiction, with mock documentaries, promodocs and tele-movie 'docudramas' that replay recent events such as the life and death of Princess Diana (e.g. *Charles and Diana: Unhappily Ever After,* 1992; *Diana: Her True Story,* 1993; *Princess in Love,* 1996; and *The Life and Death of Princess Diana,* 1998).

While contemporary pronouncements about a new or crisis state of documentary filmmaking appear to ring true, they lose much of their force when we take a closer look at both film history and historical rather than hypothetical viewers. As Bernadette Flynn has noted, for instance, the conventional division in histories of film between 'actual' (typically associated with the Lumière brothers) and 'fantastic' (typically associated with George Méliès) projects masks the long-standing use of techniques associated with fantasy to create documentaries, and vice versa. In short, documentary hybrids are not a new phenomenon, and as was argued in Chapter 2, all historical films are arguably hybrids. Méliès, for example, employed optical effects and re-enactment in *The Coronation of Their Majesties Edward VII and Queen Alexandra* (1902).[41] Conversely, Charles Chauvel's feature film *In the Wake of the Bounty* (1933) offers a mixture of scripted and ethnographic file footage. In recent years, too, computer-generated images have commanded more screen space, as with the dramatic reconstruction of the monastery at Cluny in *Crusades* (1995). As Flynn also notes, interactive documentaries have their antecedents in penny arcades, where viewers controlled the delivery of historical re-enactments by turning the handle of the mutoscope and by selecting one mutoscope over another.[42] Arguably, then, the viewer polls that dot the websites of 'fly on the wall' historical 'reality' programs like *Frontier House* (2002) simply mark a new form of viewer interaction rather than its advent.

Nor do we have solid grounds to assume that all viewers derive undemanding pleasure from, or act as the stupefied consumers of, contemporary historical documentaries. As has been argued throughout this book, the construction of viewer responses from either a psychoanalytical or a critical perspective serves to paper over differences in the experiences of people of varying histories and historical contexts. Plentiful evidence of viewer engagement may be found in both official and unofficial websites devoted to particular works. While such evidence cannot be treated as representative, or often even linked back to specific historical agents, it is enough to establish that viewers cannot be reduced to a single form of response. For instance, well over a hundred websites offer varied reactions to Michael Moore's works. These include fan fiction sites where Moore appears as a voice of warning in a lesbian Buffy adventure, as a former US president in a portrait and in a poem about presidential hopeful John Kerry.[43] Before we conclude that this is evidence of the conflation of fact and fiction in a 'post-documentary' age, it is worth noting that fan fiction excursions with Michael Moore are unusual and that he never appears in more than a cameo role. Indeed, fan fiction usages of documentary figures are so unusual that we may even have grounds to conclude that documentary can be distinguished from other forms of history making on reception alone. This is a question we will pick up again in our exploration of the commercial dimensions of historical filmmaking in Chapter 8.

Similarly, within the official websites of reality historical documentaries —the sort of programs associated by Dovey with 'Disneyfied pleasure'— one can find little evidence of a singular, consumptive stance on the part of viewers. Viewer responses in the logs for the Australian Broadcasting Corporation's *Outback House* (2005), for instance, range from comments on the physical attractiveness of various participants to a lively discussion on whether historical 'authenticity' is possible or even desirable on television. For some viewers, the program clearly slipped its moorings and wound up as '1861 Big Brother' or simply 'a camping trip in funny clothes'. Others, though, found the struggle by participants to shift from twenty-first- to nineteenth-century behaviour both interesting and informative about our own times. Furthermore, some noted that the revival of nineteenth-century practices might produce results that are far from ethical. Should we, for instance, deny present-day medical attention to an injured participant? To support their claims, viewers looked to their own experiences and to other programs with a similar format. In this way, their responses resemble those of viewers of reality and fictional programs that do not purport to be set in the past. On the other hand, some viewers also supported their claims by reference to oral and written histories such as *The Letters of Rachel Henning*.[44] This distinction will occupy more of our attention when we come to discuss viewer concepts like 'canon' again in Chapter 8.

Images and words

In many present-day theories of documentary, as well as those of history, 'reflexivity' is the hallmark of critical engagement and social emancipation. Reflexivity is said to throw into relief unquestioned assumptions, open up choices and give voice to those who have been silenced by prevailing conventions. In and of itself, however, reflexivity does not guarantee social emancipation. As Steve Woolgar and Michael Lynch have demonstrated, the concept is associated with a variety of meanings and uses, and in some cases it is seen to reinforce rather than challenge conventional practices.[45] For example, Sandra Harding's call for 'strong reflexivity' is not incompatible with the aim of objectivity. She writes:

Maximising the objectivity of our accounts requires that the conceptual frameworks within which we work—the assumed and/or chosen ones of our discipline, culture, and historical moment—be subjected to the same critical examination that we bring to bear on whatever else we are studying.[46]

Harding's interest in objectivity opens up space between 'strong objectivity' and more sceptical understandings of the concept that identify all practices as representations. Reflexivity in this sense amounts to an awareness and questioning of belief in a world independent of the mind that constructs it.[47] Belief in reflexivity as a virtue is thus undercut a little by a lack of clarity about what it entails. Additionally, the conjunction of reflexivity with the opening up of many voices—multivalency or polyphony—and the abdication of authority cannot be assumed.

In the vision of theorists like R.G. Collingwood, historians are their own authorities, subjecting all evidence to critical interpretation.[48] This vision of history is, in the words of Mikhail Bakhtin, 'monologic': historians not only impose their own interpretative framework on their texts, they also determine when the people they write about will speak and what they will say. In Bakhtin's view, monologic texts are not only unethical, they are also lacking in meaning because dialogical relationships—relationships based on dialogue—permeate 'all human speech and all relationships and manifestations of human life—in general, everything that has meaning and significance'.[49] Bakhtin explains this claim through the example of a person looking at another person. I can see things behind your back that you cannot see, and you can see things behind my back that I cannot see. We are both engaging in the act of observing, but it is different for both of us not only because our bodies occupy different spatial positions but also because we regard each other and the world with different life experiences, beliefs, values and hopes. In order to see myself more completely, I must take on the vision of others and see myself as they do. 'I' is not a discrete thing but the ever-changing product of inter-subjective communication; we determine who we are according to where we are situated in relation to other persons.[50] Thus to think about ourselves and others 'means *to talk with them; otherwise they immediately turn us to their objectivized side*; they fall silent, close up, and congeal into finished, objectified images'.[51] His point is that unless we seek to engage others in dialogue, they become objects and we are left with diminished understandings.

A quick glance at the history of history making turns up a number of works that might be considered multivalent or polyphonic. The French medieval historian Jean Froissart, for example, offers us no less that five versions of the first book of *Chronicles*, three of which may have been written simultaneously.[52] Working with a different medium over five hundred years later, Akira Kurosawa presents four largely irreconcilable accounts of an event—a rape and a murder—in *Rashomon* (1950). Readers of Froissart's book and viewers of Kurosawa's film are given little guidance as to how they should judge each of the versions of events. They thus show us that history consists of multiple voices. However, this does not mean that both of these works arose from self-reflection and the determination to bring about social and political change. Froissart's rival histories more likely arose from an interest in attracting multiple sponsors and thus financial security.

Intention alone is not enough to make a work polyphonic. Nor is there any guarantee that the use of particular textual or filmic conventions will automatically grant a voice to those who have previously been silenced. Frustrated with the lack of respect given to early modern Europeans, for example, Natalie Zemon Davis opens *Women on the Margins* with a spirited, invented exchange between herself, Glikl bas Judah Leib, Marie de L'incarnation and Maria Sibylla Merian. Likewise, an invented confrontation with Laurent Joubert, the author of a sixteenth-century book on popular medical errors, closes Davis' *Society and Culture in Early Modern France*:

NZD: Laurent Joubert, you had contempt for the midwives you knew and did not think about how they served the village women. Your *Popular Errors* was just an effort to keep the physicians on top.
LJ: That's not true. I praised the midwife Gervaise who came regularly to public dissections of female corpses at Montpellier. I was trying to give the people better health. You are incurably naïve.[53]

Here, Davis appears to embrace the opportunity to give voice to those previously silenced and to question historical methods. These dialogues, though, function as historiographical membranes, for they enclose a substantial body of argument that Davis directs and delivers in conventional ways. It is one thing to bring new historical agents into history making; it is another to allow them to change our understanding of how histories should be made. Similarly, Richard Price's use of four typefaces in *Alabi's World* (1990) to suggest a conversation between himself, eighteenth- and nineteenth-century German Moravian missionaries, Dutch settlers and colonial officials and present-day Saramakas in Suriname is arguably a cosmetic device. In the preface, he instructs us to 'hear'

the Trump Bold passages in the accent of a working-class eighteenth-century German Moravian, the Trump Bold Italics passages in the Dutch accent of a bewigged colonial governor or his soldier-administrators, and the Trump Italics passages in the speech cadences of the elderly, dignified Saramaka men, some of whose portraits grace . . . Alabi's World.[54]

The absence of any instruction on how to 'hear' Price's voice is surprising. It might spring from a desire to foreground the voices of historical agents. Combine this omission with Price's frequent interpretative interventions, however, and we arrive instead at the textual equivalent of a documentary 'voice of

God', supposedly translating the past for us in a colourless—or in this case accentless—fashion. Consider his translation of this Saramaka passage:

> At the pool, one man said to another, 'Gwinzu' [an obsolete word for 'man']. The second one answered, 'Gwinzu'. The first said, 'Gwinzu, the whites are getting close. When I tjulú you should tjalá'. The other answered, 'No way, Gwinzu, I simply can't make it'. The first said, 'Gwinzu, just keep at it, and you'll succeed'. Later, the second said, 'I can't go on'. The first said, 'Just keep going, and little by little you'll win'. And thus they passed the swamp. Captain Maáku of Kámpu used to tell us boys, 'Gwinzu, keep at it and you'll succeed'. . . . Tebini, perhaps the greatest living Saramaka historian, and Metisen, a descendant of Kaasi, described to me in elliptical fashion how they eluded a colonial army that archival records attest included seventeen whites, forty-eight slaves, and sixty-two Indians.[55]

Price unlocks the meaning of the events for us, tying oral history to what appears to be the firmer foundation of archival records and numerical evidence. In so doing, he reins in new voices to match empiricist conventions. The same criticism can be levelled at the 1996 documentary *W.E.B. Du Bois: A Biography in Four Voices*, where the views of Wesley Brown, Thulani Davis, Toni Cade Bambara and Amiri Baraka coalesce to such an extent that the result is a virtual monologue. This is despite the potential for disagreement over Du Bois' views of rival activists Booker T. Washington and Marcus Garvey.

Given these examples, it should be acknowledged that radical intentions and methodologies do not necessarily produce radical social and political outcomes. A work that appears to be multivalent may serve to reinforce conventional historical approaches. And here we take another step, asking whether the valuing of reflexivity or associated notions like polyphony itself is a radical and sceptical act. Theories of reflexivity celebrate historians and historical filmmakers who do not simply show history but also alert us to their acts of showing. These theories become 'vicious', Dick Pels argues, when they become a methodological imperative that is used to downgrade the ideas of those who are unable or unwilling to engage in self-revelation. Those who do not endorse reflexivity on the terms of the theorist can even have motives, interests and impulses imputed to them that are thought to explain their resistance. As Pels writes:

> I . . . knowing myself, also know who you are, where you come from, what your deepest interests are, why you remain unconscious of what you actually do and why you entangle yourself in performative contradictions. If you are unprepared to 'know thyself' on my theoretical conditions, you are an unreflexive bastard, and I must tutor you in my explanatory theory, which will liberate us both.[56]

Paradoxically, the call for an awareness of the conditions by which knowledge claims are formed itself becomes an unquestioned premise.

Like Grierson, and my parents, it seems that we still expect a great deal from documentary. We trust that it will foster awareness of historical phenomena, if not of history as representation. But is that trust a problem? If the call for reflexivity is unmasked as an unquestioned assumption, might all forms of documentary—not just non-reflexive forms—be seen as fostering social and political enslavement? This question serves as the focus of my next chapter.

Recommended resources

Beattie, K., *Documentary Screens: Nonfiction Film and Television*, Basingstoke: Palgrave Macmillan, 2004.

Bruzzi, S., *New Documentary: A Critical Introduction*, London: Routledge, 2000.

Cannadine, D. (ed.), *History and the Media*, Basingstoke: Palgrave Macmillan, 2004.

Lipkin, S.N., *Real Emotional Logic: Film and Television Docudrama as Persuasive Practice*, Carbondale: Southern Illinois University Press, 2002.

Middleton, J., 'Documentary comedy', *Media International Incorporating Culture and Policy*, 2002, no. 104, pp. 55–66.

Nichols, B., *Introduction to Documentary*, Bloomington: Indiana University Press, 2001.

Plantinga, C.R., *Rhetoric and Representation in Nonfiction Film*, Cambridge: Cambridge University Press, 1997.

Renov, M. (ed.), *Theorizing Documentary*, New York: Routledge, 1993.

Roscoe, J. and Hight, C., *Faking It: Mock-documentary and the Subversion of Factuality*, Manchester: Manchester University Press, 2001.

Rosen, P., 'Document and documentary: on the persistence of historical concepts', in *Change Mummified: Cinema, Historicity, Theory*, Minneapolis: University of Minnesota Press, 2001, pp. 225–64.

Notes

1 J. Grierson, 'Flaherty's poetic *Moana*' [8 February 1926], in F. Hardy (ed.), *Grierson on the Movies*, London: Faber and Faber, 1981, pp. 23–5.

2 J. Grierson, 'First principles of documentary' [1932], in I. Aitken (ed.), *The Documentary Film Movement: An Anthology*, Edinburgh: Edinburgh University Press, 1998, pp. 81–5.

3 I. Aitken, *Film and Reform: John Grierson and the Documentary Film*, London: Routledge, 1990, p. 60.

4 J. Grierson, *Grierson on Documentary*, ed. F. Hardy, Berkeley: University of California Press, 1966, p. 142.

5 P. Rotha, 'Some principles of documentary', in R.M. Barsam (ed.), *Nonfiction Film Theory and Criticism*, New York: E.P. Dutton, 1976, p. 42; and L. Jacobs (ed.), *The Documentary Tradition*, New York: Hopkinson & Blake, 1974, p. 4. For a 'transparent' view, see J.-L. Comolli, as quoted in C. Plantinga, *Rhetoric and Representation in Nonfiction Film*, Cambridge: Cambridge University Press, 1997, p. 10.

6 C. Plantinga, *Rhetoric and Representation in Nonfiction Film*, p. 15; and B. Nichols,

Introduction to Documentary, Bloomington: University of Indiana Press, 2001, p. 21.

7 L. Wittgenstein, *The Blue and Brown Books*, Oxford: Blackwell, 1958, pp. 17, 87, 124; see also *Philosophical Investigations*, ed. G.H. von Wright, R. Rhees and G.E.M. Anscombe, Oxford: Blackwell, 1992, §67; and *Philosophical Grammar*, ed. R. Rhees, trans. A. Kenny, Oxford: Blackwell, 1974, p. 75.

8 See, for example, N. Carroll, 'From real to reel: entangled in nonfiction film', *Philosophic Exchange*, 1983, no. 14, pp. 5–45; N. Carroll, 'Fiction, non-fiction and the film of presumptive assertion: a conceptual analysis', in R. Allen and M. Smith (eds), *Film Theory and Philosophy*, Oxford: Oxford University Press, 1997, pp. 173–202; and C. Plantinga, *Rhetoric and Representation in Nonfiction Film*, p. 16.

9 B. Nichols, *Introduction to Documentary*, pp. 26–32.

10 B. Nichols, 'Documentary film and the modernist avant-garde', *Critical Inquiry*, 2001, vol. 27(4), pp. 580–610.

11 D. Vertov, 'Resolution of the council of three' [1923], in P.A. Sitney (ed.), *Film Culture Reader*, New York: Praeger, 1970, p. 359.

12 S. Zizek, 'Introduction: the spectre of ideology', in S. Zizek (ed.), *Mapping Ideology*, London: Verso, 1994, p. 26.

13 J. Grierson, 'Summary and survey: 1935', in *Grierson on Documentary*, p. 183.

14 See, for example, R.G. Collingwood, *Speculum Mentis*, Oxford: Oxford University Press, 1924.

15 B. Nichols, *Introduction to Documentary*, p. 105.

16 D. Lowenthal, *The Past is a Foreign Country*, Cambridge: Cambridge University Press, 1985.

17 See also *In Search of Shakespeare* (2003), *In Search of the Trojan War* (1985), *Legacy: The Origins of Civilisation* (1991), *In Search of Ethelred the Unready* (1981) and *In Search of William the Conqueror* (1981).

18 B. Nichols, *Introduction to Documentary*, p. 107.

19 C. Lanzmann, 'De l'holocauste a Holocauste, on comment s'en debarrasser', as quoted in D. LaCapra, 'Lanzmann's "Shoah": "here there is no why" ', *Critical Inquiry*, 1997, vol. 23(2), p. 237.

20 *Ibid.*, p. 243.

21 O. Gelley, 'A response to Dominick LaCapra's "Lanzmann's Shoah" ', *Critical Inquiry*, 1998, vol. 24(3), pp. 830–2. See also D. LaCapra, 'Evocations of an autonomous art', *Critical Inquiry*, 1998, vol. 24(3), pp. 833–6.

22 Recorded in C. Lanzmann, *Shoah: An Oral History of the Holocaust*, New York: Pantheon Books, 1985, p. 7. In the book, Mordechaï Podchlebnik's responses are recorded in the third person to note the use of a translator. I have shifted his responses back into the first person to reflect the manner in which they were delivered in the film.

23 B. Nichols, *Introduction to Documentary*, p. 125.

24 On the use of performed interviews in *Far from Poland*, see J. Godmilow and A.-L. Shapiro, 'How real is the reality in documentary film?', *History and Theory*, 1997, vol. 36(4), pp. 80–101.

25 B. Nichols, *Introduction to Documentary*, p. 130.

26 *Ibid.*, pp. 34, 137.

27 B. Nichols, *Representing Reality*, p. 33.

28 C. Plantinga, *Rhetoric and Representation in Nonfiction Film*, pp. 101–3; see also C. Plantinga, 'Notes on spectator emotion and ideological film criticism', in R. Allen and M. Smith (eds), *Film Theory and Philosophy*, Oxford: Oxford University Press, 1997, pp. 372–7.

29 C. Plantinga, *Rhetoric and Representation in Nonfiction Film*, pp. 109–10.

30 *Ibid.*, pp. 18, 37.

31 *Ibid.*, p. 15.
32 S. Bruzzi, *New Documentary: A Critical Introduction*, London: Routledge, 2000, p. 154; J. Corner, *Documentary in a Post-documentary Culture*, European Science Foundation, Changing Media—Changing Europe Program, Working Paper 1, draft online at www.lboro.ac.uk/research/changing.media/John.Corner.paper.htm; and B. Winston, 'The primrose path: faking UK television documentary, "docuglitz" and docusoap', *Screening the Past*, 1999, no. 8, online at www.latrobe.edu.au/screeningthepast/firstrelease/fr1199/bwfr8b.htm
33 S.E. Ambrose, *Into the Breach:* The Making of *Saving Private Ryan*, Paramount Pictures and Dreamworks, 1999. Ambrose is the author of *D-Day: June 6 1944: The Climatic Battle of World War II*, New York: Simon & Schuster, 1995, which is recommended as a companion to the film book at www.amazon.com
34 J. Roscoe and C. Hight, *Faking It: Mock-documentary and the Subversion of Factuality*, Manchester: Manchester University Press, 2001, p. 3.
35 Y. Loshitzky, 'Holocaust others: Spielberg's *Schindler's List* versus Lanzmann's *Shoah*', in Y. Loshitzky (ed.), *Spielberg's Holocaust: Critical Perspectives on Schindler's List*, Bloomington: University of Indiana Press, 1997, p. 2.
36 J. Baxter, *Steven Spielberg: The Unauthorised Biography*, London: HarperCollins, 1996.
37 *Ibid.*, p. 67.
38 M. Renov, 'Towards a poetics of documentary', in M. Renov (ed.), *Theorising Documentary*, London: Routledge, 1993, p. 31. See also M. Renov, 'Lost, lost, lost: Mekas as essayist', in M. Renov (ed.), *The Subject of Documentary*, Minneapolis: University of Minnesota Press, 2004, pp. 84–9.
39 J. Dovey, 'Confession and the unbearable lightness of factual', *Media International Australia Incorporating Culture and Policy*, 2002, no. 104, p. 12.
40 J. Corner, *Documentary in a Post-documentary Culture*, available online at http://www.lboro.ac.uk/research/changing.media/John.Corner.paper.htm
41 A. Gaudreault, 'The cinematograph: a historiographical machine', in D.E. Klemm and W. Schweiker (eds), *Meanings in Texts and Actions: Questioning Paul Ricoeur*, London: University Press of Virginia, 1993, pp. 90–7.
42 B. Flynn, 'Factual hybridity: games, documentary and simulated spaces', *Media International Australia Incorporating Culture and Policy*, 2002, no. 104, pp. 42–4.
43 See http://glamorousrags.dymphna.net/dawninrome.html, http://www.futurama-madhouse.com.ar/fanfic/the_bot_with_the_golden_chimp.html and http://www.mudvillegazette.com/archives/001152.html
44 See the *Outback House* discussion forums at http://www.abc.net.au/tv/outbackhouse/
45 S. Woolgar (ed.), *Knowledge and Reflexivity: New Frontiers in the Sociology of Knowledge*, London: Sage, 1988; and M. Lynch, 'Against reflexivity as an academic virtue and source of privileged knowledge', *Theory, Culture and Society*, 2000, vol. 17(3), pp. 26–54.
46 S. Harding, 'Standpoint epistemology (a feminist version): how social disadvantage creates epistemic advantage', in S. Turner (ed.), *Social Theory and Sociology: The Classics and Beyond*, Oxford: Blackwell, 1996, p. 159.
47 S. Woolgar, 'Some remarks about positionism: a reply to Collins and Yearley', in A. Pickering (ed.), *Science as Practice and Culture*, Chicago: University of Chicago Press, 1992, pp. 327–42.
48 *Ibid.*, pp. 278–9.
49 M. Bakhtin, *Problems of Dostoevsky's Poetics*, ed. and trans. C. Emerson, Manchester: Manchester University Press, 1984, p. 40.
50 *Ibid.*, p. 28.
51 *Ibid.*, p. 68. Unless otherwise indicated, emphasis reflects the original.

52 J. Froissart, *Chronicles*, trans. and abr. G. Brereton, Harmondsworth: Penguin, 1968.
53 N.Z. Davis, *Society and Culture in Early Modern France*, Cambridge: Cambridge University Press, 1987, p. 267.
54 R. Price, *Alabi's World*, Baltimore: Johns Hopkins University Press, 1990, p. xx.
55 *Ibid.*, pp. 16, 18.
56 D. Pels, 'Reflexivity: one step up', *Theory, Culture and Society*, 2000, vol. 17(3), p. 9.

7 Propaganda

'Propaganda' is a pejorative term; applying it to an historical film implies disapproval, and we do not expect those who have their works so labelled to respond positively. Charges of propaganda are likely to be met with denial. As well as its function as a simple term of abuse, its definition by theorists of propaganda stresses four criteria: intention, methods or techniques, content and consequences. In this chapter, I will offer a critical assessment of each of these criteria and suggest that the view of propaganda as morally reprehensible cannot be sustained if there is a lack of clarity about what it is. Furthermore, I will note the recent expansion in applications of the term from particular historical films produced with state support during times of upheaval and war to all mass communication practices. This expansion, we will discover, rests upon the characterisation of viewers as the passive or willing recipients of what they see. This is an assumption that we have met and questioned before in this book, but in this chapter we approach it head on.

Historical films as propaganda

Undertake a search for information on historical films and propaganda and two names and contexts will appear again and again: Leni Riefenstahl and Nazi Germany and Sergei Eisenstein and the Soviet Union. Hélène Bertha Amelie ('Leni') Riefenstahl is best known for the documentaries she directed at the request of Hitler between 1933 and 1938. She began her movie career as the lead in Arnold Fanck's *Bergfilm* (mountain or glacier film) *Der heilige Berg* (*The Holy Mountain*, 1926); six years later, she directed *Das blaue Licht* (*The Blue Light*, 1932), the story of an ostracised mountain girl who dies because her ideals are shattered. Riefenstahl's thoughtful shot compositions and use of close-ups captured the attention of, among many others, Adolf Hitler, who asked her to film the 1933 Nuremberg Rally. The result was *Seig des Glaubens* (*Victory of Faith*, 1933) and later *Triumph des Willens* (*Triumph of the Will*, 1936), *Tag der Freiheit* (*Day of Freedom—Our Armed Forces*, 1935) and *Die Kamera fährt mit* (*The Camera Goes Too*, 1937). After these projects, Riefenstahl made a film about the 1936 Berlin

Olympics—*Olympia*—employing sixty camera operators, 400 kilometres of film and a variety of pioneering film techniques, including slow motion and high- and low-angle, panoramic and dolly shots. In 1938, Riefenstahl embarked on a trip to the United States to promote *Olympia*. The visit was marked by protests, not the least of which was in response to *Kristallnacht*, the burning of synagogues and the vicious persecution of Jewish shop-keepers in Germany by the Nazis on 9 November. While the response of many who saw the film was positive, the Third Reich-tainted *Olympia* failed to find a US distributor, and a dejected Riefenstahl returned to Germany. Following the end of hostilities in 1945, Riefenstahl had to face Allied charges that she was a Nazi or a Nazi sympathizer. Her close ties to Hitler and her films, most notably *Triumph of the Will*, made her an obvious target. She was submitted to a US forces 'denazification' program and released 'without prejudice' on 3 June 1945, but it was not until July 1949 that she was officially 'denazified' by a French tribunal. Even that 'final' decision was appealed against by the French military government, and the matter was only closed six months later when the Baden State Commissariat classified Riefenstahl *in absentia* as a 'fellow traveller'. But these verdicts did not mean she could resume her career as a director, as her final film project, *Tiefland* (*Lowland*, 1954), was mired by allegations that she had knowingly used gypsies imprisoned in concentration camps for some scenes and that she was Hitler's 'easy girl'.

To this day, controversy surrounds Riefenstahl's work. Opinion is divided about whether she was an artist or an agent of evil, as is apparent in these two appraisals, the first by Audrey Salkeld and the second by the historical documentary maker Jean Godmilow:

> The high profile and privileges she enjoyed in the early Hitler years guaranteed she would prove an embarrassment in a world rigorously purging itself of Nazi taint after the war. She was effectively banned for life from her profession, even though others involved in the production of infinitely more evil films were reabsorbed into the industry. . . . It is clear to me now that motivations can rarely be so neatly apportioned. The notion of guilt by association continues to cloud any rational verdict on her moral culpability for promoting Hitler's demonic Reich through her films. Hindsight telescopes those Hitler years together. Knowing where they led makes it almost impossible for us now to view Riefenstahl's work without that perception.[1]

> I read her *Memoir* during a long stay in a hospital a few years back. On every page, subtly and often not very subtly, she is rewriting her life to prove that she never had any knowledge of, or intention of supporting the practices of the Nazi party with her filmmaking. Her primary defence of this preposterous and impossible ignorance is that she was always just trying to make art—rather, pure art—and that led her to techniques and strategies that critics later claimed to be fascist.[2]

Salkeld reminds us how easy and problematic it is to judge an historical agent by outcomes. Reading Riefenstahl's *Memoir*, though, it is not hard to see why Godmilow accuses her of 'rewriting' her life. Her vision of self in that work, as Ray Müller has pointed out in his documentary *The Wonderful, Horrible Life of Leni Riefenstahl* (1993), conforms to that of Junta in *The Blue Light*, an unworldly woman who is persecuted because she is the only one who can (literally or metaphorically) scale the heights. Nowhere do her claims about persecution appear more strongly than in her written and filmed reflections on *Triumph of the Will*. Riefenstahl consistently argued that it was not propaganda for four main reasons: first, there is no commentator in the film 'telling the audience what to believe'; second, it would not have won international awards ('What interest would the directors of the World's Fair and the French Prime Minister have had in honouring Nazi propaganda?'); third, she did not organise the Nuremberg rallies; and fourth, she had the composition of images, not political messages, at the top of her mind.[3]

Describing Sergei Eisenstein's films as propaganda appears to be easier, for in many places he portrayed his works as helping to define the Soviet state. Eisenstein claimed that the October Revolution of 1917 first drew him to film art:

> The revolution gave me the most precious thing in life—it made an artist out of me. If it had not been for the revolution I would never have broken the tradition, handed down from father to son, of becoming an engineer. . . . The revolution introduced me to art, and art, in its own turn, brought me to the revolution.[4]

Eisenstein's hope for the instruction of the masses in the history and theory of their political movement could be realised, he believed, in the creation of a 'purely intellectual film', the mainspring of which was 'montage' or the juxtaposition of conflicting shots, sounds, tempos and light levels.[5] His three films about the 1905 and February and October 1917 revolutions—*Stachka* (Strike, 1925), *Bronenosets Potemkin* (*Battleship Potemkin*, 1925) and *Oktiabr* (*October*, 1928)—all employ montage and focus on either collectives or the activities of individuals within collectives. This was in stark contrast to the continuity editing and 'boy meets girl' formula he associated with contemporary 'bourgeois cinema'.[6] After working unsuccessfully to produce a film in Hollywood between 1928 and 1932, Eisenstein returned to the USSR to find a very different political climate under the leadership of Joseph Stalin. He produced two stylised historical films that showed how medieval history could be used to support contemporary political views: in *Aleksandr Nevski* (*Alexander Nevsky*, 1938), Russian knights valiantly defend their homeland against Teutonic invaders, and in *Ivan Grozni* (*Ivan the Terrible I*, 1944), the protagonist battles against internal enemies involved in a conspiracy. After a near fatal heart attack in 1946, he completed a working print of *Ivan Grozni*

II Boyarski Zagorov (*Ivan the Terrible II*, 1958), but poor critical reviews delayed its public release until 1958, a decade after his death.

The conventional treatment of Riefenstahl's and Eisenstein's historical films as propaganda by film scholars reflects the assumed limitation of the concept to state or state-sponsored articulations of national community during times of war and social upheaval. All Nicholas Reeves' case studies in *The Power of Film Propaganda*, for instance, fit that bill. However, media and communication theorists have sought to broaden the term to cover the work of all organisations or groups that seek to move recipients to a desired view.[7] The Disney Corporation's global reach, for instance, has led scholars to warn of the social effects that might result from its purported construction of conservative, sexist, racist, nationalist and even imperialistic histories. Henry Giroux has argued that:

> The strategies of entertaining escapism, historical forgetting, and repressive pedagogy in Disney's books, records, theme parks, movies and TV programs produce a series of identifications that relentlessly define America as white and middle class. Pedagogy in Disney's texts functions as a history lesson that excludes the subversive elements of memory. Reduced to vignettes of childhood innocence, adventure and chivalry, memory is removed from the historical, social and political context that defines it as a process of cultural production that opens rather than closes down history. It is precisely this pedagogical policing of memory that undercuts its possibility as a form of critical remembrance.[8]

Giroux sees in *Good Morning, Vietnam* (1987)—a partly fictionalised drama about a disc jockey (Adrian Cronauer, played by Robin Williams) who is sent to Vietnam in 1965 to boost morale—the expunging of historical, political and ethical discourses in favour of rock 'n' roll nostalgia and the 'narcissistic assertion of whiteness as the singular referent for intelligence, manhood, and sensuality'. Tran, for instance, is a Vietnamese 'Tonto' who serves Cronauer, only to betray him and Western notions of culture and civility through membership of the Vietcong, and his sister, Tuan, is present only as an object of Cronauer's patriarchal gaze.[9] Interestingly, too, Cronauer's engagement with the Vietnamese is entirely structured by the American popular culture elements of street slang (taught in an English class) and a baseball game. For Giroux, *Good Morning, Vietnam* is at one with other contemporary US Vietnam combat films that shed the big historical picture in favour of small stories of North American masculine virtue and suffering. As with Desser and Studies' reading of *Rambo*, it is an 'aversion' to history. We will have more to say on this opposition of Disney films and history when we come to delineate the criteria for 'propaganda'.

Gary Edgerton and Kathy Jackson see in the animated Disney feature *Pocahontas* (1995) a similar expurgation of political and historical discourses in favour of imperialist romantic fantasy. Pocahontas' screen image is an exotic synthesis of the physical features of paintings of Pocahontas, Native American consultant Shirley 'Little Dove' Custalow McGowan, the Filipina model Dyna Taylor and white supermodel Christy Turlington (see Figure 7.1).[10] And although Pocahontas echoes Chief Seattle's arguments for cross-cultural sensitivity and respect for the environment in the song 'Colors of the Wind', these ideals are ultimately subordinated to her quest for a 'true path' in love and their realisation with the first white man she sees, John Smith.[11] Though not a Disney animation, 20th Century Fox's *Anastasia* (1997) fits a related pattern. Set in the wake of the Russian Revolution of October 1917 in which, to quote

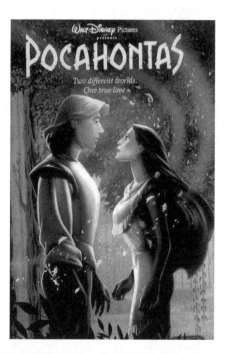

Figure 7.1 Synthesising and deconstructing the past: Disney's *Pocahontas* (© 1995, Disney Enterprises) and 20th Century Fox's *Anastasia* (© 1998)

one of the songs, 'since the revolution our lives have been so grey', *Anastasia* reworks the popular myth of a surviving Romanov child into a romantic travel narrative in which the protagonist declares that she will not be 'complete' until she finds 'Home, Love, Family'.[12] In the process, Lenin, Trotsky and the mass action of the collective are purged from the screen in favour of the explanation that the revolution and the death of the Romanovs was due to the machinations of a long-dead, disassembling Rasputin who resides in a kind of purgatory with a talking bat (see Figure 7.1). Clearly, this literal and metaphorical deconstruction of the mainsprings of the October revolution serves a very different function to that of Eisenstein's revolution films.

The appeal of animated films to children as well as to adults marks them out among film critics as being of special concern. This is due to the fear that 'Disney history' may become definitive history—or in Giroux's words 'close down history'—if viewers are too young to have developed critical analytical skills. For many more film theorists, though, concerns about indoctrination ought to be extended to *all* viewers of historical films, irrespective of age and educational attainment. Anxieties about the dangers of film may be dated back to the earliest days of production. Some of these anxieties focused on the darkened environments in which films were seen, while others looked to the impact on audiences of the images offered. Before long, these anxieties were codified in film censorship policies and in the 'direct effects' theory of communication. Both these activities shared the view of film as having a potentially narcotic and dangerous effect, particularly on working-class, immigrant and female viewers.[13] Film theorists today may not write so openly about morally vulnerable audiences, but anxieties about the social impact of film viewing remains. Their anxiety stems not from the threat of moral and social disorder, however, but its opposite: social order.

Throughout this book, we have caught glimpses of various theorists' characterisations of film as a potential instrument of social regulation. In Barthes' view, we recall, film 'naturalises' the constructedness of its meaning, encouraging viewers to accept its 'reality' and to surrender an opportunity for resistance against socio-cultural mores. For Baudrillard, the 'absolute realistic verisimilitude' of 'hyperreal' historical films has dulled our ability to distinguish reality from artifice and reduced us to passive consumers. Debord sees filmic spectacle as serving the economy as a tool of regulation and depoliticisation. And for Godard and Benjamin, cinema peddles the dream and logic of the nineteenth century, one that enshrines either a particular form of masculine identity or a culture of consumption. The psychoanalytical film theories of Jean-Louis Baudry, Jean-Pierre Oudart, Christian Metz, Daniel Dayan and Stephen Heath paint a similarly bleak picture of film viewers as either the passive victims of, or vulnerable to, the 'illusion' of cinema.[14]

Psychoanalytical film theories owe much of their form to a combination of the neo-Marxist writings of Louis Althusser, Jacques Lacan's psychoanalytical account of the stages of human development and Julia Kristeva's semiotics. In the main, they are characterised by the premise that the illusive reality of cinema deceives viewers about themselves and the societies they live in. All knowledge and truth is wrought by the systems of concepts of which they are a part. The 'empiricist' impression of reality generated by many historical films, though, is one of seeing the world in a way that is unmediated. In the apparent 'transparency' of empiricism, the presuppositions that cement society together pass unnoticed and serve to suture viewers in specific social roles. Viewer acceptance of those roles is explained by Lacan's 'imaginary' or 'mirror' stage of human development, when infants transfer the visual integrity of their figure reflected in a mirror to an ontological belief that they are unified, discrete and autonomous selves.[15] From the mirror stage onwards, individuals are tugged between impressions of themselves as unified selves and fragmented experiences. Anxieties, and more specifically castration anxiety, however, impel viewers into seeking and accepting coherence, even at the cost of social freedom.[16] The cinema screen does not reflect, as a mirror does, but projects on to viewers a structure of cognition, desire and selfhood. Viewers think of themselves as autonomous free agents who are able to discriminate truth from falsehood, but this conception is a product of presuppositions that they do not see because of the assumed transparency of empiricism. This misunderstanding is sustained by society in order to discourage true social change. Due to this apparent deception of the viewer, psychoanalytical film theorists identify cinema with the perpetuation of ideology. Therefore, cinema can become a tool for social change only through the creation of films, including historical films, that challenge the cinematic conventions of realism or that employ nonstandard techniques of editing or narration and so on. This is because deviation can make viewers aware of convention, of the cement that holds society together in its current form, and offer them the chance to prise open cracks in that cement through revolutionary activities.

Defining propaganda

The varying ideas and applications of 'propaganda' described above—ranging from overtly political films to all historical films—seems to affirm Leonard Doob's assertion that a clear-cut definition of the term is not possible.[17] However, underlying these views is a common stock of four conceptual criteria that, alone or in combination, serve to secure a pejorative appraisal of propaganda that, in Barthes' words, 'goes without saying'. I will examine and question these criteria under the labels of method, content, intention and outcome.

Method

Looking first to method, Riefenstahl and Eisenstein share the assumption that propaganda is a particular means of bringing about a state of belief.

Beyond that, though, their opinions diverge, with voiceover narration, mont-age and its opposite continuity editing, narration and verisimilitude variously identified as instruments of propaganda. This is the first problem with the method criterion. Furthermore, it is not specified whether any use of these methods, or only a certain sufficient amount of use, corresponds to propa-ganda. What proportion of continuity and verisimilitude is needed to make a film an appendage of bourgeois ideology? How much voiceover is needed? How much montage? Any response to these questions is at worst arbitrary and at best points to other criteria. Eisenstein's work bears this point out, for he used non-continuity editing to raise support for Soviet ideals. If psy-choanalyst film theorists have difficulty associating his filmic techniques with propaganda, then we have highlighted the point that for them, propaganda is *capitalist, bourgeois* propaganda. Similarly, few scholars would agree that it is voiceover alone that determines whether *Triumph of the Will* or indeed any historical documentary is propaganda. It seems, then, as Reeves and Carl Plantinga have argued, that method of filmmaking is not a sufficient criterion for propaganda, since we must ask not only 'How is the film presented?' but also 'What ideas and ideals are being presented?'[18]

Content

It might be argued then that it is the content that an historical film presents that determines whether it is propaganda. This is a view that informs all but Riefenstahl's account of *Triumph of the Will* in the above section. We recall, for instance, that criticisms about Disney animations and Fox's *Anastasia* concerned their purported promotion of North American fantasies of white-ness, colonial domination and romantic love. An obvious objection to the simple link of propaganda with content is that even in what seem to be hall-mark cases (i.e. images showing Western imperialism), there might be ways of treating the content that encourage questions and critical reflection. An his-torical film that demonstrates this point is Yervant Gianikian and Angela Ricci Lucchi's *Dal Polo All'Equatore* (*From the Pole to the Equator*, 1987), which is composed of filmic travelogues produced by Luca Comerio between 1900 and 1920. Working without sound, Gianikian and Lucchi use short introductory titles, editing, tinting and out-takes to highlight and critique Comerio's celebration of the dominance of European civilisation over nature and 'natives'. In two juxtaposed shots filmed in Africa, for instance, perform-ing natives and exotic game animals are paraded before the camera like items to be collected by viewers, and in other sequences lingering shots of war casualties and hunted polar bears drive home the cruelty of European enlightenment. The filmmakers did not add any new footage; they simply used arrangement and emphasis to read Comerio against the grain.[19] Comerio and Gianikian are of course promoting their own message, but that message is unlikely to attract the label of propaganda on the part of theorists. Why? On its own, content, like method, seems an insufficient criterion for propaganda.

Intention

This brings us to intention, which is often taken as the sole or chief measure of propaganda in theories of communication. Garth Jowett and Victoria O'Donnell, for instance, characterise propaganda as the 'deliberate', 'wilful' and 'premeditated' shaping of human activities.[20] On this view, an historical film is propaganda if its maker clearly expresses the aim to shift viewer activities in a favoured direction. Eisenstein's work seems to best fit this account, for he clearly stated his aim to use film as an instrument to raise revolutionary awareness. However, intention is far too problematic a concept to function as the basis for propaganda. A first, methodological objection is that historical films are rarely the product of a single individual, let alone a single cohesive plan. Paul Wells, for instance, has argued that the heterogeneous process of creating a Disney text undercuts ideological coherence. As with many historical films, the production of an animated history often begins with primary or secondary historical sources. Aspects of the sources are selected and arranged into a script that is informed by collective suggestion and negotiation between budget, casting, historical consultant, storyboard, design, animation, compositing and editing teams. That script remains fluid during production as everyone from voice artists to compositors 'works through' the aural and visual personality of characters and puts their results to test audiences.[21] We recall from Chapter 3, too, that the heterogeneous nature of *mise en scène*, editing and scripting in historical films highlights the fact that they are the product of collaboration and negotiation.

Second, even if we are looking to the claims of individual filmmakers like Eisenstein and Riefenstahl, there is still the question of how we might distinguish intentions from authorial intentions. That is, are we able to discriminate between intentions that are 'the meaning the utterance has for its author at the point of [making] the work' and those that are prior to or even outside of it?[22] Or is a film scholar bound to accept all the filmmaker's activities and expressions as in some way connected to their works, as Jean Godmilow and Susan Sontag have done in reading Riefenstahl's images of tropical fish and the Nuba people in Africa as an affirmation of the fascist views that purportedly underpin *Triumph of the Will* and *Olympia*?[23] On what criteria are we able to regard or disregard a filmmaker's activities? Must we consider a filmmaker's activities as a coherent body, or (as was argued in Chapter 3) is the very idea of a filmmaker as a single, coherent self, suspect?

This brings us to a third objection to the connection of propaganda with intentions, one expressed through the literary theory catchphrase of 'there is no "outside" to the text'.[24] In the wake of pronouncements by writers such as Roland Barthes that 'a text is not a line of words releasing a single "theological" meaning (the "message" of the Author-God)' historians have struggled to establish that the subject matter of intellectual history is external to textual analysis.[25] 'Weak' intentionalists like Mark Bevir, for instance, have conceded that historians cannot gain direct access to the intentions of historical agents and that they simply 'postulate them as part of their interpretation of the texts before them'. R.G. Collingwood, whose views I canvassed in Chapter 4, also holds that the re-enactment of thoughts and emotions is made possible through reading the public language that shapes artefacts (e.g. writing and material evidence). Hence the intentions of an historical agent are those expressed by a work. Bevir and Collingwood are also open to overturning agent statements of intent and invoking notions of deception, insincerity and irrationality to 'make sense' of a work.[26] Bevir's and Collingwood's arguments support the conventional treatment of Riefenstahl's statements about *Triumph of the Will* as deceptive or insincere. But this conventional reading, and that of psychoanalytical film theory in which filmmakers affirm bourgeois ideology, is ontologically problematic. In particular, can we call the work of a filmmaker 'propaganda' if they work within a setting in which certain ideas—like empiricism—are generally accepted as beyond question and they sincerely believe that they are helping viewers to think for themselves? On what grounds are the historian's imputed intentions to be given preference over any historically stated intentions? Intentions alone cannot carry the meaning of 'propaganda'.

Outcome

The appeal to intentions as an explanation for propaganda is further undercut by the simple point that filmmakers can aim to persuade viewers but fail in the task. Too often, as Reeves has argued, conclusions are made about the power of films without evidence to show that they reached and had an impact on their target audiences. So while, for instance, *Battleship Potemkin* topped box office earnings in Germany in 1925–6 and was shown in thirty-eight countries outside the Soviet Union, in the Soviet Union more viewers went to see Buster Keaton's *Our Hospitality* (1923) and Douglas Fairbanks' *Robin Hood* (1923) and *The Thief of Bagdad* (1924).[27] This example affirms the observation I made in Chapter 4, that viewers may seek different stories and imagined communities than those advanced in the public political historical films often favoured by historians and film scholars. Similarly, while *Triumph of the Will* was awarded the German National Film Prize and gold medals at the Venice Film Festival and the Paris World Exhibition of 1937, it did not achieve a run of more than a week in most German cinemas. Indeed, *Triumph of the Will* has been seen by more viewers since the Second World War as a part of democracy education programs. This afterlife shows us that judgements about the use and impact of an historical film need to be considered over time and in historical context.

Even if an historical film does secure a large audience at the time it is first released, there is no guarantee that exhibitors and viewers will receive it in the same way. A good case in point is *Battle of the Somme*, which was seen by around twenty million people in Britain in 1916. In his introduction to the film, Prime Minister Lloyd George expressed the hope that it would reinforce commitment to the war. Some of the audience responded to the film in this way, while others used it to work through the loss of friends and family in the conflict. Still others might have found the work a welcome source of entertainment, as the dean of Durham complained in a contemporary letter to *The Times* that some viewers clearly had 'feasted' their eyes on the 'hideous tragedy' of war.[28] This seems to have been the case for a number of the children surveyed in 1917 about their wartime film preferences by the National Council of Public Morals. Both *Battle of the Somme* and *Battle of Ancre* (1917) were ranked in the top four popular films, and comments written about them show how they were drawn into everyday life. One boy described a battle sequence in *Battle of Ancre* in this way:

> Now the whistle shrills, and they leap over the parapet, rat, tap, tap, go the German machine guns, but nothing daunts our soldiers. Crack! And their gallant captain falls. This enrages the men to fury. At last they reach the German lines. Most of the Germans flee for their lives shouting 'Kamerad! Kamerad!' etc. Now the British and German wounded are brought in, some seriously, some slightly. Soon after follow the German prisoners, some vicious looking scoundrels that I should not like to meet on a dark night, others young boys, about sixteen years of age.

As Reeves has noted, this synopsis bears almost no relationship to the film itself and is clearly a synthesis of other visual, written and oral accounts in circulation and elements of imaginative play that he and his peers might have enjoyed.

Even exhibitors parted company with Lloyd George's reading of the film, using it to highlight the barbarity and pointlessness of war. A screening supported by the Red Cross in the Hague, for instance, was intercut by slides drawing attention to the number of casualties and the activities of the anti-war league.[29] Beyond the boundaries of Reeves' study, other examples demonstrate the complex and variable relations of film production, exhibition and reception. Sometimes an explanation for the reception of films might, as Reeves assumes, be linked to a public political context. The screening of *Ireland, a Nation* (1914)—a film given clearance by the press censor—in Dublin in 1918 was cut short to two days when audiences sang 'rebel' songs and cheered the on-screen killing of British soldiers.[30] But sometimes no public political explanation is apparent or even relevant, as with a preview screening of Orson Welles' *The Magnificent Ambersons* (1942) in Pomona, California, in which the audience laughed in the 'wrong places', talked back at the screen and expressed their disdain for its 'artiness' in their preview card comments.[31]

A place for wonder?

Propaganda, as Terence Qualter has emphasised, 'must be seen, remembered, understood, and acted upon'.[32] Yet scholars routinely bypass the study of historical audiences, settling instead for implied or hypothetical viewers who are characterised variously as 'hypnotised', 'deceived', 'credulous', 'undemanding' and 'transfixed'. As Tom Gunning has provocatively argued:

> Contemporary film theorists have made careers out of underestimating the basic intelligence and reality-testing abilities of the average film viewer and have no trouble treating previous audiences with similar disdain.[33]

Gunning has played a leading role in arguing for the recognition of many different and even competing viewing positions in the era of early cinema, which he labels the 'cinema of attractions'. The mode of exhibition of many early films undermined a naïve experience of realism and fostered instead a conscious appreciation of them as illusions. The opening of many films with frozen images, for example, militated against the reading of the images as reality and encouraged instead an appreciation of the novelty of projected motion. This form of reading is at work in a description by George Méliès, who went on himself to demonstrate mastery of cinematic effects in works like *Joan of Arc* (1899):

> A still photograph showing the place Bellecour in Lyon was projected. A little surprised. I just had time to say to my neighbour: 'They got us all stirred up for projections like this? I've been doing them for over ten years'. I had hardly finished speaking when a horse pulling a wagon began to walk towards us, followed by other vehicles and then pedestrians, in short all the animation of the street. Before this spectacle we sat with gaping mouths, struck with amazement, astonished beyond all expression.[34]

The withholding of moving images heightened suspense and fostered an appreciation of the technological novelty of the *cinématographe*. Reports from early North American screenings highlight another important theatrical feature: lectures that connected and stressed the novelty and amazing properties of the images about to be revealed. These lectures, like the frozen images, served to build viewer expectations about the thrills to come. Furthermore, the juxtaposition of moving images with live action undercut the possibility of becoming absorbed in the illusion.[35]

Michele Pierson has noted how lecturers in nineteenth-century public science and phantasmagoria displays also utilised a combination of conjuring techniques and explanatory narratives to elicit surprise, curiosity and an appreciation of illusions. But she also notes that few exhibitors and viewers relied on what was presented in theatres alone. Rather, supporting print publications were expected to play an important part in the cultivation of human inquiry and reflection. In periodicals like *Scientific American* (1845–) there emerged communicative practices that not only demanded but also rewarded the attention of the 'connoisseur'. Unlike amateurism, which connoted the use of technical literature to produce home-grown displays, 'connoisseurship' was a form of technical know-how that would contribute to the aesthetic appreciation of public displays. People thus read about special effects in *Scientific American* not to make them but to enhance their understanding and aesthetic enjoyment of them. Connoisseurship was the vehicle for wonder, the 'taking of delight in having one's expectations met'.[36]

Science periodicals were a source for wonder, but there is reason to believe that it was also fostered in performative spaces and performances themselves. The London Polytechnic, as Helen Groth has pointed out, was a heterogeneous space in which those who paid the entry fee gained access to hands-on experiments and gadgetry, an illuminated 'cosmorama' (a form of panorama),[37] a library containing periodicals and newspapers, and a program of twice-daily lectures and pantomimes. Audiences could consult technical literature before and after performances. But, she further argues, performances themselves could elicit wonder without the external buttress of technical literature. They did so through literary allusions. The example Groth cites is that of Dr John Pepper and Henry Dirck's 'A Strange Lecture' (1862), a phantasmagorical stage adaptation of Charles Dickens' *The Haunted Man*. The centrepiece of Pepper and Dirck's show was an optical illusion that used magic lantern light, mirrors, glass sheets and a concealed stage to make an intangible ghostly figure appear and 'touch' an actor on stage. Both Pepper and Dircks appreciated the visual literacy of their audience, and perhaps also that they were jaded by the contemporary abundance of visual spectacles and optical illusions. Additionally, Pepper and Dircks knew that the selection of Dickens' tale would resonate with the audience, given contemporary reports of audiences mouthing the words in time at public readings by or of Dickens. The embedding of the illusion within a web of readings and live action depictions of Dickens was an incisive move, for it brought a novel twist to the story and to the performance, and coherence and intellectual legitimation to the latter. In the combination of the two lay the seeds of wonder, which Groth defines not as the meeting of expectations but as 'a differential tension between the known and the unknown, the ordinary and the extraordinary . . . [being] surprised into a new understanding of the familiar'.[38]

In their studies of pre- and early cinema performances, Gunning, Pierson and Groth highlight the knowingness of audiences. This finding is important to us for three reasons. First, while they acknowledge that practices of appreciation and connoisseurship could be consumerist and politically conservative, they suggest that wonder—the aesthetic, critical appreciation of different ways of seeing, knowing and remembering—also had a part to play in nineteenth-century visual culture. Wonder, Pierson argues, could foster demanding and utopian thought.[39] The consideration of wonder highlights the reductiveness of Benjamin's characterisation of the dream of the nineteenth-century as the domination of capital and leads us to question the adequacy of his and other theorists' portrayals of film as simply affirming bourgeois consumer culture. Second, Gunning, Pierson and Groth connect the reflexive responses of connoisseur audiences with special effects. This challenges the claims of Thomas Doherty, J. Robert Craig and Sean Cubitt— first aired in Chapter 5—that special effects are a powerful means of indoctrinating naïve or even knowing audiences into accepting the views of demagogues or the role of passive consumers. Third, Groth shows us that intertextuality is not simply a medium of social regulation, and that in the bringing together of written texts and images (even for commercial reasons) the aesthetic desire for new forms of expression may arise.

Buoyed by this broader view of nineteenth-century visual culture, we might reasonably ask whether there was and is a place for wonder in twentieth- and twenty-first-century responses to historical films. Drawing on Gunning, we might answer with a qualified yes, for he sees awareness of the act of looking as in tension with narrative and diegetic realism and cohesion. However, I believe that a range of non-filmic elements in screening spaces provided more opportunities for audience participation and even rebellion than Gunning credits. We have noted that early cinema included lectures, and that tradition has continued, albeit in modified form, in various times and places. The premiere of Akira Kurosawa's *Rashomon* (1950) in Japan, for example, included a *benshi* or lecturer-commentator. *Benshi* were first employed in Japanese film screenings during the time of silent film production, where they offered cultural explanations for phenomena in foreign films, narration to connect discontinuous images and dialogue in different voices.[40] *Benshi* are used infrequently at live screenings now, but they have been replaced in Japan and elsewhere with the director's commentaries that are now a reasonably standard feature on DVDs. Live directors' commentaries are also sometimes offered at premieres or 'art cinema' screenings of historical films.

Music has also functioned to foster the conscious appreciation of films as illusions. Before the introduction of talking pictures in the 1930s, music was a staple at screenings. This was because it allowed exhibitors to both mask the obtrusive sounds of projection technologies and to offer what seemed to be a 'natural' or even 'realistic' aural accompaniment to screen images. Some exhibitors initially opted for mechanical musical technologies like player pianos, which could be controlled from the projection booth. While clearly cheaper and less prone to fingering errors than live performers, incidents where projection and musical technologies landed out of sync could mean the delivery of ragtime or 'chase' tunes during close-up love scenes. To stem the flow of complaints and unintended laughter, most exhibitors eventually replaced player pianos with pianists and organists.[41] Projection technologies were also liable to malfunction, with film strips jamming, drifting after sprocket hole damage, slowing down or speeding up and even catching fire. And projection technologies might also be put to aberrant extra-filmic uses, as with the handwritten 'Please pass your coffee cups to the centre aisle' plastic overlay that always seemed to appear at diegetically inappropriate moments (such as the death of a character) in screenings that I attended in a Hobart cinema in the late 1980s.

No film screening is ever likely to be identical to the next. To revisit a point made earlier in this chapter, film watching was—as it continues to be for most people—a social occasion characterised by negotiated receipt. Film viewers have read inter- and subtitles aloud for illiterate companions, talked back at the screen (as with the three Holocaust survivors I sat behind at a screening of *The Last Days* (1998)), displayed courtship rituals, joined in the songs, danced, fallen asleep, thrown food and sent mobile phone text messages. These various activities demonstrate that neither images nor screening spaces can automatically deliver control over the attention of viewers.[42] But is this wonder, or simply capitalism delivering the impression that we have opportunities for interaction and expression? In agreement with Pierson, I do not believe that consumerism exhausts the social and cultural significance of contemporary film. In Pierson's view, the aesthetic response of wonder has not become an undercurrent—as Gunning argues—but is to be found in new channels such as repeat viewings and DVD special features.[43] As we establish in more depth in the next chapter, the special features that accompany most DVDs are not just marketing tools but discourses that may allow for more informed, reflexive and aesthetically attentive forms of viewing than cinema attendance. For the moment, though, I would like to explore another communication space that has opened up: the Internet.

Since the earliest days of film production, viewers have communicated their grievances about various aspects of film productions. Philip Rosen has named this activity 'Everett's game' in honour of the author of a 1938 letter to Warner Bros about a confusion in *The Life of Emile Zola* (1937): 'If I am wrong I should much like to know it, but I am still convinced that those were lobsters and not craw-fish [*langoustes*] as advertised by the fish wife'.[44] Many more communications of this sort are available for perusal via Movie Mistakes (www.moviemistakes.com), ranging from the observation of a viewer who spotted a gas cylinder in the back of one of the chariots in *Gladiator* (2000) to this comment on the manner of restraining dogs in the opening scene of *Titanic* (1997):

> A small one and probably only noticed by dog trainers like me. When the dogs are being brought on board, they are on leather leashes made by J&J Dog Supplies, invented in the 1970s. It is the type of leash preferred by professional trainers, who probably supplied the dogs for the movie, and is distinguished by the 'braid' near the snap, rather than by a sewn or riveted section. J&J's website is www.jandjdog.com. You can see the leashes there.[45]

Rosen reads communications like this as moves in a game built on a basic rule: 'that every detail of the film must be gotten "right" or else [the viewer] can assert a victory, consisting in a claim of knowledge of the detail superior to that of the film'. Moreover, he sees the game as being prompted by the claims to knowledge and accuracy in details that have been promoted by the North American makers of historical films since the 1910s.[46] We recall from the examples set out in Chapter 5 that claims to verisimilitude in detail are indeed a feature of publicity materials for historical films. However, Rosen's explanation for the activities of those who post to forums like Movie Mistakes requires revision and expansion.

At first sight, there does appear to be a relationship between the degree of emphasis placed on verisimilitude of historical details and viewer point scoring: in Movie Mistakes, for instance, *Titanic* is connected with 172 mistakes, nearly the highest total on the site, whereas *Dogville* (2003) has attracted only seven postings by a single viewer. Even more popular with viewers though, are science fiction films like *Star Wars* (1977) and *The Matrix* (1999), which have a higher count of mistakes and which occupy five of the top ten spots in the 'most popular' browser's poll. Playing 'the game' is thus not a simple reaction to publicity rhetoric, for science fiction films are more often promoted on the basis of their special effects than on verisimilitude. Combine that point with the fact that James Cameron has a strong track record in science fiction film production and made generous use of the same effects technologies in *Titanic* and it is then worth asking whether special effects and not historical details are the focal point for critical observation. If so, this would further undermine Doherty, Craig and Cubitt's assumptions about the social function and impact of special effects. Further complicating any account of 'Everett's game' we might construct is the observation that most of the errors identified in Movie Mistakes are not factual. This was evidently recognised by the introduction of seven new categories to the site in 2003: 'factual errors', 'continuity errors', 'visible crew or equipment', 'plot holes', 'revealing mistakes', 'audio problems' and 'deliberate "mistakes"'. A great many of the 'mistakes' in Movie Mistakes are continuity errors, including those for *Titanic*, suggesting perhaps that repeat viewings can undermine the impression of diegetic coherence.

It is the categories of 'visible crew or equipment', 'plot holes' and 'deliberate "mistakes"', though, that are significant for our purposes, because they include expressions of wonder, as Pierson and Groth would define it. Consider these two examples, the first concerning a scene in the VHS version of *Raiders of the Lost Ark* (1981) and the second *Saving Private Ryan* (1998):

> While Indy and Marion are in the Well of Souls, and they encounter the snakes, Indy falls to the ground only to get confronted by a cobra rearing its head and hissing. Look carefully and you'll see the reflection of the snake on the safety glass between it and Indy. Briefly you can also see the torch's reflection while he's waving it around.
>
> In the scene where the medic gets shot, watch the shot where Upham brings the bags up to the injured medic. The next shot there is some fog which then reveals the injured medic. In this shot, watch carefully as

the cast rips away the medic's shirt. If you look near the neck, you can see the fake stomach vest he is wearing for a split second—when the actor realises he ripped too far up, he quickly covers it back up.[47]

In both cases, the message posters take the role of special effects connoisseurs, inviting viewers to take another look—'Look carefully' and 'If you look'—and to adopt a stance of reflexive seeing rather than illusionistic absorption. They differ from Everett's letter, then, in that their composers have adopted for a moment the mantle of lecturer, preparing others for the viewing of a scene. These lecturers may talk the effects down, rather than up, but they may still elicit suspense, surprise and appreciation among those who do go and look. This point is borne out by the category of 'deliberate mistakes' and other posted comments, like that of a viewer who declared the disguise of Soviet T-34 as US tiger tanks in *Saving Private Ryan* to be excellent. We cannot therefore explain away Movie Mistakes as picky point scoring about historical details. The examples I have included are more suggestive of viewers who are critically aware of how film art is and might be done.

Movie Mistakes is hardly representative of Internet users' receptions of historical films. Nor is it free from consumerist discourses: postings vie for attention with advertisements, and the aggregation of diverse mistakes into one site is perhaps akin to the display of items in the shopping arcades described by Benjamin in his account of the 1851 Crystal Palace exhibition in London. But within those structures, I have suggested, there is still space for browsers to explore the act of seeing and to engage in aesthetic appreciation. Perhaps, therefore, the focus of 'Everett's game' lies not with studios and their publicity departments but with viewer agents who use spaces like websites to express their views and invite other viewers to see as they do.

Images and words

It is often assumed by historiographers that professional historians differ from other people in their recognition of the mediated nature of history. And within the profession, some practitioners have further recognised the intertwining of history and ideology. Keith Jenkins, for instance, has argued that 'in the end, history is theory and theory is ideological and ideology just is material interests. Ideology seeps into every nook and cranny of history'.[48]

History is thus a form of politics, because there is no unmediated access to a past that can be used to judge between various accounts of it. Yet, Jenkins further claims, the ostensible 'transparency' of empirical histories encourages historians and history readers to believe that access to reality is possible. In so doing, it masks the bourgeois values that give it shape and projects on to writers and readers ways of thinking and selfhood that they think are the hallmark of autonomy but which really serve to enslave them in a commodity culture as passive consumers. Emancipation, Jenkins believes, lies with the end of 'History' as we know it and the creation of 'histories' that challenge cherished notions of realism by eschewing 'reality effects' like footnotes, talk of historical agents' intentions and third person address.[49]

As with many other 'postmodernist' theories of history, Jenkins' view springs from many of the same sources that have shaped the film theories described in this chapter. And like those, Jenkins' vision of society rests upon two problematic assumptions: 'Historians' and 'History' readers as the consumers of bourgeois ideology; and the collapse of ideology into material interests. As I hope this chapter has demonstrated, historical research demonstrates the inadequacies of monolithic theories of history reception. Individuals and society may encourage a view of the world, but that does not guarantee its acceptance. Furthermore, there might be more to that view of the world than material interests. We have begun to search for aesthetic expressions of wonder as well as activities of consumption in historical film watching. It is worth asking what opportunities for wonder there are for the readers of histories too.

Recommended resources

Allen, R., *Projecting Illusion: Film Spectatorship and the Impression of Reality*, Cambridge: Cambridge University Press, 1995.

Baudry, J.-L., 'Ideological effects of the basic cinematographic apparatus' and 'The apparatus: metapsychological approaches to the impression of reality in cinema', in P. Rosen (ed.), *Narrative, Apparatus, Ideology*, New York: Columbia University Press, 1986, pp. 286–318.

Dayan, D., 'The tutor-code of classical cinema', in B. Nichols (ed.), *Movies and Methods*, Berkeley: University of California Press, 1976, pp. 438–50.

DeCordova, R., *Picture Personalities: The Emergence of the Star System in American Film*, Urbana: University of Illinois Press, 1990.

Giroux, H.A., 'Memory and pedagogy in the "Wonderful World of Disney": beyond the politics of innocence', in E. Bell, L. Haas and L. Sells (eds), *From Mouse to Mermaid: The Politics of Film, Gender and Culture*, Bloomington: University of Indiana Press, 1995, pp. 43–61.

Gunning, T., 'An aesthetic of astonishment: early film and the (in)credulous spectator', in L. Williams (ed.), *Viewing Positions: Ways of Seeing Film*, 1995, pp. 114–33.

Heath, S., 'Narrative space', in *Questions of Cinema*, Bloomington: University of Indiana Press, 1981, pp. 19–75.

Jenkins, K., *Re-thinking History*, London: Routledge, 1992.

Jenkins, K., *Refiguring History*, London: Routledge, 2003.

Metz, C., *The Imaginary Signifier*, Bloomington: University of Indiana Press, 1982.

Oudart, J.-P., 'Cinema and suture', trans. K. Hanet, *Cahiers du Cinéma 1969–1972: The Politics of Representation*, ed. N. Browne, Cambridge, Mass: Harvard University Press, 1990, pp. 35–47.

Pierson, M., *Special Effects: Still in Search of Wonder*, New York: Columbia University Press, 2002.

Reeves, N., *The Power of Film Propaganda: Myth or Reality?*, New York: Cassell, 1999.

Taylor, R., *Film Propaganda: Soviet Russia and Nazi Germany*, London: I.B. Tauris, 1998.

Welch, D., *Propaganda and the German Cinema, 1933–1945*, London: I.B. Tauris, 2001.

Wells, P., 'I wanna be like you-oo-oo': Disnified politics and identity from *Mermaid* to *Mulan*' in P.J. Davies and P. Wells (eds), *American Film and Politics from Reagan to Bush Jr*, Manchester: Manchester University Press, 2002, pp. 139–54.

Notes

1 A. Salkeld, *Leni Riefenstahl: A Portrait*, London: Pimlico, 1997, pp. vii–viii.

2 J. Godmilow with A.-L. Shapiro, 'How real is the reality in documentary film?', *History and Theory*, 1997, vol. 36(4), p. 97.

3 *The Wonderful, Horrible Life of Leni Riefenstahl* (1997), directed by Ray Muller; and L. Riefenstahl, *A Memoir*, p. 209.

4 S. Eisenstein, *Beyond the Stars: The Memoirs of Sergei Eisenstein*, London: BFI, 1995, p. 45.

5 S. Eisenstein, *Film Form*, London: Dobson, 1951, pp. 39, 63; and S. Eisenstein, *The Film Sense*, London: Faber and Faber, 1943, p. 17.

6 S. Eisenstein, *Film Form*, p. 16.

7 N. Reeves, *The Power of Film Propaganda*, London: Cassell, 1999. For communication theories, see, for example, G.S. Jowett and V. O'Donnell, *Propaganda and Persuasion*, London: Sage, 3rd edn, 1999, p. 7; J.M. Sproule, *Channels of Propaganda*, Bloomington, Ind.: Edinfo, 1994, p. 8; and J. Ellul, *Propaganda: The Formation of Men's Attitudes*, New York: Knopf, 1965, p. xv.

8 H. Giroux, 'Memory and pedagogy in the "Wonderful World of Disney": beyond the politics of innocence', in E. Bell, L. Haas and L. Sells (eds), *From Mouse to Mermaid: The Politics of Film, Gender and Culture*, Bloomington: University of Indiana Press, 1995, p. 47.

9 *Ibid.*, p. 51. On 'Tonto', see T. Morrison, *Playing in the Dark: Whiteness and the Literary Imagination*, Cambridge, Mass.: Harvard University Press, 1992, p. 82.

10 J. Cochran, 'What becomes a legend most?', *Entertainment Weekly*, 16 June 1995, p. 42.

11 G. Edgerton and K.M. Jackson, 'Redesigning Pocahontas: Disney, the "White man's Indian", and the marketing of dreams', *Journal of Popular Film and Television*, 1996, vol. 24(2), pp. 90–100.

12 Lyrics to the songs in *Anastasia* are available online at http://www.foxhome.com/anastasia

13 See, for example, D. Czitrom, *Media and the American Mind: From Morse to McLuhan*, Chapel Hill: University of North Carolina Press, 1990, pp. 114–19; and K.H. Fuller, 'Boundaries of participation: the problem of spectatorship and American film audiences, 1905–1930', *Film and History*, 1990, vol. 20(4), pp. 76–7.

14 J.-L. Baudry, 'Ideological effects of the basic cinematographic apparatus' and 'The apparatus: metapsychological approaches to the impression of reality', in P. Rosen (ed.), *Narrative, Apparatus, Ideology*, New York: Columbia University Press, 1986, pp. 286–98, 299–318; C. Metz, *The Imaginary Signifier*, Bloomington: University of Indiana Press, 1982; J.-P. Oudart, 'Cinema and suture', trans. K. Hanet, in N. Browne (ed.), *Cahiers du Cinéma 1969–1972: The Politics of Representation*, Cambridge, Mass.: Harvard University Press, 1990, pp. 45–57; D. Dayan, 'The tutor-code of classical cinema', in B. Nichols (ed.), *Movies and Methods*, Berkeley: University of California Press, 1976, pp. 438–50; and S. Heath, 'Narrative space', in *Questions of Cinema*, Bloomington: University of Indiana Press, 1981, pp. 19–75.

15 J. Lacan, 'The mirror stage as formative of the function of the I', in *Ecrits*, trans. A. Sheridan, New York: Tavistock, 1977, pp. 1–7.

16 A number of critics have taken issue with the theorisation of film viewers as male or masculine. See, for example, T. de Laurentis, 'Through the looking glass', in P. Rosen (ed.), *Narrative, Apparatus, Ideology*, New York: Columbia University Press, 1986, pp. 360–72; D. Pribham (ed.), *Female Spectators: Looking at Film and Television*, London: Verso, 1988; F. Jameson, *The Political Unconscious*, Ithaca, NY: Cornell University Press, 1981; and G. Deleuze and F. Guattari, *Anti-Oedipus: Capitalism and Schizophrenia*, Minneapolis: University of Minnesota Press, 1983.

17 L.W. Doob, 'Propaganda', in E. Barnouw, G. Gerbner, W. Schramm, T.L. Worth and L. Gross (eds), *International Encyclopedia of Communications*, New York: Oxford University Press, 1989, vol. 3, p. 375.

18 C. Plantinga, 'Notes on spectator emotion and ideological film criticism', in R. Allen and M. Smith (eds), *Film Theory and Philosophy*, Oxford: Oxford University Press, 1997, p. 377.

19 D. Sipe, '*From the Pole to the Equator*: a vision of a wordless past', in R. Rosenstone (ed.), *Revisioning History: Film and the Construction of a New Past*, Princeton, NJ: Princeton University Press, 1995, pp. 174–87.

20 For an account of these theories, see G.S. Jowett and V. O'Donnell, *Propaganda and Persuasion*, pp. 1–46.

21 P. Wells, '"I want to be like you-oo-oo": Disnified politics and identity from *Mermaid* to *Mulan*', in *American Film and Politics from Reagan to Bush Jr*, Manchester: Manchester University Press, 2002, pp. 144–8.

22 V. Brown, 'On some problems with weak intentionalism for intellectual history', *History and Theory*, 2002, vol. 41(2), p. 199.

23 J. Godmilow, 'How real is the reality in documentary film?', p. 97; and S. Sontag, 'Fascinating fascism', in *Under the Sign of Saturn*, New York: Anchor, 1980, pp. 73–108.

24 J. Derrida, *Of Grammatology*, trans. G. Spivak, Baltimore: Johns Hopkins University Press, 1976, p. 158.

25 R. Barthes, 'The death of the author', *Image, Music, Text*, trans. S. Heath, London: Fontana, 1977, p. 146.

26 M. Bevir, 'How to be an intentionalist', *History and Theory*, 2002, vol. 41(2), pp. 209–17; M. Bevir, *The Logic of the History of Ideas*, Cambridge: Cambridge University Press, 1999, pp. 70–1, 142–71, 265–86; and R.G. Collingwood, 'The principles of history' and 'Inaugural: rough notes', in W.H. Dray and W.J. van der Dussen (eds), *The Principles of History and Other Writings in the Philosophy of History*, Oxford: Oxford University Press, 1999, pp. 48n and 144–6.

27 On the reception of *Battleship Potemkin* and Soviet film styles, see R. Taylor, 'A "cinema for the millions": Soviet socialist realism and the problem of film comedy', *Journal of Contemporary History*, 1983, vol. 18 (2), pp. 439–61.

28 N. Reeves, *The Power of Film Propaganda*, pp. 33–5, quote at p. 33.

29 *Ibid.*, pp. 36–8, quote at p. 37.

30 K. Rockett, 'Emmet on film', *History Ireland*, 2003, vol. 11(3), p. 46.

31 J. Staiger, *Perverse Spectators: The Practices of Film Reception*, New York: New York University Press, 2000, p. 20.

32 T.H. Qualter, *Propaganda and Psychological Warfare*, New York: Random House, 1962, p. xii.

33 T. Gunning, 'An aesthetic of astonishment: early film and the (in)credulous spectator', in L. Williams (ed), *Viewing Positions: Ways of Seeing Film*, New Brunswick, NJ: Rutgers University Press, 1996, p. 115.

34 George Méliès, as quoted in *ibid.*, pp. 118–19.

35 *Ibid.*, p. 120; and S. Kracauer, 'The cult of distraction', *New German Critique*, 1987, no. 40, p. 96.

36 M. Pierson, *Special Effects: Still in Search of Wonder*, New York: Columbia University Press, 2002, pp. 19, 22, 33, 41, 46.

37 On the different forms of panorama, see S. Oetterman, *The Panorama: History of a Mass Medium*, Boston: Zone Books, 1997, ch. 2.

38 H. Groth, 'Wonder, memory and nineteenth century phantasmagoria', paper presented at Embodied Memory, Action, History: An Interdisciplinary Conference, Macquarie University, Sydney, 2 December 2004. See also Groth's exploration of the interplay of literary allusion and photography in *Victorian Photography and Literary Nostalgia*, Oxford: Oxford University Press, 2003.

39 M. Pierson, *Special Effects*, p. 9.

40 J.A. Dym, *Benshi, Japanese Silent Film Narrators, and their Forgotten Art of Setsumei: A History of Japanese Silent Film*, Lewiston, NY: Edwin Mellen, 2003.

41 K.H. Fuller, 'Boundaries of participation: the problem of spectatorship and American film audiences, 1905–1930', *Film and History*, 1990, vol. 20(4), pp. 77–8.

42 See, for example, Annette Kuhn on cinema courtship rituals: A. Kuhn, 'This loving darkness', in *Dreaming of Fred and Ginger: Cinema and Cultural Memory*, New York: New York University Press, 2002, pp. 138–67. On social interaction among Indian film viewers, see L. Srinivas, 'The active audience: spectatorship, social relations and the experience of cinema in India', *Media, Culture and Society*, 2002, vol. 24(2), pp. 155–74.

43 T. Gunning, 'An aesthetic of astonishment', pp. 121, 123; and M. Pierson, *Special Effects*, pp. 164–6.

44 P. Rosen, *Change Mummified: Cinema, Historicity, Theory*, Minneapolis: University of Minnesota Press, 2001, p. 156.

45 Mistake 54/172 for *Titanic*, www.moviemistakes.com

46 P. Rosen, *Change Mummified*, pp. 156–8.

47 Mistake 19/30 in Most Popular Mistakes and mistake 5/78 for *Saving Private Ryan*, www.moviemistakes.com

48 K. Jenkins, *Re-thinking History*, London: Routledge, 1992, p. 19.

49 *Ibid.*, and see also K. Jenkins, *Refiguring History*, London: Routledge, 2003.

8　Selling history

Relive the opening scene just as you remember it.
　　　　　Advertisement for 'The Official *Titanic* Porcelain Portrait Doll',
　　　　　　　　　　　　　　　　　　　http://www.franklinmint.com

Jack Lives! I refuse to believe otherwise.
　　　　Jack Lives Fan Fiction, http://www.sparkling-horizon.net/odyssey/
　　　　　　　　　　　　　　　　　　　　　　　　jacklives.html

Historical films commonly invite criticism. In Chapter 1, I traced that criticism to the assumption that films cannot deliver information about the past as effectively as written text. Filmmakers take liberties: they leave out details, avoid competing explanations of the same phenomenon, telescope events and offer a pastiche of the past and present. They do so, a number of theorists further assume, in the service of capitalist ideology. While I have questioned the hierarchical arrangement of written and visual histories and the portrayal of viewers as passive, it remains for us to explore the extent to which capitalist ideology shapes practices of historical film production, promotion and reception.

If we were to think of the prime reason why visual histories differ from written ones, Frank Sanelo argues, then we should look no further than one word: money. He explains:

> Never . . . let historical truth get in the way of a good, two-hour blockbuster that earns $200 million domestic. . . . Commercial imperatives most often fuel cinematic rewrites of history. Complex economic and social issues are puréed into easily digestible bits of information intended for consumption by Hollywood's most sought-after demographic: the lowest common denominator.[1]

But not all historical films are like this, just those produced in Hollywood. This is a relatively common assumption, one undercut by Justin Wyatt's account of varying marketing practices in Hollywood. It is with Wyatt's account of 'high-concept' Hollywood films that we begin our analysis of the relationship between the producers, promoters and viewers of historical films, an analysis that takes us via the concepts of 'patina' and nostalgia' to the twofold conclusion that neither the makers nor the audiences of historical films singlehandedly shape their meaning and that historical film studies require the combined consideration of material, commercial and cultural practices.

High concept and patina

High-concept films, which Justin Wyatt sees as constituting a significant portion of US film production, are 'narrated as much by their marketing as by their ostensible story'.[2] High-concept films combine three elements: pre-sold premises, music and advertising aesthetics. Looking at a range of US historical films that have performed well at box offices around the world, it is not hard to see what Wyatt means. As I noted in Chapter 2, advertising and marketing research campaigns for a number of historical films tap into previous successes through the citation of novels, stage shows and a producer's, director's or musical director's other projects. Thus, for example, *The Shipping News* (2001) is billed as 'Based on the Pulitzer Prize winning novel by E. Annie Proulx' and 'From the Director of *Chocolat* and *The Cider House Rules*'. The most commonly cited 'pre-sold premise' in film market research and advertising post-1910 is the 'star'. Stars—actors who embody desired values and identities—sell movies, as the vice president of Paramount makes clear in his description of concept testing for *Titanic*:

> In our original concept testing—when we read the concept of the movie over the phone and who was in it—we mentioned Leonardo DiCaprio, and there was a lot of interest in him among girls. . . . When we tested the first trailers, the young girls were the highest quadrant in their interest in seeing the film. And when we screened, the girls were one of the highest-testing groups who enjoyed the movie.[3]

This strategy appeared to work, for the high rate of repeat viewings by young girls was mostly credited to DiCaprio.

Music is also an important marketing and merchandising element. In the silent era, live performers and song slides were promoted as special features in films, and sheet music, lyric booklets and pianola rolls were offered for sale.[4] With the arrival of recorded music consumer technologies, new marketing opportunities were sought through the production of soundtrack albums and theme song singles. Given the role of music as a cross-promotional vehicle, airplay has often been as much desired as sales. Film companies tend to secure saturation airplay by commissioning several recordings of a song, even if they are not all available for purchase. So, for example, while Celine Dion's recording of 'My Heart Will Go On', the 'theme song' for *Titanic*, was played largely in chart programs, additional performances were achieved in adult contemporary and dance formats through cover versions recorded by Kenny G and Déjà Vu, the first of which was not available for individual purchase. Staggered releases of difference mixes can also maintain airplay, as was the case with a re-release of the Dion version intercut with audio from the film. Timing is also considered important, with film companies tending to favour the release of singles, video clips and soundtracks about a month before a film's release to foster circulation of its title through radio and retail outlets. Similarly, new or remixed music can be used to signal the imminent release of a film in video or DVD format: the release of *Titanic* in VHS format, for example, was preceded by that of a soundtrack sequel, *Return to Titanic* (1998; Figure 8.1).

High-concept films are in Wyatt's view also characterised by a particular aesthetic, one commensurate with contemporary consumer goods advertising. As with corporate communications campaigns, for example, film-advertising campaigns are characterised by the economical use of graphics and text. So, for example, an 'X' on a baseball hat advertises *Malcolm X* (1992), a neon 'C' announces *Chicago* (2002) and a pair of hands on a keyboard and an illuminated star of David armband signal the diegesis of *Le Pianiste* (*The Pianist*, 2002). Film advertising is also structured by a preference for text and images that are concise and transferable to other media, including merchandise. Clean, relatively simple images are needed, for example to communicate in the

Figure 8.1 Going back to *Titanic* with Sony Classical's soundtrack sequel (© 2000, Sony Classical BMG)

low-density format of print newspapers. Importantly, Wyatt sees the aesthetics of consumer advertising also infusing film production design. High-concept films, he argues, are characterised by 'perfect images': 'a set of production techniques composed of extreme back-lighting, a minimal (often almost black-and-white) colour scheme, a pre-dominance of reflected images, and a tendency toward settings of high technology and industrial design'.[5] It should therefore be of little surprise to us to learn that many high-concept film directors like Ridley Scott started their careers making television commercials.

The images of historical films, Julian Stringer, Mark Carnes and Robert Rosenstone contend, are 'perfect', but in a different sense to Wyatt's definition.[6] Opportunities to showcase high-tech industrial design within historical diegeses are obviously limited, so 'perfection' is conveyed instead through a combination of digital design and material 'patina'. Patina denotes the value placed on material objects that show evidence both of age and of being maintained with care, because as Grant McCracken puts it, 'patina serves as a kind of visual proof of status. . . . The greater the patina on certain objects, the longer the owner has enjoyed certain status'.[7] Historical films play upon this perception and fetishise objects to such an extent that their narratives are mediated through objects. Opening up the patina system to mass consumption through the production of tie-in merchandise allows viewers the chance to buy into desired elements of a film. On a basic level, the materiality of historical films is obvious: movie prints and cells, posters and booklets have long been collected, exchanged and sold. But production and distribution companies and 'promotional partners' have also used merchandise—both free and for sale—to raise and maintain awareness of historical films. Film merchandise is commonly connected with children's films, like Disney's campaign to sell *Pocahontas* (1995) with colouring-in books, Burger King meal toys, moccasins and Barbie-like dolls and Fox's agreements with Burger King, Hershey, Chesebrough-Ponds and Shell to promote *Anastasia* (1997). T.L. Stanley's report for *Brandweek* on the Shell–Fox deal to promote *Anastasia* provides us with a clear example of the economic significance of tie-in deals for promotional partners, even with young audiences:

> The gas-station category has been through several rounds of aggressive advertising and promotion of late, with chains spiffing up their stations and looking for more and better ways to reach people with messages that stress convenience, savings and speed. The competition is fierce because consumers have so many choices. Often, a buying decision, based on a child's influence, comes down to how nifty the mini-mart is, or what the giveaway is. . . . To reach the 4–11 year old demographic, Shell execs decided to offer a premium with purchase, a $2.99 travel game with five Anastasia-themed figurines. More than two million of the premiums were ordered, and as an early indicator of acceptance around the property, stations reported selling through cases of them before the movie even premiered.[8]

Film-inspired products are not just for children. Viewers of *Titanic*, for instance, had the opportunity to purchase replicas of Rose's 'Heart of the Ocean' necklace and a Rose doll from Franklin Mint (Figure 8.2). Merchandising is even available for R-rated features, with viewers of *Rambo First Blood Part II* (1985) able to buy an action doll. Historical films aimed at adult audiences, though, more commonly promote ancillary tie-ins. In 1953, for example, MGM encouraged cinema operators to sell scarves with the tag 'Make a wish when you wear one of these attractive scarfs [*sic*], and you, too, like Ava Gardner, might find a "Dream Knight" '. Images from *The Great Gatsby* (1974) were used in advertisements for Ballantine's scotch, Glenby hairstyling studios, Robert Bruce's men's sportswear and DuPont cookware. Bloomingdale's was the 'alpha point' for a *Moulin Rouge* (2001) campaign, selling 'inspired-by-Moulin' evening gowns and accessories and Christian Dior 'Satine' lipstick. Beauticians were even trained to do 'Moulin Rouge makeovers' at counters designed 'to "feel" like "Moulin Rouge", with red velvet chairs and themed tester-stands'.[9] Similarly, advertisements intercut with footage from *Chicago* promoted Max Factor's 'Lipfinity' lipstick, a company that five years earlier offered consumers six *Titanic*-inspired lipstick shades and the chance to exchange proof of purchase for a copy of the book

Figure 8.2 Franklin Mint's Rose doll (© 2000, Franklin Mint)

James Cameron's Titanic (Figure 8.3). Indeed, Max Factor's origins as a producer of stage and film make-up has meant that it has long had both formal and informal opportunities for promotion.

Other important elements of the marketing-driven aesthetics of historical films are image production and exhibition technologies. In the mid-1950s, film studios sought to differentiate their products from television by conjoining the wide-angle sets of 'swords and sandals' films set in the ancient world with widescreen technologies like Cinerama, CinemaScope and VistaVision. Even after the passing of those technologies, the association of the ancient world with wide-angle shots remains, as *Gladiator* (2000), *Troy* (2004) and *Alexander* (2004) attest. Today, the visual locus of film marketing is thought to be CGI, and again films set in the ancient world have been used to showcase its capabilities. Features set in the modern world, by contrast, are more likely to rely upon a combination of digital technologies and patina.

Selling what?

It would be naïve to deny that historical film production and exhibition are shaped at least in part by marketing principles and goals. However, we are unable to conclude that historical films are commercial products without an assessment of how and why they are so. Historical films may sell, but what do they sell, and how are they received? Are they simply products that are bought and consumed, like a pair of jeans or a chocolate bar? As was outlined in

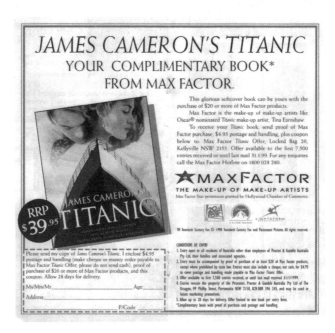

Figure 8.3 Max Factor's *Titanic* tie-in (© 2000, Max Factor Cosmetics)

Chapter 5, a number of commentators portray digital technologies as vehicles for the advancement of late capitalist, consumerist ideologies. As we shall see in this section, conventional treatments of film promotion and exhibition advance a similar conclusion. In response to these claims, I want to re-articulate the chief argument of the previous chapter, that the nature and impact of historical films cannot be summarised so simply.

In Wyatt's view, we recall, high-concept films are organised by an aesthetic akin to that used in consumer advertising. And like advertisements, he further argues, many films 'manipulate the consumer' into buying not just a product but also a lifestyle—often wrapped up with a 'star'—into which the product permits entry.[10] While Wyatt does not see the lifestyles promised by films as necessarily utopian, other commentators disagree. Vivian Sobchack for one sees the combination of stars, digital images and object fetishisation in *Titanic* as supplying viewers with a 'prosthetic' experience such as loss, an 'authentic emotion' from an 'age of innocence' never personally suffered and untainted by contemporary irony. Similarly, Alexandra Keller sees *Titanic* as exemplifying the formula 'obsessive detail + grand emotion = ideological stupefication'. She explains:

> *Titanic*'s narrative and visual coding are weighted down with an apparently never-ending succession of accurate details, and this has the paradoxical effect of buoying up spectators, allowing them to float with ease through an experience without any attendant historical anxiety. When this lack of anxiety is enhanced by emotional catharsis on an epic scale, it is particularly easy to sway an audience to a particular ideological position, since they have no idea that any ideological argument is being made at all.[11]

In both Sobchack's and Keller's estimation, *Titanic* is a 'protective' device that keeps 'real trauma, but not real emotion, at bay' and as such is symptomatic of what Susan Stewart calls 'the social disease of nostalgia':

> A sadness which creates a longing that of necessity is inauthentic because it does not take part in lived experience. . . . Hostile to history . . . and yet longing for an impossibly pure context of lived experience as a place of origin, nostalgia wears a distinctly utopian face, a face that turns towards a future-past, a past which has only ideological reality.[12]

Nostalgia is predicated on a preference for emotional attachment over intellectual abstraction and distance.

Stewart's pejorative appraisal of nostalgia is echoed in other film and cultural studies, most notably those of Frederic Jameson and Christopher Lasch.[13] Jameson reads late capitalist society's preoccupation with a nostalgic past as a desperate attempt to prop up the illusion 'that things still happen, that events still exist, that there are still stories to tell' and that the human subject or self is something other than an ideological, imaginary assemblage that society utilises to elicit subjection.[14] Nostalgia testifies to our inability to make representations of our own current experience.[15] Lasch has a similarly bleak view, portraying nostalgia as the evasion of memory and history. He writes:

> Nostalgia appeals to the feeling that the past offered delights no longer obtainable. Nostalgic representations of the past evoke a time irretrievably lost and for that reason timeless and unchanging. Strictly speaking, nostalgia does not entail the exercise of memory at all, since the past it idealizes stands outside time, frozen in unchanging perfection. Memory too may idealize the past, but not in order to condemn the present. It draws hope and comfort from the past in order to enrich the present and to face what comes with good cheer. It sees past, present, and future as continuous. It is less concerned with loss than with our continuing indebtedness to a past the formative influence of which lives on in our patterns of speech, our gestures, our standards of honour, our expectations, our basic disposition toward the world around us.[16]

Nostalgia, these various commentators assume, is a pathological affective activity that has as its goal the replacement of the present with a desired past.[17]

Chapter 4 gave us philosophical reasons to doubt whether the emotions can be sequestered from historical understanding. Sobchack's and Keller's criticism of *Titanic* on the grounds that it fosters emotional engagement is not sufficient to rule it out as 'history'. As Linda Hutcheon has noted, too, cultural theories of nostalgia are often undercut by their protagonists' own nostalgic inclinations. Is Jameson's call for 'genuine historicity', for instance, a symptom of an inability or even unwillingness to represent the present?[18] The nostalgic inflection of Jameson's work and current studies of nostalgia suggest perhaps that nostalgic practices are not simple and that they are not necessarily problematic. It is possible, for instance, that historical films may elicit different stances towards nostalgia among viewers. Todd Hayne's fusion of potentially nostalgic elements from 1950s melodramas with a hypervisual style in *Far from Heaven* (2002), to take just one example, clearly announces that his work is a re-presentation of other cinematic works.[19] This opens up, as Haynes puts it, 'an ignited, electrified distance' between viewers and films and encourages a combined intellectual and emotional response. This Haynes likens to John Kelly's performance as the singer Joni Mitchell:

> He sounds just like Joni Mitchell, he imitates her stage banter, he's in drag and looks like a ghoulish version of the little pixie Joni Mitchell from the 1960s. You're laughing, but you're laughing at yourself, at your own intensely serious investment in Joni Mitchell when you were in high school. But you're also crying, at the beauty of the music, and for that person in high school who loved those songs and who you feel rekindled.

There's this freedom to go from one emotion to the next, neither one undermining the other. If the real Joni Mitchell was up there, you'd be going, oh god she's older, oh she can't hit that same note—you get caught up in all the discrepancies of the real. There's something about a beautiful surrogate that opens up this wealth of feeling that you wouldn't have with the real thing. And to me, the best kind of cinema is not about the real—it's about a distance that you fill in, participate in with your life experiences, your memories, and your associations.[20]

Similarly, in *Far From Heaven* artificial sets and forms of acting collide with the socio-historical prejudices of sexism, homophobia and racism. These prejudices are no less painful for being represented, but we do not expect that they have been captured 'as they were or are' and thus dealt with by the filmmaker on our behalf. Haynes sees viewers as active partners in the making of meaning. Both his film and the examples he offers, though, are limited because they treat periods of history that he and some of his viewers have experienced. What room is there for reflection on investment in historical films that treat events prior to living memory, or outside a viewer's experiences? What can viewers bring to 'fill in' films of that sort? Will they slip simply into accepting a 'prosthetic experience', and is that a problematic act?

Reception: wonder and collaboration

As was argued in the previous two chapters, not all viewers can be described as passive consumers. Similarly, close study of viewer interactions with the material and ideational elements of 'high-concept' films—merchandise, tie-ins, visual technologies, intertextual references and plotlines—reveals activities of poaching, appropriation and refashioning. As we shall also see, however, any celebration of viewer agency we might be tempted to engage in must be tempered by the acknowledgement of, first, activities of regulation by viewers and, second, commercial appropriation of viewer practices. Historical film viewing affords opportunities for wonder but also grounds for commercial collaboration.

Merchandise and tie-ins

As writers like Sobchack and Jameson suggest, audiences may adopt on-screen and tie-in objects and activities in order to evade the present. However, this claim can be questioned in two ways: first by asking whether viewers simply emulate or adopt what they see and second by asking whether viewer responses to historical films are necessarily escapist. Dealing with the first point, a number of studies of film merchandise and tie-ins encourage us to see viewer behaviour as better characterised by the concept of 'adaptation'. Writing on film fashions and female viewers, for example, Jackie Stacie and J. Craik have argued for the recognition of 'bottom-up' adaptive processes or, put simply, 'selective borrowings'.[21] Annette Kuhn has stressed the same point in her study of 1930s filmgoers. For many of the male informants in her study, film was the raw material for imaginative play: for example, many recalled pretending to be Douglas Fairbanks' character in *The Black Pirate* (1926) with improvised swords. Film also prompted improvisation on the part of female viewers, but their memories were focused on their adolescent experiments with make-up, hair and costume. Few of the women interviewed could afford to emulate what they saw on screen, so they 'made do'. Consequently, magazines like *Film Fashionland* and *Women's Filmfair* tried to capitalise on filmgoers' improvisations of fashions they saw on screen by giving away dress patterns and advertising dresses or paper patterns by order. Even so, copying screen costumes by order or sewing called for more money or sewing prowess than many filmgoers could muster. Women's memories of adaptations therefore focus more on hats, make-up and hairstyling. With make-up or hairstyling, women could opt to purchase products given prominent advertising space in magazines like *Filmfair*, or they could again make do, using household products like bleach, for instance, to achieve the look of a blonde streak or sugar and water to fix curls.[22]

Go forward in time sixty years and viewers are still making do. Viewers of *Titanic*, for instance, can fashion 'inspired by' costumes with the help of a Simplicity paper pattern (Figure 8.4). But the Internet also details many cases of viewers ordering or making outfits and engaging in adaptive practices. At the website '*Titanic* Show and Tell', for example, 'Helen' tells us that 'I am going to take a more lenient attitude towards accessories than to the dresses themselves: the dresses have to be accurate but it's all right for the accessories to be "in the style of" ' and 'Lexi' suggests the use of sari material to make the 'dinner dress' from the film. Making do, as Michel de Certeau has argued, is a form of counter-hegemonic production, an art of using by poaching.[23] Viewers 'make do', but some also engage in the critical, aesthetic appreciation of film costumes. The claims that film costumes make upon viewer attention cannot be understood if we describe them purely in terms of realism or simulation. Some viewers, whom we might call 'connoisseurs', display a detailed knowledge of how costumes are made, the styles of different designers and an appreciation of costumes as an aesthetic effect. The creator of the '*Titanic* on Tour: Costume Photos' website, for instance, offers a detailed, critical pictorial and textual account of fabrics, draping techniques and designer decisions in support of their decision to 'get to work', 'play with' and 'try out' new sewing techniques and *Titanic*-inspired patterns.[24] Similarly, 'Jenny-Rose' justifies her decision to remove the gloves that came with the 'boarding outfit' for her Franklin Mint 'Rose' doll on the grounds that they were 'poorly made. . . . ugly and detract[ed] from the outfit' and asks other browsers of the 'Costume Dolls' site to tell her whether the running stitch used in that outfit is the same as that for the film costume.[25] Whether discussing costumes for dolls or people, contributors to *Titanic*-related sites display knowledge of designers and the sources for their creations (e.g. historical

Figure 8.4 'Making do': *Titanic* costumes courtesy of Simplicity (© 2000, Simplicity)

designs and fabric types) and do not refrain from judgement, even when it is clear that they have an emotional investment in the film.

Sarah Berry has argued that consumer film fashion is potentially subversive because it can encourage fantasies of self-transformation.[26] That may be so, but it is also important to note that film fashion can be drawn into and transformed by viewer uses. Film viewing is therefore not a straightforward act of escapism. '*Titanic* Show and Tell', to take just one example, includes a gallery of photographs of costumes made to wear at home, on cruises, to parties, *Titanic* exhibitions and weddings, and even to meetings with survivors of the accident. So while, for instance, the description of 'Sabine' wearing her 'dinner dress' costume to a *Titanic* exhibition as 'the greatest moment of her life' might be read as her buying into a desired persona or even lifestyle, it is also clear that the 'moment' is meaningful because of the presence of her boyfriend. As with the reminiscences of the 1930s filmgoers detailed in Chapter 4, film is drawn into everyday life and used to articulate and secure memories of experiences with family, friends and lovers.[27]

Poaching words: fan fiction

It is not only the material elements of films that are drawn into the fabric of viewers' lives. Plots can also be used to support fantasies of self-transformation and understandings of past and present relationships and rituals. Fan fiction—stories written by viewers that extend and/or alter the diegeses of films—like fan fashion demonstrates that viewers are not the passive recipients of consumerist ideologies. Words, like fabrics, can be part of 'bottom-up' adaptive processes. Fan fiction can be created for personal use (e.g. a diary entry) or shared with a limited peer group, as with the fantasies played out by the 1930s film viewers interviewed by Kuhn. But fanzines and the Internet websites have also been used by viewer-writers to garnish wider reception and review. FanFiction.net, for instance, is an online archive of around 50,000 stories that extend or rewrite *anime*, books, television programs and films, including historical films, although interestingly not documentaries. Most commonly, fan fiction exists as a platform for exploring underdeveloped and perhaps even unlikely relationships between characters. In the sub-genre of 'slash', for example, writers posit emotional and sexual encounters between characters of the same gender, as with 'Amatia's' suggested relationship between Oskar Schindler and Itzhak Stern from *Schindler's List* in 'Night after Night' and 'The Thickness of the Rain'.[28] Fiction may also posit a relationship between film characters and a 'Mary Sue', a perfect character (who seems to be gendered female) whom moderators of fan fiction sites assume is a stand-in for the author. Sometimes, historical details or setting are incidental to the story, or even changed to accommodate the author's aims. For example, some of the '*Titanic* Continued' stories see Rose breaking off her engagement with Cal and either marrying Jack on the ship or when they reach New York safely.[29] As the moderator of one site makes clear, 'Jack lives! I refuse to believe otherwise'.[30] Evidently, these writers have taken the instruction of promoters like Franklin Mint to relive a film 'just as you remember it' quite literally. 'Gina's' continuation of *Anastasia* with a Thanksgiving dinner also displays scant regard for the historical setting and events that 'inspired' the film.[31] However, it might be argued that these viewer-writers display in their compositions an awareness of the contemporary discourses of romantic love and 'home, heart and family' that shape *Titanic* and *Anastasia*.

It is also not the case that fan fiction is simply a form of communication in which 'anything goes', for contributions to fanzines and Internet archives are open to review. One of the most frequently used words in reviews of fan fiction is 'canon'. Many of the reviews posted on 'The Thickness of the Rain', for instance, opine that people could be easily offended and even defamed by the story because it concerns 'real people'. Slash fiction about the Holocaust, 'Leigh-Anne' concludes, 'is just not right': it is 'not canon'. As with our analysis of Holocaust comedy in Chapter 2, it is worth exploring why this might be so. As Caroline Picart and Jason McKahan have argued, homosociality and even homoeroticism are instantiated in many filmic representations of Nazi masculinity.[32] Might these elements also be present in Holocaust films and written histories? And what might our reluctance to connect the Holocaust with sexualities say about our understandings of the nature and functions of history? 'Canon' in this case might be suggestive of an orthodoxy in which the mediated nature of history and the relationship of history with narrative are either downplayed or denied. Thus as 'Anonymous' argues, 'This is [*sic*] real people you are dealing with . . . you can't twist it into fiction', where the 'real people' are those of the historical record, not the characters in the film. However, a closer look at fan fiction reviews complicates this equation of canon with what might be called an 'empiricist' orthodoxy. The same reviews that dismiss 'The Thickness of the Rain' as wrong or offensive see it as 'canonical' in the sense of displaying a consistency of style and characterisation. Hence 'astartea' writes, 'I think this feeling was totally canon in the movie' and 'Khanele' and 'Leigh-Anne' acknowledge the use of a 'good' and 'lovely' writing style. Canon is thus as much about the style of the truth as it is about the truth itself.

In reviews of fan fiction for other historical films, we see at least one other major meaning of 'canon' in play, one in which connections and consistency with an historical record that is larger than the diegesis of a film are evoked. The diverse body of fan fiction connected with *Saving Private Ryan*, to take just one example, might be read as critical judgement about the historical and stylistic limitations of the film. Fan fiction for *Ryan* explores, for example, the experiences of British troops on D-Day, the struggles families encounter before and after combatants return home and the difference that the addition of a character or a musical number can have upon the diegesis. These efforts are supported by reference not only to film style but also to primary and secondary works on D-Day.[33] Bringing all of these elements together, it may be concluded that as with fan fashion, 'canonical' fan fiction cannot be reduced to a discourse on realism or simulation. Viewer-writers can also be 'connoisseurs', highlighting and sharing perceived aesthetic and historical limitations and qualities in films. What is perhaps more clear in the case of fan fiction, though, is that viewers engage in regulatory practices, defending both a filmmaker's creative work and the historical record from perceived misuse and even disrespect.

Connoisseurs and sequel makers: computer games and DVD special features

In Theodor Adorno's estimation, cinema works to produce consumers without giving them any influence upon future productions. Nowhere is that clearer, he argues, than in films that make extensive use of special and now digital effects.[34] In the last chapter, I drew upon the writings of Gunning, Pierson and Groth to show that the reception of special effects on stage and on film is shaped by both appreciations of photorealism and aesthetic decisions. Evidence for that is to be found in records of film viewing—as with Méliès' description—and in critical discussions of effects in print texts such as *Scientific American*. In this chapter, I would like to revisit this dual treatment of viewers as connoisseurs and consumers through a consideration of computer games and DVD special features.

Contemporary discussions on movie-to-game tie-ins are dominated by considerations of marketing power and thus possibilities for enhanced financial returns. As marketing manager Pete Snyder has noted, for instance, a clear majority of gamers prefer to rent or buy games related to films, and around a quarter of gamers are happy to play a tie-in game before they see the related film.[35] Clearly, games can have an impact both on box office and rental returns and on the overall financial return of a title. In some cases, games sales can even outstrip box office and rental returns. Consequently, there has been a dramatic growth in the production of computer games that are closely tied to the characters, situations and settings of films. As marketers also recognise, though, gamers are far from passive consumers. Jim Wilson, for example, has observed that game producers see little advantage in producing works that are firmly tied to a movie's plot. This is not simply to protect gaming revenue when a film does poorly at the box office. Rather, he argues, 'Consumers don't want a rehash of a movie. Kids want a rehash, but gamers don't'.[36] Successful games expand both the collection of characters and their experiences and thus work like a sequel or a parallel story. When this recipe for success is applied to historical films, counterfactuals— alternative histories that result from pursuing questions of the form 'What if?'—can be the main result. That is clearly the expectation communicated in this review of *Pearl Harbor: Ground Zero* (2001):

> The attack upon Pearl Harbor was both a horrendous day in United States history, and a date that propelled the nation into the forefront of power upon Earth. It pushed the U.S. into World War II, brought the nation together in a single-mindedness of purpose, and served notice to the rest of the world that you don't mess with this country. This game is trying to capitalize on that recognition without delivering anything that is remotely connected with the true world of gaming—a chance to strategize, to avenge or stop that initial devastation. Games that have faithfully tried to recreate World War II scenarios, to give gamers an opportunity to redraw history, have little in common with this title.[37]

Pearl Harbor: Zero Hour is not at fault because of its connection with an historical event; rather, the problem lies with the lack of latitude it gives to players. A game should allow you to 'remake' history. The same principle might be applied to fan fiction. And like fan fiction, it is not the case that player latitude simply means 'anything goes'. Games can offer players the opportunity to look to the experience of historical agents and experiences excluded from a film, as with the British soldiers written into *Saving Private Ryan* fan fiction. Furthermore, gamers share with fan fiction writers and reviewers regulatory practices and concepts. The review of *Pearl Harbor: Ground Zero* above does not include the word 'canon', but the game is nonetheless measured against the criterion of a 'true' game. Where it differs from fan fiction is in the source of that criterion. Fan fiction is 'canon' if it is consistent with other phenomena in a film or history. A game, on the other hand, is 'true' if it offers opportunities for decision making to players. Forms of agency in fashion and fan fiction making are thus not the same as those for gaming.

DVD special features have also been viewed primarily through the lenses of promotion and consumption. Language and subtitle options, 'chapter-by-chapter' access, 'making of' profiles, special commentaries, film stills, cast and crew biographies, music videos and trailers are increasingly included as routine items in DVD releases of films. These features can be cast as 'collector's items' and promoted by appealing to viewer desire to establish or support a hierarchy of fandom. What makes these claims difficult to sustain is that these features are available to all potential buyers. Film distributors have thus embraced other means of appealing to consumer collectors. 'Easter eggs'—undocumented features found through key sequences on a computer keyboard or DVD controls—are a good case in point. The first Easter eggs were used by computer software engineers to draw attention to their contribution to the generation of an application or system. As they were not formally documented or in some cases even known to software distributors, there grew up an oral and online culture of telling and finding that could be framed as the search for creative expression within corporate spaces. Viewer ability to watch DVDs on a computer monitor made the transfer of the activity of hiding and finding Easter eggs to another medium possible. In addition to their use for credits, Easter eggs now unlock 'behind the scenes' and 'making of' clips, out-takes, songs, gags and excluded footage, like the 'rhino fight' in *Gladiator*, the gag reel for *Pearl Harbor* and Kamahl's performance of 'Danny Boy' in *Harvie Krumpet*. Easter eggs may still be expressions within and against corporate spaces, but their proliferation in recent releases like *Moulin Rouge* points to corporate attempts to build affiliation through the appropriation of fan activities and discourses.[38]

Much of what is 'special' about a DVD is promotional. The documentary form of the 'Into the Breach' featurette packaged with *Saving Private Ryan*, for example, barely masks an introspective and circular endorsement of the film and Stephen Ambrose's writings on D-Day. For at least some viewers, though, DVD provides an opportunity for more studied and varied forms of viewing than cinemas currently allow. Repeat viewings and close scrutiny of scenes through the use of different speeds of fast forward and rewind may foster connoisseurship and wonder in the sense that Pierson and Groth describe: the understanding and enjoyment of aesthetic decisions and effects.[39] In distinction from their studies of nineteenth-century cultures of connoisseurship, though, we find support for a culture of connoisseurship not through print materials or the London Polytechnic but in the heterogeneous spaces of DVD discs and the Internet. Easter eggs may be hidden to support the promotion of a film, but they can deliver both production information and expanded or parallel narratives that might change a viewer's understanding of a film. As Wyatt has also noticed, bundled music video clips can generate a 'dense textual network' that can expand and even redraw a film's diegesis.[40] The film clip for Celine Dion's 'My Heart Will Go On', for instance, rearranges the diegesis of *Titanic* and allows for viewer construction of a parallel diegesis in which the shipping disaster is even further sidelined. In line with Roland Barthes' claim, it thus appears that 'Re-reading is no longer consumption, but play (that play is the return of the different). If then, a deliberate contradiction in terms, we immediately reread the text, it is in order to obtain, as though under the effect of a drug (that of recommencement, of difference), not the real text, but a plural text: the same and new'.[41]

Over the course of this chapter, a picture of viewer agency and resourcefulness has emerged. Clearly, the meaning of historical films cannot be reduced to the activities of multinationals cynically exploiting emotionally vulnerable audiences in the cause of corporate profit. In saying this, however, I am not offering an unequivocal endorsement of audience studies that champion viewers as either resisters or 'autonomous' agents engaged in 'creative critical work'.[42] Rather, the relationship between viewers and film and tie-in producers and distributors is, as Simone Murray suggests, more like 'an uneasy dance' in which corporate desire for maximum circulation of content 'chafes uncomfortably against fans' resourcefulness in eluding the prescribed legal and economic frameworks for the circulation of that content'.[43] Three factors complicate conventional accounts of the relationship between film producers and promoters and viewers.

First, historical film producers confront a paradox: on the one hand, they want their works to circulate as widely as possible, but on the other, circulation outside the control of the corporate rights holder can mean missed revenue and the possibility of content being 'redrawn'.[44] Between the twin historiographical shoals of viewer resistance and passivity lies a relationship in which viewers appropriate media texts to their own ends, but producers also work with viewer practices if they detect means to promote their works. As Murray's study of the *Lord of the Rings* trilogy has shown, scholars have yet to come to grips with the activities of film producers and promoters who seek out, feed material to and foster hierarchies within viewer communities. New Line's use of a small number of inner-ring fan websites to deliver production information proved effective in both promoting and controlling use of film materials. Their selective non-enforcement of intellectual property rights was not a clear victory for public domain usage, because inner-ring webmasters become non-salaried marketing collaborators and regulators of intellectual property that they saw as 'canon' with J.R.R. Tolkien's endeavours. Cases like this show us the need for the combined consideration of activities of material production, corporate management and marketing strategy and viewer agency in historical film studies. Although Murray assumes that this is a recent trend in film promotion and reception, I believe that historical analysis of promotion and viewer activities will bring many more examples to light.

Murray's findings break down any notions we might have of a clear opposition between producers and viewers and of a united group of viewers. A second feature that further complicates our account of the relationship between producers, promoters and viewers is that it is not organised simply around the axis of photorealism and thus issues of deception and consumption. While a number of scholars have talked of film as an ideological apparatus that fosters stupefaction, depoliticisation and consumption rather than production, a number of examples in this chapter have supported Pierson's and Groth's arguments for the recognition of viewer interest in the aesthetic dimensions of films. Albert La Valley has argued that science fiction and fantasy films appear to 'hover between being about the world their special effects imply—i.e. about future technology and its extensions—and about the special effects and the wizardry of the movies themselves'. That is, effects are simultaneously part of the diegesis and a cinematic spectacle. But, as he continues, science fiction film producers and viewers 'demand more realism from their special effects than fantasy does, which permits greater stylisation and whim'.[45] Ostensibly, this makes sense, and we would expect the producers and viewers of historical films to demand 'more realism' from both special and routine effects such as CGI, costumes and soundtrack. Still, the history of historical or even science fiction film production and reception cannot be collapsed into photorealism or 'reality effects'. Not all viewers want an historical film in which all the military insignia are right; some also want film craft that offers new vistas on historical phenomena. Science fiction fans and devotees of special effects may not be the only connoisseurs of art, and the 'wonder' Pierson speaks of is thus perhaps not particular to their experiences.

Clearly, there is a need for more work on modes of aesthetic engagement and criticism among viewers of historical films. This brings me to a third facet of the producer, promoter and viewer relations, a facet about which we speak with least confidence because of its neglect among scholars. The dominant stream of historical film research proffers decontextualised concepts of domination and agency. I am not complaining simply that models of the relations of producers and viewers are implicitly Western in focus, for the term 'Western' also masks cultural and historical differences that are worthy of study.

Images and words

Histories—visual and written—are complex sites of relation, negotiation and even conflict among producers, promoters and audiences. Traditionally, however, studies of histories have been author- and auteur-(director)oriented. In recent years, however, 'intentionalist' studies have been questioned by literary theorists and historiographers, who have called for greater attention to audiences. As Michel De Certeau argues, textual meaning is impossible without readers:

> Whether it is a question of newspapers or Proust, the text has a meaning only through its readers; it changes along with them; it is ordered in accord with codes of perception that it does not control. It becomes only a text in its relation to the exteriority of the reader, by an interplay of implications and ruses between two sorts of 'expectation' in combination: the expectation that organises a *readable* space (a literality), and one that organises a procedure necessary for the *actualisation* of the work (a reading).[46]

Similarly, it can be argued that the meaning of historical films is not inscribed and fixed without viewers.

Much of what has been written in the burgeoning field of reception studies can inform our understanding of both viewers and readers, including the readers of histories. Jonathon Rose's identification of five assumptions that can hamper the study of readers, for example, provides much for historical film scholars to think about. Scholars often take it for granted, he writes, that

> first, all literature is political, in the sense that it always influences the political consciousness of the reader; second, the influence of a given text is directly proportional to its circulation; third, 'popular' culture has a much larger following than 'high' culture, and therefore it more accurately reflects the attitudes of the masses; fourth, 'high' culture tends to reinforce acceptance of the existing social and political order (a presumption widely shared by both the left and right); and, fifth, the canon of 'great books' is defined solely by social elites. Common readers either do not recognise that canon, or else they accept it only out of deference to elite opinion.[47]

Rose's observations are important: we must, for instance, seek evidence for the influence of a film or a book beyond sales and not assume that its influence was solely political. Furthermore, these observations all point to a more fundamental assumption: that readers are passive recipients of whatever authors put into their texts. Rose and Janice Radway have provided us with evidence to the contrary, showing readers responding to texts in fashions that were unintended and using them to their own ends.[48] We too have found a number of examples of viewers poaching, appropriating and refashioning historical films and drawing them into their lives. As we have also discovered through our analysis of film, though, viewer activities of regulation and the intertwining of commercial and connoisseur activities have yet to register as themes in historical film studies. Furthermore, there is a shortage of studies on film producer, promoter and viewer relationships in specific historical and cultural contexts.

So, too, studies of the relations between the producers, promoters and readers of written histories are in short supply. Keith Jenkins has noted the commercial pressures on historians to produce texts according to the time-tables and ideas of market that publishers hold.[49] However, we still await the delivery of extensive historical studies on readers' uses of histories, and we are yet to chart the depths of how commercial, material and cultural factors shape our understanding of what 'history' is and what it is for.

Recommended resources

Dika, V., *Recycled Culture in Contemporary Art and Film: The Uses of Nostalgia*, Cambridge: Cambridge University Press, 2003.

Dwyer, R. and Patel, D., *Cinema India: The Visual Culture of Hindi Film*, London: Reaktion Books, 2002.

Eckert, C., 'The Carole Lombard in Macy's window', in J. Gaines and C. Herzog (eds), *Fabrications: Costume and the Female Body*, London: Routledge, 1990, pp. 100–21.

Fischer, L. and Landy, M. (eds), *Stars: The Film Reader*, London: Routledge, 2004.

Glenhill, C. (ed.), *Home is Where the Heart Is: Studies in Melodrama and the Woman's Film*, London: BFI, 1987.

Jameson, F., *Postmodernism, or, the Cultural Logic of Late Capitalism*, Durham, NC: Duke University Press, 1991.

Kuhn, A., *Dreaming of Fred and Ginger: Cinema and Cultural Memory*, Washington Square, NY: New York University Press, 2002.

Lasch, C., *The True and Only Heaven: Progress and its Critics*, New York: W.W. Norton, 1991.

McCracken, G., *Culture and Consumption: New Approaches to the Symbolic Character of Consumer Goods and Activities*, Bloomington: University of Indiana Press, 1990.

Pierson, M., *Special Effects: Still in Search of Wonder*, New York: Columbia University Press, 2002.

Ricoeur, P., *Memory, History, Forgetting*, trans. K. Blamey and D. Pellauer, Chicago: University of Chicago Press, 2004.

Stacey, J., *Star Gazing: Hollywood Cinema and Female Spectatorship*, London: Routledge, 1994.

Stewart, S., *On Longing: Narratives of the Miniature, the Gigantic, the Souvenir, the Collection*, Baltimore: Johns Hopkins University Press, 1984.

Sweeney, R.C., *Coming Next Week: A Pictorial History of Film Advertising*, London: Thomas Yoseloff, 1973.

Wyatt, J., *High Concept: Movies and Marketing in Hollywood*, Austin: University of Texas Press, 1994.

Notes

1 F. Sanello, *Reel vs Real: How Hollywood Turns Fact into Fiction*, Lanham, Md: Taylor Trade, 2003, pp. xi–xii.

2 J. Wyatt, *High Concept: Movies and Marketing in Hollywood*, Austin: University of Texas Press, 1994, p. 20.

3 B. Weinraub, 'Who's lining up at the box office? Lots and lots of girls', *New York Times*, 23 February 1998, E1, E4.

4 J. Smith, 'Selling my heart: music and cross-promotion in *Titanic*', in K.S. Sandler and G. Studlar (eds), *Titanic: Anatomy of a Blockbuster*, New Brunswick, NJ: Rutgers University Press, 1999, pp. 47–8. On the sale of song lyrics at Indian film screenings, see R. Dwyer and D. Patel, *Cinema India: The Visual Culture of Hindi Film*, London: Reaktion Books, 2002, p. 101.

5 J. Wyatt, *High Concept*, p. 28.

6 M. Carnes (ed.), *Past Imperfect: History According to the Movies*, New York: Henry Holt, 1996, p. 9; R. Rosenstone, *Visions of the Past: The Challenge of Film to Our Idea of History*, Cambridge, Mass.: Harvard University Press, 1995, pp. 59–60; and J. Stringer, ' "The china had never been used!": on the patina of perfect images in *Titanic*', in K.S. Sandler and G. Studlar (eds), *Titanic*, pp. 205–19.

7 G. McCracken, *Culture and Consumption: New Approaches to the Symbolic Character of Comsumer Goods and Activities*, Bloomington: University of Indiana Press, 1990, pp. 32, 35.

8 T.L. Stanley, 'Pumping ana-stations', *Brandweek*, 1997, vol. 38(44), p. 16.

9 Promotion Marketing Association [USA], '2002 Reggie Award Winners', online at http://www.pmalink.org/awards/reggie/2002reggiewinners1.asp; and D. Finnigan, 'Dior, Bloomies paint it red with Fox's rouge—Christian Dior and Bloomingdale's Inc. Promote 'Moulin Rouge', *Brandweek*, 2001, vol. 42(14), p. 3.

10 J. Wyatt, *High Concept*, p. 26.

11 V. Sobchack, 'Bathos and bathysphere: on submersion, longing and history in *Titanic*', in K.S. Sandler and G. Studlar (eds), *Titanic*, pp. 189–204; and A. Keller, ' "Size does matter": notes on *Titanic* and James Cameron as blockbuster auteur', in K.S. Sandler and G. Studlar (eds), *Titanic*, p. 148. Although a little less critical, Robert Rosenstone sees the foregrounding of individuals' experiences in historical films as a way of avoiding difficult or insoluble problems suggested by the historical setting. See *Visions of the Past: The Challenge of Film to our Idea of History*, Princeton, NJ: Princeton University Press, p. 57.

12 S. Stewart, *On Longing: Narratives of the Miniature, the Gigantic, the Souvenir, the Collection*, Baltimore: Johns Hopkins University Press, 1984, p. 23.

13 On this point, see also L. Williams, 'Melodrama revisited', in N. Browne (ed.), *Refiguring American Film Genres: Theory and History*, Berkeley: University of California Press, 1998, pp. 42–88; and T. Elsaesser, 'Tales of sound and fury: observations on the family melodrama', in *Home is Where the Heart Is: Studies in Melodrama and the Woman's Film*, London: BFI, 1987, pp. 43–69.

14 F. Jameson, *Signatures of the Visible*, New York: Routledge, 1990, p. 87.

15 *Ibid.*, pp. 84–5; F. Jameson, *Postmodernism, or the Cultural Logic of Late Capitalism*, Durham, NC: Duke University Press, 1991, pp. 19–21.

16 C. Lasch, *The True and Only Heaven: Progress and Its Critics*, New York: W.W. Norton, 1991, pp. 82–3.

17 See also R.A. Reeves, 'Nostalgia and the nostalgic', *Southwest Philosophical Studies*, 1992, vol. 14(2), pp. 92–7.

18 L. Hutcheon, 'Irony, nostalgia, and the postmodern', *Iowa Journal of Cultural Studies*, 2005, no. 5, pp. 5–6.

19 A. DeFalco, 'A double-edged longing: nostalgia, melodrama and Todd Hayne's *Far From Heaven*', *Iowa Journal of Cultural Studies*, 2005, no. 5, p. 34. Problematically, DeFalco also distinguishes intellectual spectatorship from emotional investment.

20 T. Haynes, as quoted in D. Lim, 'Heaven sent', *Village Voice*, 30 October–5 November 2002, online at http://www.villagevoice.com/news/0244,lim,39523,1.html. On the connection between active engagement by viewers and nostalgia, see also P. Brooker and W. Brooker, 'Introduction', *Postmodern After Images: A Reader in Film, Television and Video*, London: Edward Arnold, 1997, p. 7.

21 J. Stacey, *Star Gazing: Hollywood Cinema and Female Spectatorship*, London: Routledge, 1994; and J. Craik, *The Face of Fashion: Cultural Studies in Fashion*, London: Routledge, 1994. See also C. Eckert, 'The Carole Lombard in Macy's window', in *Fabrications: Costume and the Female Body*, London: Routledge, 1990, pp. 100–21.

22 A. Kuhn, *Dreaming of Fred and Ginger: Cinema and Cultural Memory*, Washington Square, NY: New York University Press, 2002, pp. 107, 100, 112–23.

23 M. de Certeau, *The Practice of Everyday Life*, trans. S. Rendall, Berkeley: University of California Press, 1984, p. 31.

24 *Titanic* on Tour: Costume Photos, online at http://www.sensibility.com/titanic/titanictour

25 'Costumed Dolls', http://www.sensibility.com/titanic/showandtell/dolls.com

26 S. Berry, *Screen Style: Fashion and Feminity in 1930s Hollywood*, Minneapolis: University of Minnesota Press, 2000, p. 185.

27 *Titanic* Show and Tell, online at http://www.sensibility.com/titanic/showandtell/dolls.com

28 The term 'slash' refers to the forward slash '/' that is used to identify 'male/female' or 'male/male' romances.

29 *Titanic* Continued, online at http://www.geocities.com/Hollywood/Academy/9204/storypage.html

30 Jack Lives Fan Fiction, http://www.sparkling-horizon.net/odyssey/jacklives.html

31 'Warm Thanksgiving Memories', online at http://www.geocities.com/Paris/Arc/1142/storythanks.html?200522

32 C.J.S. Picart and J.G. McKahan, '*Apt Pupil's* misogyny. Homoeroticism and homophobia: sadomasochism and the Holocaust film', *Jump Cut*, 2002, no. 45, online at http://www.ejumpcut.org/archive/jc45.2002/picart/index.html

33 *Saving Private Ryan* Fan Fiction, online at http://www.fanfiction/net

34 T. Adorno, 'The schema of mass culture', in J.M. Bernstein (ed.), *The Culture Industry*, London: Routledge, 1991, pp. 47, 54.

35 P. Snyder, 'Hollywood tie-ins mean greater sales: and bigger branding challenges', *Electronic Gaming Business*, 2 July 2003, online at http://www.electronicgamingbusiness.com.

36 As quoted in K. Thompson, 'Fantasy, franchises, and Frodo Baggins: *The Lord of the Rings* and modern Hollywood', *The Velvet Light Trap*, 2003, no. 52, p. 59.

37 M. Lafferty, 'Review of *Pearl Harbor: Zero Hour*', 14 June 2001, online at http://pc.gamezone.com/gzreviews/r18517.htm

38 Easter eggs for *Gladiator* (regions 2 and 4), *Harvie Krumpet* (region 4), *Pearl Harbor* (region 1) and *Moulin Rouge* (regions 1, 2 and 4) are described in 'Hidden DVD Easter Eggs', online at http://wwwhiddendvdeasteregges.com/films/33873.html

39 M. Pierson, *Special Effects: Still in Search of Wonder*, New York: Columbia University Press, 2002, pp. 19, 22, 33, 41, 46.

40 J. Wyatt, *High Concept*, pp. 44–6. See also Barbara Klinger, 'Digressions at the cinema: reception and mass culture', *Cinema Journal*, 1989, vol. 28(4), p. 10.

41 R. Barthes, *S/Z*, trans. R. Miller, New York: Hill & Wang, 1974.

42 On fan resistance, see J. Fiske, 'The cultural economy of fandom', in L.A. Lewis (ed.), *The Adoring Audience: Fan Cultures and Popular Media*, London: Routledge, 1992, pp. 30–49. On fans as engaged in creative work, see J. Hartley, *Popular Reality: Journalism, Modernity, Popular Culture*, London: Edward Arnold, 1996.

43 S. Murray, ' "Celebrating the story the way it is": cultural studies, corporate media and the contested utility of fandom', *Continuum: Journal of Media and Cultural Studies*, 2004, vol. 18(1), p. 9.

44 H. Jenkins, 'Digital land grab', *Technological Review*, 2000, March–April, pp. 103–5.

45 A.J. La Valley, 'Traditions of trickery: the role of special effects in the science fiction film', in G.S. Slusser and E.S. Rabkin (eds), *Shadows of the Magic Lamp: Fantasy and Science Fiction in Film*, Carbondale: Southern Illinois University Press, 1985, p. 144, as quoted in M. Pierson, *Special Effects*, p. 107.
46 M. de Certeau, 'Reading as poaching', in *The Practice of Everyday Life*, trans. S.F. Rendell, Berkeley: University of California Press, 1984, pp. 170–1.
47 J. Rose, 'Rereading the English common reader: a preface to a history of audiences', *Journal of the History of Ideas*, 1992, vol. 53(1), p. 48.
48 *Ibid.*, and J. Radway, *Reading the Romance: Women, Patriarchy, and Popular Literature*, Chapel Hill: University of North Carolina Press, 1984.
49 K. Jenkins, *Re-thinking History*, London: Routledge, 1991, pp. 22–4.

Conclusion

Beyond 'historiophoty': film as history

Since it permits seeing the past directly, it will eliminate, at least at certain important points, the need for investigation and study.[1]

In a 1988 paper for *The American Historical Review*, Hayden White coined the term 'historiophoty'. He did so in the first instance to recognise that the evidence historians work with now is as much visual as written or oral. But he also did so to support his claim that visual evidence needs to be read with 'a lexicon, grammar, and syntax' that is 'quite different' from that used for written evidence. 'We are inclined', he argued:

To use pictures primarily as 'illustrations' of the predications made in our verbally written discourse. We have not on the whole exploited the possibilities of using images as a principal medium of *discursive* representation, using verbal commentary only diacritically, that is to say, to direct attention to, specify, and emphasise a meaning conveyable by visual means alone.[2]

Images are not ancillary to words; they can convey meaning in their own right. Exactly ninety years earlier, Boleslas Matuszewski also argued for the recognition of film as a source of meaning in his pioneering call for the creation of a visual histories repository in Paris. Matuszewski and White both value film as a source for historians, but beyond that, their views appear to diverge, in a way that suggests the dramatic development of historical film studies over the last century. While White sees the meaning of film as available only through a special form of reading, Matuszewski assumes its transparency. White sees a need to train historians to help them to make better use of visual materials in their investigations, whereas for Matuszewski, film minimises the need for historical study altogether. As I hope this book has shown, film is not a transparent window on to the past. Films are sculpted by techniques, and these techniques are conventions that have their own histories. On this count, White's vision of film needing to be read rings true and perhaps helps to support a view that understanding and appreciation of film is better in the present than in the past. But the gap between White and Matuszewski is not as big as we might first suppose. Vestiges of both transparency and a belief in the sufficiency of film as a source connect White, and other present-day historical film scholars, with that rallying cry over one hundred years ago.

White's treatment of the analysis of images as different from that of words echoes the arguments of many other historical film scholars. Marc Ferro, for instance, sees cinema as 'a new form of expression' for history, Richard White sees film as a distinct form of historical narrative, and Natalie Zemon Davis holds that as long as we appreciate the differences between film and prose, 'we can take film seriously as a source of valuable and even innovative historical vision'.[3] In Chapter 1, I argued that claims like these may do little to challenge the hierarchical arrangement of written history over 'other' or 'nearly' histories. Here we revisit the idea of historical film studies being distinct from other historical studies, but this time from a methodological perspective. When historical film scholars mark their efforts off as different from those of other historians, are they signalling the use of particular methodologies? We learned above that White sees 'historiophoty' as a form of reading, a form that he describes in more detail in this excerpt:

> I do not know enough about film theory to specify more precisely the elements, equivalent to the lexical, grammatical and syntactical dimensions of spoken or written language, of a distinctly filmic discourse. Roland Barthes insisted that still photographs do not and could not predicate—only their titles or captions could do so. But cinema is quite another matter. Sequences of shots and the use of montage or close-ups can be made to predicate just as effectively as phrases, sentences, or sequences of sentences in spoken or written discourse.[4]

This form of reading is equivalent to, but distinct from, that entailed in historiography. Extrapolating, it might be thought that all forms of historical study are organised by their own distinct methodologies. Even if this appeals as a way of indicating the 'seriousness' of historical film studies, we must be wary of the problems to which it gives rise. Writers like Gregory Currie, for instance, have argued that there is no evidence to suggest that film possesses its own linguistic structure.[5] This is an interesting area of debate, but there are two other problems that I want to focus on here.

I alluded to the first above when I suggested that vestiges of transparency remain in historical film studies. The transparency referred to here is not just the one between the past and film but also that between film and historical film scholars. In Chapter 2, you may recall, I noted a gap between the views of historical film scholars and the promoters of films. The former have shown a persistent interest in identifying films that epitomise an 'historical' genre, while the latter have a commercial interest in presenting individual films as offering a mixture of genres ('something for everyone'). This example alerts us to the important idea that films are read in different ways for different reasons. Just as films are not the privileged property of their producers, historical film scholars have no proprietorial hold over films, and their readings are not transparent registrations of filmic reality. Nor can they singlehandedly inscribe and fix meaning, regardless of how much effort they have put into outlining and justifying their methodologies. Their methods for reading film, like those detailed by Hayden White above, are timebound conventions that have their own functions and histories, and these conventions are not universal. Recognising historical film scholars as a varied group of readers highlights the diversity beneath the apparent homogeneity of a single film print. Historical film studies is thus historical not simply because we may view a film as representing the past but because our view of it as history is itself historically located.

This point about multiple readers brings us back to the second problem with present-day historical film methodologies: the assumption that the discursive meaning and functions of films can be deduced from their diegeses alone. A number of scholars, like White, have complained about the treatment of films as transparent recordings of reality or as plots. Yet their solution to this problem, in the main, has been to conjoin an analysis of film plot with filmic techniques such as editing and to treat that combination as sufficient; for example, White talks of sequences of shots and the use of montage and close-ups. Davis argues a similar line in her *Slaves on Screen* (2000):

> Reviewers of historical films often overlook techniques in favour of a chronological summary of the plot or story line and the overall look of the moving picture in terms of costumes and props. These aspects of the film are necessary, to be sure. But viewers respond as well to the film's modes of narration, just as viewers respond to the organization and rhetorical disposition of a history book.[6]

Viewers do not respond only to modes of narration or filmic techniques. As I have argued at a number of points in this book, they also respond to print and online reviews and information about 'stars', the physical environment in which they see a film, merchandise, and the friends they share their film-watching experiences with. Any one of these things may be more important than editing, say, in shaping their understanding of a film, yet none of these activities is captured in that viewed film. Thus film alone does not tell us how others—past and present—view it and make use of it.

Reframing historical film studies and 'the historical film'

Recognising the role of context in historical film studies is nothing new. A number of writers have parted company with Matuszewski's view of films as sufficient markers of meaning and now formulate studies that analyse 'the symbiotic relationship between film technologies and industrial relations, marketing and advertising, filmmakers' intentions and audience reception'.[7] The range of evidence I have both drawn upon and pointed to in this work, though, shows how much further historical film studies may be expanded. In addition to film company documents, financial and production records, film scripts, inter-office memos, film publicity materials, industry trade periodicals, legal files, distribution records and mass observation surveys,[8] we may now consider merchandise, DVD 'special features', fanzines, the records of 'amateur' cine clubs, websites and online discussion forums, computer games, viewer costumes, and fan fiction. Films are embedded in extensive networks of relations and products, and those networks may be studied using multiple and intertwined methodologies from fields such as historiography, psychology, literary and film studies, aesthetics, economics, and marketing. The logical consequence of these points is that the activities of isolating historical films *and* historical film studies must come under scrutiny.

Moreover, I believe that this holistic methodology for studying films should shape our very definition of an historical film. At the opening of this book, I declared my reluctance to offer a definition and argued for the concept to be opened up. What I mean by 'opening up' should now be clearer but may be clarified further through an example. You and I might watch a film together. After seeing it, and my telling you how much I enjoyed it as an historical film, you may look at me puzzled. The film could be *Catch Me if you Can* (2002), and your puzzlement may be due to the apparent lack of distance between the costumes used to represent the 1960s and what people wear today. The film could be *Donnie Darko* (2001), and our difference of opinion may come down to 1988 being too recent a setting for you to count as 'history'. The film could be *Distant Voices, Still Lives* (1989), and my interest in what it says about relationships in the past may not sit well with your demand that history be about 'events'. Here we have three films that I see as historical, but you disagree with my judgement about each for different reasons. My point is a simple but fundamental one: history is in the eye of the viewer, not inscribed on the film itself. More people may agree about the status of some films than others, but as we recall from the introduction, multitudinous agreement is not the same as homogeneous agreement. It is unlikely that communities in different places will produce a canonical list of 'historical' films. Similarly, the view of a particular film as historical may persist for a long period, but that does not mean that it will or ought to be regarded so permanently. Views of history may be debated and are subject to change. How we handle disagreements about history is important. Our response should not be to ignore them or to engage in defensive acts of boundary drawing and retreat but to recognise the value of that discussion for exploring the assumptions that people hold about what history is and what it is for.

A little over a hundred years after Matuszewski argued for the recognition of film as history, Robert Rosenstone advanced that what makes a film historical 'is its willingness to engage the discourse of history—that is, the facts, the issues, and the arguments raised in other historical works'.[9] Film on its own, we now see, does not engage history; filmmakers and viewers do. Historical film studies is thus no longer simply about reading and analysing films. With a few tweaks, though, this definition may be reframed in a way that recognises the location of films in networks of makers and viewers, and this will serve as my working definition. What makes a film historical, I believe, is its location in a timebound network of discussions—more or less explicit—on what history is and what it is for. On this definition, any film may be historical because it is viewed as offering indexical markers—on-screen phenomena seen as capturing or connected with past phenomena—or because it suggests something about how and why histories are made.

The challenges of historical film research

Undertaking research according to this expanded notion of historical film studies is a tall order. The body of evidence we might look to is in theory huge, perhaps beyond the time and resource constraints of researchers. Historians, though, are familiar with problems of selection, and the inclusion of even some evidence of historical reception would be enough to shift historical film studies away from its transparent stance and almost exclusive focus on diegetic analysis. Moreover, it is important to note that there is not a uniform superfluity of evidence available for analysis in practice. Why not? The disjunction between a field that is enormous in theory and the realities of available evidence can be explained in this case by considering the fragility of evidence, decisions of valuation and access arrangements.

Film evidence is fragile. Motion picture film consists of emulsions (developed images) that are fixed to a transparent support base. Both cellulose nitrate supports (used from 1890 to approximately 1950) and cellulose acetate plastic 'safety' supports (used from 1950) are prone to chemical degradation, particularly in warm and humid environments. Emulsions may also degrade, with colour fading now well documented in 'Eastmancolor' stocks. Preservation studies suggest that black and white films appear to have a longer life.[10] Additionally, film may deteriorate as a result of physical damage: for example, perforation tears, called 'crowsfooting'; scratches; water damage; or staining by particles, including rust. The materials used for film merchandise may also degrade, with poster and handbill dyes fading, plastics becoming brittle and papers vulnerable to oxygen burning. The increasingly rapid obsolescence of production, screening and discussion technologies is also a problem, as anyone with home movies in Betamax and now VHS format can appreciate. You will have noted too that I made use of some portions of a currently abundant body of Internet evidence in Chapters 5 to 8. How much of that evidence will be archived and still available ten or even five years from now? Similarly, film viewers wrote letters to other viewers in the past; now viewers send emails or SMS messages. Will historians of the future have access to those viewers' responses?

Preservation is not determined solely by the longevity of media. More important, arguably, are human decisions. Some kinds of film have been the focus of stronger preservation efforts than others. Sound features, for instance, have generally been treated with more value than newsreels, actualities, documentaries, home movies, instructional films, and independent and *avant-garde* works. Fears about the loss of nitrate stock have in some cases steered attention away from equally fragile post-1950 safety stock. Sometimes films are preserved because they are thought to epitomise forms of film art, or because they say something about the features and changing contours of a community.[11] In other cases, though, preservation is undertaken as a result of economic imperatives: the upgrading of film storage facilities at some production companies, for example, reflects the increased revenues achieved through cable, free-to-air and DVD rights. Conservators have also tended, like historical film scholars, to treat films as separate from the viewing communities that give them meaning. Few collection policies explicitly specify an interest in merchandise or viewer responses. The combined impact of fragility and valuation can be dramatic. In a report submitted to the US Congress in 1993, to take just one example, it was noted that 50 percent of feature films produced before 1950, 20 percent of the films made in the 1920s and just 10 percent of the films made before 1910 survive. Survival rates for other kinds of film are even lower, such as home movies, 16mm news film, kinescopes of early broadcasts and VHS recordings.[12] As a reflection of how little attention has been accorded to film-related activities, there has been no national inquiry into survival rates for evidence or issues of access.

Finally, accessing films and evidence of film networks can be difficult. Conservators may be reluctant to project films or allow access to materials that are fragile. Moreover, most films and film products are privately owned and subject to cascading arrangements of rights, which can make gaining access, let alone public screening, difficult. Concerns about piracy and policies of cyclical access and withdrawal—undertaken to sustain market interest in a work—may limit access. Libraries and repositories may hold copies of films but not the rights to allow viewers to copy segments. In combination, these three factors may slow efforts to expand the parameters of film research. Any difficulties associated with this expanded vision of historical film studies are in my view outweighed by the advantage it brings in foregrounding parallel, intersecting and sometimes competing visions of history.

I want to close by returning to where we started. In the Introduction, I cited two surveys that give us good cause to believe that a significant fraction of people come into contact with the past through film. Film, we now assume, is a medium that reaches billions around the world. What we must not take for granted, though, is that those viewers have visions of history that are identical to those of historical film scholars. The next step for historical film studies is to use film as an entry point to explore and understand those varied visions of history, and I hope that this work has suggested not only directions for that research but also some of the things that we might learn. When we do that, I believe, we will have made a start at re-visioning history.

Recommended resources

Billington, J.H. and the National Film Preservation Board (US), *Redefining Film Preservation: A National Plan*, Washington: Library of Congress, 1994, online at http://www.loc.gov/film/plan.html

British Film Institute, *Collecting Policy for Moving Images*, London: BFI, 2004.

Davis, N.Z., *Slaves on Screen: Film and Historical Vision*, Cambridge, Mass.; Harvard University Press, 2000.

Film History: An International Journal, 1987, vols 1–

Historical Journal of Film, Television and Radio, 1980, vols 1–

Matuszewski, B., 'A new source of history: the creation of a depository for historical cinematography (Paris 1898)', trans. J.B. Frey, *Screening the Past*, 1997, no. 1, online at http://www.latrobe.ed.au/screeningthepast/classics/clasjul/mat.html

Melville, A., Simmon, S. and the National Film Preservation Board (US), *Film Preservation 1993: A Study of the Current State of American Film Preservation*, Washington: Library of Congress, 1993, online at http://www.loc.gov/film/study.html

Rosenstone, R., 'Film reviews', *American Historical Review*, 1992, vol. 97(4), pp. 1138–9.

White, H., 'Historiography and historiophoty', *American Historical Review*, 1988, vol. 93(5), pp. 1193–4.

Notes

1 B. Matuszewski, 'A new source of history: the creation of a depository for historical cinematography (Paris 1898)', trans. J.B. Frey, *Screening the Past*, 1997, no. 1, online at http://www.latrobe.ed.au/screeningthepast/classics/clasjul/mat.html

2 H. White, 'Historiography and historiophoty', *American Historical Review*, 1988, vol. 93(5), pp. 1193–4.

3 M. Ferro, 'Does a filmic writing of history exist?', *Film and History*, 1987, vol. 17(4), p. 82; R. White, 'History, the *Rugrats*, and world championship wrestling', *Perspectives*, April 1999, online at http://www.historians.org/Perspectives/Issues/1999/9904/index.cfm; and N.Z. Davis, *Slaves on Screen: Film and Historical Vision*, Cambridge, Mass.: Harvard University Press, 2000, p. 15.

4 H. White, 'Historiography and historiophoty', p. 1196.

5 G. Currie, 'Plot synopsis', *Philosophical Studies*, 1998, vol. 89(2), pp. 319–21.

6 N.Z. Davis, *Slaves on Screen*, p. 8. For a similar view, see B. Toplin, 'Review of *Revisioning History: Film and the Construction of a New Past*', *Historical Journal of Film, Radio and Television*, 1996, vol. 16(2), pp. 279–80.

7 J.-C. Horak, 'Using Hollywood film stills as historical documents', *Historical Journal of Film, Radio and Television*, 1990, vol. 10(1), p. 93.

8 For examples of studies that utilise these kinds of materials, see G.F. Custen, *Bio/Pics: How Hollywood Constructed Public History*, New Brunswick, NJ: Rutgers University Press, 1992; and S. Harper, 'The scent of distant thunder: Hammer films and history', in T. Barta (ed.), *Screening the Past: Film and the Representation of History*, Westport, Conn.: Praeger, 1998, pp. 109–25.

9 R. Rosenstone, 'Film reviews', *American Historical Review*, 1992, vol. 97(4), p. 1138.

10 P.Z. Adelstein, J.M. Reilly, D.W. Nishimura and C.J. Erbland, 'Stability of cellulose ester base photographic film: Part II practical storage considerations', *Journal of Society of Motion Picture and Television Engineers*, 1992, vol. 101(5),

pp. 347–53; J.M. Reilly, *The IPI Storage Guide for Acetate Film*, Rochester, NY: Image Permanence Institute, 1993; and R. Patterson, 'The preservation of color films', *American Cinematographer*, 1981, vol. 62(2), pp. 694–720 and vol. 62(3), pp. 792–822.

11 See, for example, the collection policies of the British Film Institute, *Collecting Policy for Moving Images*, London: BFI, 2004; and the National Film Preservation Board (US), *National Film Register 1994–2004*, online at http://www.loc.gov/film/study.html

12 See L. Slide, *Nitrate Won't Wait: A History of Film Preservation in the United States*, Jefferson, NC: McFarland, 1992, p. 5; A. Melville, S. Simmon and the National Film Preservation Board (US), *Film Preservation 1993: A Study of the Current State of American Film Preservation*, Washington: Library of Congress, 1993, online at http://www.loc.gov/film/study.html; and British Film Institute, *Collecting Policy for Moving Images*, p. 13.

Glossary

Academy ratio film   Frame shape 1.85 times as wide as it is high (1.85:1), as approved by the Academy of Motion Picture Arts and Sciences (US).

auteur A term used to credit directors as the primary makers of films.

Bergfilm A term used to describe German films set on mountains or glaciers.

CGI (computer-generated imagery)   The use of digital technologies to add, remove, substitute or enhance elements of film images.

close-up   A shot in which an object, event or person is seen up close, such as a shot that shows only a person's face.

continuity editing   Editing that matches actions and temporal relations from shot to shot in as seamless a manner as possible.

cross-cutting   Alternating shots between two sequences of action that are meant to be read as simultaneous.

desaturated colour   Leached or subdued emulsion colour.

diegesis   Events, persons and phenomena, as shown on screen, or within a 'film's world'.

discontinuity editing   Mismatching of action and temporal relations from shot to shot.

dissolve   The move between two shots in which the first gradually disappears and the second takes its place.

docudrama   A term usually applied to television movies that offer depictions of occurrences or people.

dolly shot   A shot produced with a camera mounted on a wheeled platform ('dolly').

editing   The selection and arrangement of shots in a film.

elliptical editing   The omission of parts of an event or phenomenon, which creates an ellipsis in the film diegesis.

emulsion   A layer of gelatin and light-sensitive particles that form a photo-graphic image. Emulsion is fixed on a transparent film base.

fade   The gradual replacement of a shot with a darkened screen.

film stock   Emulsions fixed to a transparent support base.

flashback   A shot, scene or sequence of scenes that are understood by viewers as representing temporal occurrences chronologically prior to those in the shots or scenes that preceded them.

flashforward   A shot, scene or sequence of scenes that are understood by viewers as representing temporal occurrences chronologically after those in the shots or scenes that preceded them.

freeze-frame   A succession of identical film images that generate the impression of the suspension of action.

high angle   A shot produced with a camera above and trained below on the event, person or phenomenon filmed.

hyperreality   Representations of historical reality that acquire more legitimacy than past phenomena themselves.

intertitle   A card or sheet of plastic that offers printed information that appears between two shots.

iris   The closing of a shot in a circular or oval manner, as a camera aperture closes.

jump cut   An elliptical cut that signals the deletion of parts of an event or phenomenon from a film's diegesis.

low angle   A shot produced with a camera below and trained up on the event, person or phenomenon filmed.

match on action   An editing cut that splices two different views of the same action together in such a way that viewers understand it as being uninterrupted.

merchandise   Objects produced for viewers that either advertise film details, are replicas of on-screen objects or are objects produced in a style suggestive of a relationship with a film.

mise en scène   All of the elements seen on screen, including settings and property ('props'), lighting, costumes, make-up, actors and action.

mock documentary   (mockumentary) A film that imitates or parodies documentary subjects or filmic techniques.

montage   The use of editing to suggest discontinuity between shots.

panoramic shot   A shot in which a camera is pivoted horizontally (also known as 'panning').

promotional documentary   ('promo doc') 'Making of' or 'behind the scenes' featurettes that are either screened on television, bundled with a DVD or available on a film website.

slow motion   Projection or display of motions at a slower speed than that at which the camera filmed.

special features   Items other than a film included in a DVD.

stop-motion animation   Filming a two- or three-dimensional object, stopping the camera, changing something about the object, starting the camera over, and so on. Put together, these suggest the movement of otherwise inanimate objects such as clay models.

tie-ins   The use of commercial products on screen or the connection of a movie with commercial products.

trailer   An advertisement for a film, VHS or DVD release.

wipe   The gradual, horizontal replacement of one shot by another.

zoom in and out   The use of a zoom lens to suggest the increase or decrease in size of represented events, phenomena and persons.

Filmography

1492 Conquest of Paradise (1992)
   directed by Ridley Scott, Percy Main
1900 (1976)
   directed by Bernardo Bertolucci P.E.A., Produzioni Europée Associate
24 Hour Party People (2002)
   directed by Michael Winterbottom, 24 Hour Films Ltd
A dunai exodus (*The Danube Exodus*) (1999)
   directed by Péter Forgács
A History of Britain (2000–2002)
   directed by Martin Davidson, History Channel
A Night to Remember (1958)
   directed by Roy Ward Baker, Rank Organisation Film Productions Ltd
Adventures of Barry McKenzie, The (1972)
   directed by Bruce Beresford, Longford Productions
Alexander (2004)
   directed by Oliver Stone, Internationale Medien und Film GmbH & Co. 3
   Prod
Aleksandr Nevski (*Alexander Nevsky*) (1938)
   directed by Sergei M. Eisenstein, Mosfilm
Alvin Purple (1973)
   directed by Tim Burstall, Hexagon Productions
Amistad (1997)
   directed by Steven Spielberg, DreamWorks SKG
Anastasia (1997)
   directed by Don Bluth, Twentieth Century Fox Film Corporation
Anthony Adverse (1936)
   directed by Mervyn LeRoy, Warner Bros.
Atlantic (1929)
   directed by E.A. Dupont, British International Pictures
Back to the Future (1985)
   directed by Robert Zemeckis, Amblin Entertainment
Back to the Future II (1989)
   directed by Robert Zemeckis, Amblin Entertainment

Back to the Future III (1990)
    directed by Robert Zemeckis, Universal City Studios, Inc.
Bakha Satang (*Peppermint Candy*) (1999)
    directed by Lee Chang-Dong, East Film Company
Band of Brothers (2001)
    directed by David Frankel and Tom Hanks, DreamWorks SKG
Barry Lyndon (1975)
    directed by Stanley Kubrick, Warner Bros
Battle of Ancre (1917)
    directed by Geoffrey Malins and John McDowell, British Topical Committee for War Films
Battle of Elderbush Gulch, The (1913)
    directed by D.W. Griffith, Biograph Company
Battle of the Somme, The (1916)
    directed by Geoffrey Malins and John McDowell, British Topical Committee for War Films
Before the Rain (1994)
    directed by Milcho Manchevski, PolyGram Filmed Entertainment
Ben-Hur (1959)
    directed by William Wyler, Loew's Inc.
Ben-Hur: A Tale of the Christ (1925)
    directed by Fred Niblo, Metro-Goldwyn-Mayer Pictures Corporation
Bill and Ted's Excellent Adventure (1988)
    directed by Stephen Herek, Nelson Films, Inc.
Black Hawk Down (2001)
    directed by Ridley Scott, Revolution Studios Distribution LLC
Black Pirate, The (1926)
    directed by Albert Parker, Elton Corporation
Bontoc Eulogy (1995)
    directed by Marlon Fuentes and Bridget Yearian, Independent Television Service (ITVS)
Bowling for Columbine (2002)
    directed by Michael Moore, Iconolatry Productions Inc.
Boys Don't Cry (1999)
    directed by Kimberly Peirce, 20th Century Fox Film Corporation
Braveheart (1995)
    directed by Mel Gibson, B.H. Finance CV
Bride of Vengeance (1949)
    directed by Mitchell Leisen, Mitchell Leisen Prods
Bronenosets Potemkin (*Battleship Potemkin*) (1925)
    directed by Sergei Eisenstein, First Studio Goskino
Buccaneer, The (1958)
    directed by Anthony Quinn, Paramount Pictures Corporation
Cabiria (1914)
    directed by Giovanni Pastrone, Itala Film

Cat's Meow, The (2001)
    directed by Peter Bogdanovich, Cats Gbr
Catch Me If You Can (2002)
    directed by Steven Spielberg, Dreamworks SKG
Ceddo (1976)
    directed by Sembène Ousmane, Filmi Doomireev
Charge of the Light Brigade, The (1936)
    directed by Michael Curtiz, Warner Bros.
Charles and Diana: Unhappily Ever After (1992)
    directed by John Power, Konigsberg/Sanitsky Company
Charlie's Angels (1976)
    directed by John Llewellyn Moxey, Spelling-Goldberg Productions
Charlie's Angels (2000)
    directed by McG, Global Entertainment Productions GmbH & Co.
    Movie
Charlie's Angels Full Throttle (2003)
    directed by McG, Columbia Pictures Industries, Inc.
Chicago (2002)
    directed by Rob Marshall, KALIS Productions GmbH & Co. KG
Chinatown (1974)
    directed by Roman Polanski, Long Road Productions
Chocolat (2001)
    directed by Lasse Hallström, Miramax Film Corporation
Chopper (2000)
    directed by Andrew Dominik, Australian Film Finance Corporation
Christopher Columbus: The Discovery (1992)
    directed by John Glen, Peel Enterprises, Christopher Columbus Pro-
    ductions
Cider House Rules, The (1999)
    directed by Lasse Hallström, Miramax Film Corporation
Citadel, The (1938)
    directed by King Vidor, Metro-Goldwyn-Mayer British Studios
Citizen Kane (1941)
    directed by Orson Welles, RKO Radio Pictures
Civil War, The (1990)
    directed by Ken Burns, American Documentaries Inc.
Civilisation (1969)
    directed by Peter Montagnon and Michael Gill, British Broadcasting
    Corporation (BBC)
Cleopatra (1934)
    directed by Cecil B. DeMille, Paramount Pictures
Cleopatra (1963)
    directed by Joseph L. Mankiewicz, 20th Century Fox Productions Ltd
Conquistadors (2000)
    directed by David Wallace, British Broadcasting Corporation (BBC)

Coronation of Edward VII, The (1902)
  directed by Georges Méliès and Charles Urban, Warwick Trading Company
Count of Monte Cristo, The (1934)
  directed by Rowland V. Lee, Reliance Pictures
Courage Under Fire (1996)
  directed by Edward Zwick, 20th Century Fox Film Corporation
Course of Irish History, The (1966)
  Radio Telefís Èireann
Crusades, The (1995)
  directed by Alan Ereira and David Wallace, BBC Entertainment
Dal Polo All'Equatore (*From the Pole to the Equator*) (1987)
  directed by Yervant Gianikian, Zweites Deutsches Fernsehen
Dallas (1978–1991)
  directed by David Jacobs, Lorimar Television
Dancer in the Dark (2000)
  directed by Lars von Trier, Zentropa Entertainments ApS
Das Blaue Licht (*The Blue Light*) (1932)
  directed by Leni Riefenstahl, H.R. Sokal-Film
De Tweeling (*Twin Sisters*) (2003)
  directed by Ben Sombogaart, IdtV Film
Der Heilige Berg (*The Holy Mountain*) (1926)
  directed by Arnold Fanck, Ufa
Der Name Der Rose (*The Name of the Rose*) (1986)
  directed by Jean-Jacques Annaud, Constantin Film AG
Diana: Her True Story (1993)
  directed by Kevin Connor, Martin Poll Productions
Diane (1955)
  directed by David Miller, Loew's Inc.
Distant Voices, Still Lives (1988)
  directed by Terence Davis, British Film Institute Production Board
Dogville (2003)
  directed by Lars von Trier, Zentropa Entertainments ApS
Donnie Darko (2001)
  directed by Richard Kelly, Pandora, Inc.
Dorothy Vernon of Haddon Hall (1924)
  directed by Marshall Neilan, Mary Pickford Productions
Down With Love (2003)
  directed by Peyton Reed, Mediastream Dritte Film GmbH & Co.
  Beteiligungs
Du Barry was a Lady (1943)
  directed by Roy Del Ruth, Loew's Inc.
E La Nave Va (*And the Ship Sails On*) (1983)
  directed by Federico Fellini, RAI Radiotelevisione Italiana
Edwardian Country House, The (2002)
  Channel 4 Television Corporation, Wall to Wall Television Ltd

Eijanaka (1981)
  directed by Shohei Imamura, Imamura Productions, Shochiku Co. Ltd
Electrocution of an Elephant (1903)
  directed by Thomas Edison, Edison Manufacturing Company
Eliza Fraser (1976)
  directed by Tim Burstall, Hexagon Productions
Elizabeth (1998)
  directed by Shekhar Kapur, PolyGram Filmed Entertainment, Inc.
Empire (2003)
  Channel 4
English Patient, The (1996)
  directed by Anthony Minghella, Tiger Moth Productions
Eve's Bayou (1997)
  directed by Kasi Lemmons, Trimark Pictures
Far from Heaven (2002)
  directed by Todd Haynes, Vulcan Productions
Far from Poland (1984)
  directed by Jill Godmilow, Beach Street Films
Forrest Gump (1994)
  directed by Robert Zemeckis, Paramount Pictures
Frontier House (2002)
  directed by Nicolas Brown and Maro Chermayeff, Public Broadcasting
  Service (PBS)
Full Monty, The (1997)
  directed by Peter Cattaneo, 20th Century Fox Film Corporation
Gallipoli (1981)
  directed by Peter Weir, Associated R & R Films
Gandhi (1982)
  directed by Richard Attenborough, Carolina Bank Ltd
Girl with a Pearl Earring (2003)
  directed by Peter Webber, Archer Street (Girl) Ltd
Giron (*Bay of Pigs*) (1974)
  directed by Maneul Herrera, Instituto Cubano del Arte e Industrias
  Cinematograficos ICAC
Gladiator (2000)
  directed by Ridley Scott, DreamWorks LLC
Good Morning, Vietnam (1987)
  directed by Barry Levinson, Touchstone Pictures
Great Dictator, The (1940)
  directed by Charles Chaplin, Charles Chaplin Corporation
Great Gatsby, The (1974)
  directed by Jack Clayton, Newdon Company
Guns of Navarone, The (1961)
  directed by J. Lee Thompson, Open Road Films

Hadashi no gen (*Barefoot Gen*) (1983)
    directed by Mori Masaki, Gen Productions
Harvie Krumpet (2003)
    directed by Adam Elliot, Melodrama Pictures
Heimat (1984)
    directed by Edgar Reitz, Edgar Reitz Film, Sender Freies Berlin, Westdeutscher Rundfunk
Hiroshima, Mon Amour (1959)
    directed by Alain Resnais, Argos Films
History of the World Part I (1981)
    directed by Mel Brooks, Brooksfilms Ltd
Hitler: The Rise of Evil (2003)
    directed by Christian Duguay, Alliance Atlantis Communications
Hotaru no Haku (*Grave of the Fireflies*) (1988)
    directed by Isao Takahata, Studio Ghibli
Hours, The (2002)
    directed by Stephen Daldry, Miramax Films
Il Casanova Di Federico Fellini (*Casanova*) (1976)
    directed by Federico Fellini, Kapustan Industries N.V.
Il Etait Une Fois Un Pays (*Underground*) (1995)
    directed by Emir Kusturica, CiBy 2000
In the Footsteps of Alexander the Great (1998)
    directed by David Wallace, Maryland Public Television
In the Wake of the Bounty (1933)
    directed by Charles Chauvel, Expeditionary Films Production
Into the Breach: 'Saving Private Ryan' (1998)
    directed by Chris Harty, Dreamworks SKG
Intolerance (1916)
    directed by D.W. Griffith, Wark Producing Corporation
Ireland, a Nation (1914)
    directed by Walter MacNamara and P.J. O'Bourke, Gaelic Amusement Co.
Ivan Grozni (*Ivan the Terrible*) (1945)
    directed by Sergei M. Eisenstein, Mosfilm
Ivan Grozni II Boyarski Zagorov (*Ivan The Terrible II*) (1958)
    directed by Sergei M. Eisenstein, Mosfilm
Jakob, der Lügner (1975)
    directed by Frank Breyer, DEFA-Studio für Spielfilme, Deutscher Fernseh-funk, Filmové Studio Barrandov, Westdeutscher Rundfunk
Jakob the Liar (1999)
    directed by Peter Kassovitz, Global Entertainment Productions GmbH & Co.
Jeanne d'Arc (*Joan of Arc*) (1899)
    directed by Georges Méliès, Star Film
JFK (1991)
    directed by Oliver Stone, Warner Bros.

Julius Caesar (1953)
    directed by Joseph L. Mankiewicz, Loew's Inc.
King Arthur (2004)
    directed by Antoine Fuqua, Touchstone Pictures
L'albero delgi zoccoli (*Tree of Wooden Clogs*) (1978)
    directed by Ermanno Olmi, Rai
La Haine (*The Hate*) (1995)
    directed by Mathieu Kassovitz, Productions Lazennec
La Vita è bella (*Life is Beautiful*) (1997)
    directed by Roberto Benigni, Melampo Cinematografica srl (Rome)
Land of the Pharaohs (1955)
    directed by Howard Hawks, Warner Bros.
Last Days, The (1998)
    directed by Jim Moll, Survivors of the Shoah Visual History Foundation
Lawrence of Arabia (1962)
    directed by David Lean, Ace Films Productions
Le Jour ou le clown pleura (*The Day the Clown Cried*) (1972)
    directed by Jerry Lewis, Capitole Films (Paris)
Le Marseillaise (1937)
    directed by Jean Renoir, Société de Production et d'Exploitation du film
Le Pianiste (*The Pianist*) (2002)
    directed by Roman Polanski, RP Productions
Le Retour de Martin Guerre (1982)
    directed by Daniel Vigne, Société Française de Production de Cinéma
Life and Death of Peter Sellers, The (2004)
    directed by Stephen Hopkins, Home Box Office
Life and Death of Princess Diana, The (1998)
    MSNBC Television Network
Life of an American Fireman, The (1903)
    directed by Edwin S. Porter, Edison Manufacturing Company
Life of Emile Zola, The (1937)
    directed by Wilhelm Dieterle, Warner Bros.
Lord of the Rings: The Fellowship of the Ring, The (2001)
    directed by Peter Jackson, New Line Cinema
Lord of the Rings: The Return of the King, The (2003)
    directed by Peter Jackson, New Line Cinema
Lord of the Rings: The Two Towers, The (2002)
    directed by Peter Jackson, New Line Cinema
Macht der Bilder: Leni Riefenstahl, Die (*The Wonderful, Horrible Life of Leni Riefenstahl*) (1993)
    directed by Ray Müller, Channel Four Films, Nomad Films, Omega Film GmbH, Without Walls, Zweites Deutsches Fernsehen (ZDF) arte
Madame Curie (1943)
    directed by Mervyn LeRoy, Loew's Inc.

Madonna of the Seven Moons (1944)
  directed by Arthur Crabtree, Gainsborough Pictures
Magnificent Ambersons, The (1942)
  directed by Orson Welles, Mercury Productions
Majestic, The (2001)
  directed by Frank Darabont, Warner Bros.
Malcolm X (1992)
  directed by Spike Lee, 40 Acres and a Mule Filmworks
Man in Grey, The (1943)
  directed by Leslie Arliss, Gainsborough Pictures
Marie Antoinette (1938)
  directed by W.S. Van Dyke, Loew's Inc.
Matewan (1987)
  directed by John Sayles, Cinecom Entertainment Group
Matrix, The (1999)
  directed by Andy Wachowski and Larry Wachowski, Warner Bros.
Maytime (1937)
  directed by Robert Z. Leonard, Metro-Goldwyn-Mayer Corporation
Medieval Lives (2004)
  directed by Nigel Miller, BBC Television Centre, Oxford Film and
  Television Production
Meet Me in St. Louis (1944)
  directed by Vincente Minnelli, Loew's Inc.
Memento (2000)
  directed by Christopher Nolan, Remember Productions LLC
Men of Our Time: Mussolini (1970)
  narrated by A.J.P. Taylor, ITV
Mister Prime Minister (1966)
  Australian Broadcasting Corporation
Moana – A Romance of the Golden Age (1926)
  directed by Robert Flaherty, Famous Players-Lasky Corporation
Monarchy of England, The (2004)
  Channel 4 Television
Monster (2003)
  directed by Patty Jenkins, Film and Entertainment VIP Medienfonds 2
  GmbH & Co.
Monty Python's Flying Circus (1969–1974)
  directed by John Howard Davies and Ian MacNaughton, British Broad-
  casting Corporation (BBC)
Moulin Rouge (2001)
  directed by Baz Luhrmann, 20th Century Fox Film Corporation
Mutters Courage (*Mother's Courage*) (1995)
  directed by Michael Verhoeven, Sentana Filmproduktion
Navigator: A Medieval Odyssey, The (1988)
  directed by Vincent Ward, Arenafilm

Ned Kelly (1970)
  directed by Tony Richardson, Woodfall Film Productions
Ned Kelly (2003)
  directed by Gregor Jordan, Kelly Gang Films Pty Ltd
Nixon (1995)
  directed by Oliver Stone, Cinergi Productions N.V. Inc.
Nuit et brouillard (*Night and Fog*) (1955)
  directed by Alain Resnais, Argos Films
Ogniem i Mieczem (*With Fire and Sword*) (1999)
  directed by Jerry Hoffman, Zespol Filmowy 'Zodiak'
Oktiabr (*October*) (1928)
  directed by Sergei M. Eisenstein, Sovkino
Olympische Spiele Fest Der Schönheit (*Olympia*) (1938)
  directed by Leni Riefenstahl, Olympia Film
Olympische Spiele Fest Der Völker (*Olympia*) (1938)
  directed by Leni Riefenstahl, Olympia Film
On a Clear Day You Can See Forever (1970)
  directed by Vincente Minnelli, Paramount Pictures Corporation
Our Hospitality (1923)
  directed by Buster Keaton, Joseph M. Schenck Productions
Outback House (2005)
  Produced by Ivo Porum, Australian Broadcasting Corporation
Patriot, The (2000)
  directed by Roland Emmerich, Global Entertainment Productions GmbH
  & Co.
Peacemaking 1919 (1971)
  directed by David Mingay, VPS
Pearl Harbor (2001)
  directed by Michael Bay, Touchstone Pictures
People's Century (1995)
  directed by Angus MacQueen, British Broadcasting Corporation (BBC)
People's Century, The (1995)
  directed by Angus MacQueen, British Broadcasting Corporation (BBC),
  WGBH Boston
Perry Mason (1957–1966)
  directed by Jack Arnold and Earl Bellamy, CBS Television, Paisano
  Productions, TCF Television Productions Inc.
Picnic at Hanging Rock (1975)
  directed by Peter Weir, Picnic Productions
Pocahontas (1995)
  directed by Michael Gabriel, Walt Disney Pictures
Pride and Prejudice (1940)
  directed by Robert Z. Leonard, Loew's Inc.
Pride and Prejudice (1952)
  directed by Campbell Logan, British Broadcasting Corporation (BBC)

Pride and Prejudice (1958)
  directed by British Broadcasting Corporation (BBC)
Pride and Prejudice (1967)
  directed by Joan Craft, British Broadcasting Corporation (BBC)
Pride and Prejudice (1980)
  directed by Cyril Coke, British Broadcasting Corporation (BBC)
Pride and Prejudice (1995)
  directed by Simon Langton, A&E Television Networks Inc., British Broadcasting Corporation (BBC), Chestermead Ltd
Pride and Prejudice (2005)
  directed by Joe Wright, Working Title Films
Prince and the Pauper, The (1937)
  directed by William Keighley, Warner Bros.
Princess in Love (1996)
  directed by David Greene, CBS Television
Producers, The (1968)
  directed by Mel Brooks, Embassy Pictures Corporation
Purple Rose of Cairo, The (1985)
  directed by Woody Allen, Orion Pictures Corporation
Quiet American, The (2002)
  directed by Philip Noyce, Internationale Medien und Film GmbH & Co.
Quo Vadis (1951)
  directed by Mervyn LeRoy, Loew's Inc.
Rabbit-proof Fence (2002)
  directed by Philip Noyce, Australian Film Finance Corporation
Radio Bikini (1987)
  directed by Robert Stone, Crossroads
Raiders of the Lost Ark (1981)
  directed by Steven Spielberg, Lucasfilm
Rambo First Blood Part II (1985)
  directed by George Pan Cosmatos, Carolco Pictures Inc.
Rashomon (1950)
  directed by Akira Kurosawa, Daiei
Rasputin and the Empress (1932)
  directed by Richard Boleslavsky, Metro-Goldwyn-Mayer Distributing Corporation
Ray (2004)
  directed by Taylor Hackford, Unchain My Heart Louisiana LLC
Robe, The (1953)
  directed by Henry Koster, 20th Century Fox Film Corporation
Robin Hood (1923)
  directed by Allan Dwan, Douglas Fairbanks Pictures Corporation
Russki Kovcheg (*Russian Ark*) (2002)
  directed by Alexsandr Sokurov, Hermitage Bridge Studio

Rutles: All you Need is Cash, The (1978)
    directed by Eric Idle and Gary Weis, Above Average Productions Inc.,
    Broadway Video, Rutle Corp.
Sans Soleil (*Sunless*) (1982)
    directed by Chris Marker, Argos Films
Saving Private Ryan (1998)
    directed by Steven Spielberg, DreamWorks SKG
Scarlet Empress, The (1934)
    directed by Josef von Sternberg, Paramount Productions
Schindler's List (1993)
    directed by Steven Spielberg, Universal Pictures
Seven Ages of Britain (2003)
    directed by Paul Sen, Wildfire Television
Shipping News, The (2001)
    directed by Lasse Hallström, Miramax Film Corporation
Shoah (1985)
    directed by Claude Lanzmann, Films Aleph
Sieg des Glaubens: Der Film vom Reichs-Parteitag der NSDAP (*Victory of
Faith*) (1933)
    directed by Leni Riefenstahl, Reichspropagandaleitung der NSDAP
Smultronstallet (*Wild Strawberries*) (1957)
    directed by Ingmar Bergman, Svensk Filmindustri
Snow Falling on Cedars (1999)
    directed by Scott Hicks, Universal Pictures Company
Sommersby (1993)
    directed by Jon Amiel, Regency Enterprises
Sound of Music, The (1965)
    directed by Robert Wise, Argyle Enterprises
Spartacus (1960)
    directed by Stanley Kubrick, Universal Pictures Company
Spartans, The (2002)
    Channel 4 Television
Stachka (*Strike*) (1925)
    directed by Sergei Eisenstein, Proletkult
Star Wars (1977)
    directed by George Lucas, Lucasfilm
Staroye i Novoye (*The General Line*) (1929)
    directed by Sergei Eisenstein, Sovkino
Stork (1971)
    directed by Tim Burstall, Tim Burstall & Associates
Story of Alexander Graham Bell, The (1939)
    directed by Irving Cummings, 20th Century Fox Film Corporation
Story of Dr. Erhlich's Magic Bullet, The (*Dr Erhlich's Magic Bullet*) (1940)
    directed by Wilhelm Dieterle, Warner Bros.

Story of Louis Pasteur, The (1936)
    directed by Wilhelm Dieterle, Warner Bros.
Story of the Kelly Gang, The (1906)
    directed by Charles Tait, J&N Tait, Johnson and Gibson
Surname Viet, Given Name Nam (1989)
    directed by Trinh T. Minh-ha, Idera Films
Tag Der Freiheit Unsere Wehrmacht (*Day of Freedom – Our Armed Forces*)
(1935)
    directed by Leni Riefenstahl, Nazionalsozialistische Deutsche
    Arbeiterpartei
Ten Commandments, The (1956)
    directed by Cecil B. DeMille, Paramount Pictures
Terminator 2: Judgment Day (1991)
    directed by James Cameron, Carolco Pictures, Inc.
Thief of Bagdad, The (1924)
    directed by Raoul Walsh, Douglas Fairbanks Pictures Corporation
Tiefland (*Lowland*) (1954)
    directed by Leni Riefenstahl, Riefenstahl-Film
Titanic (1953)
    directed by Jean Negulesco, 20th Century Fox Film Corporation
Titanic (1997)
    directed by James Cameron, 20th Century Fox Film Corporation
Tom Jones (1963)
    directed by Tony Richardson, Woodfall Film Productions
Train de vie (*Train of Life*) (1998)
    directed by Radu Mihaileanu, Noe Productions
Triumph Des Willens: Das Dokument vom Reichsparteitag 1934 (*Triumph of
the Will*) (1936)
    directed by Leni Riefenstahl, Nazionalsozialistische Deutsche
    Arbeiterpartei
Triumph of the West, The (1985)
    ITV
Trouble with Merle, The (2002)
    directed by Marée Delofski, Film Australia
Troy (2004)
    directed by Wolfgang Petersen, Helena Productions Ltd
U-571 (2000)
    directed by Jonathan Mostow, Universal Pictures Company
Villin Pohjolan salattu laakso (*The Secret Valley of the Wild North*) (1963)
    directed by Aarne Tarkas, Keskus-Elokuva
Virgin Queen, The (1955)
    directed by Henry Koster, 20th Century Fox Film Corporation
Walker (1987)
    directed by Alex Cox, Walker Film Productions

War Walks (1997)
 British Broadcasting Corporation Television (BBC)
WEB DuBois: A Documentary in Four Voices (1996)
 Directed by Louis Massiah, Public Broadcasting Service
We Are History (2000)
 directed by Sean Grundy and Alex Walsh-Taylor, BBC Entertainment
We Were Soldiers (2002)
 directed by Randall Wallace, Motion Picture Production GmbH & C Erste KG
Windtalkers (2002)
 directed by John Woo, Metro-Goldwyn-Mayer
Wo Hu Zang Long (*Crouching Tiger Hidden Dragon*) (2000)
 directed by Ang Lee, United China Vision Inc.
World at War, The (1974)
 directed by Ted Childs and Michael Darlow, Imperial War Museum, Thames Television
Xena: Warrior Princess (1995–2001)
 directed by John Schulian and Robert G. Tapert, MCA Television Entertainment Inc.,
 Renaissance Pictures, Studios USA Television, Universal TV
Ying Xiong (*Hero*) (2002)
 directed by Zhang Yimou, Elite Group Enterprises

Index

Related titles from Routledge

Historics

Martin L. Davies

From a published author at the forefront of research in this area comes this provocative and seminal work that takes a unique and fresh new look at history and theory.

Taking a broadly European view, the book draws on works of French and German philosophy, some of which are unknown to the English-speaking world, and Martin L. Davies spells out what it is like to live in a historicised world, where any event is presented as historical as, or even before, it happens.

Challenging basic assumptions made by historians, Davies focuses on historical ideas and thought about the past instead of examining history as a discipline. The value of history in and for contemporary culture is explained not only in terms of cultural and institutional practices but in forms of writing and representation of historical issues too.

Historics stimulates thinking about the behaviours and practice that constitute history and introduces complex ideas in a clear and approachable style. This important text is recommended not only for a wide student audience but for the more discerning general reader as well.

ISBN10: 0–415–26165–1 (Hb)
ISBN10: 0–415–26166–X (Pb)

ISBN13: 978–0–415–26165–4 (Hb)
ISBN13: 978–0–415–26166–1 (Pb)

Available at all good bookshops
For ordering and further information please visit:
www.routledge.com

Related titles from Routledge

Making History

Peter Lambert and Philip Schofield

Making History offers a fresh perspective on the study of the past. It is an exhaustive exploration of the practice of history, historical traditions and the theories that surround them. Discussing the development and growth of history as a discipline and of the profession of the historian, the book encompasses a huge diversity of influences and is organised around the following themes:

- the professionalisation of the discipline, looking at methodology, 'scientific' history and the problem of objectivity

- the most significant movements in historical scholarship in the last century, including the *Annales* School, and the development of social and economic history

- the increasing interdisciplinary trends in scholarship, showing interconnections between history, archaeology, psychoanalysis, sociology, anthropology and literature. Scholars from non-historical disciplines have contributed to provide a unique approach to a controversial debate

- theory in historical practice, looking at the social movements and ideologies that propelled its increased importance, including Marxism, postmodernism and gender history

- historical practice outside the academy with reference to film, 'amateur' history, heritage and popular culture.

The volume offers a coherent set of chapters to support undergraduates, postgraduates and others interested in the historical processes that have shaped the discipline of history.

ISBN10: 0–415–24254–1 (Hb)
ISBN10: 0–415–24255–X (Pb)

ISBN13: 978–0–415–24254–7 (Hb)
ISBN13: 978–0–415–24255–4 (Pb)

Available at all good bookshops
For ordering and further information please visit:

www.routledge.com

Related titles from Routledge

Film as Social Practice

Graeme Turner

This fourth edition of a bestselling classic text has been comprehensively updated and revised to bring it up to date with contemporary film analysis and new material published.

Film as Social Practice follows on the heels of the wide–selling third edition and presents an introduction to cinema as an industry and entertainment form.

Primarily focusing on contemporary popular cinema with examples from classical Hollywood cinema too, Graeme Turner examines the social and cultural aspects of film culture such as audiences, exhibition, technology, and issues including race and gender.

This fourth edition now contains:

- an expanded treatment of special effects and spectacle
- inclusion of film theory's discussion of the representation of race and ethnicity
- a thorough updating of individual film references
- a revised applications chapter that includes new contemporary examples
- added new illustrations from contemporary popular cinema.

Students of film studies, film practice and film theory will find this a welcome addition to their degree course studies.

ISBN10: 0415–37513–4 (Hb)
ISBN10: 0415–37514–2 (Pb)

ISBN13: 978–0–415–37513–9 (Hb)
ISBN13: 978–0–415–37514–6 (Pb)

Available at all good bookshops
For ordering and further information please visit:

www.routledge.com

Related titles from Routledge

The Film Cultures Reader
Edited by Graeme Turner

This companion reader to *Film as Social Practice* brings together key writings on contemporary cinema, exploring film as a social and cultural phenomenon.

Key features of the reader include:

- thematic sections, each with an introduction by the editor
- a general introduction by Graeme Turner
- sections: understanding film, film technology, film industries, meanings and pleasures, identities, audiences and consumption.

Contributors include Tino Balio, Sabrina Barton, Tony Bennett, Jacqueline Bobo, Edward Buscombe, Stella Bruzzi, Jim Collins, Barbara Creed, Richard Dyer, Jane Feuer, Miriam Hansen, John Hill, Marc Jancovich, Susan Jeffords, Isaac Julien, Annette Kuhn, P. David Marshall, Judith Mayne, Kobena Mercer, Tania Modleski, Steve Neale, Tom O'Regan, Stephen Prince, Thomas Schatz, Gianluca Sergi, Ella Shohat, Jackie Stacey, Janet Staiger, Robert Stam, Chris Straayer, Yvonne Tasker, Stephen Teo, Janet Wollacott, Justin Wyatt.

ISBN10: 0–415–25281–4 (hb
ISBN10: 0–415–25282–2 (pb)

ISBN13: 9–78–0–415–25281–2 (hb)
ISBN13: 9–78–0–415–25282–9 (pb)

Available at all good bookshops
For ordering and further information please visit:

www.routledge.com

Related titles from Routledge

Screening the Past

Pam Cook

This lively and accessible collection explores film culture's obsession with the past, offering searching and provocative analyses of a wide range of titles from *Mildred Pierce* and *Brief Encounter* to *Raging Bull* and *In the Mood for Love*.

Screening the Past engages with current debates about the role of cinema in mediating history through memory and nostalgia, suggesting that many films use strategies of memory to produce diverse forms of knowledge which challenge established ideas of history and the traditional role of historians. The work of contemporary directors such as Martin Scorsese, Kathryn Bigelow, Todd Haynes and Wong Kar-wai is used to examine the different ways they deploy creative processes of memory, arguing that these movies can tell us much about our complex relationship to the past, and about history and identity.

Pam Cook also investigates the recent history of film studies, reviewing the developments that have culminated in the exciting, if daunting, present moment. Classic essays sit side by side with new research, contextualised by introductions which bring them up to date and provide suggestions for further reading. The result is a rich and stimulating volume that will appeal to anyone with an interest in cinema, memory and identity.

ISBN10: 0–415–18374–X (Hb)
ISBN10 : 0–415–18375–8 (Pb)

ISBN13: 978–0–415–18374–1 (Hb)
ISBN13: 978–0–415–18375–8 (Pb)

Available at all good bookshops
For ordering and further information please visit:
www.routledge.com